D0928209

WEST ORANGE LIBRARY
46 MT. PLEASANT AVENUE
WEST ORANGE, NJ 07052
(973) 736 – 0198

Reconstruction Era
Primary Sources

Reconstruction Era
Primary Sources

Bridget Hall Grumet

Lawrence W. Baker,
Project Editor

U·X·L

*An imprint of Thomson Gale,
a part of The Thomson Corporation*

Detroit • New York • San Francisco • San Diego • New Haven, Conn. • Waterville, Maine • London • Munich

Reconstruction Era: Primary Sources

Bridget Hall Grumet

Project Editor
Lawrence W. Baker

Permissions
Margaret Abendroth, Denise Buckley,
Margaret Chamberlain

Imaging and Multimedia
Lezlie Light, Dan Newell, Denay Wilding

Product Design
Pamela A. E. Galbreath, Kate Scheible

Composition
Evi Seoud

Manufacturing
Rita Wimberley

©2005 by U•X•L. U•X•L is an imprint of Thomson Gale, a division of Thomson Learning, Inc.

U•X•L® is a registered trademark used herein under license. Thomson Learning™ is a trademark used herein under license.

For more information, contact:
Thomson Gale
27500 Drake Rd.
Farmington Hills, MI 48331-3535
Or you can visit our Internet site at
http://www.gale.com.

ALL RIGHTS RESERVED
No part of this work covered by the copyright hereon may be reproduced or used in any form or by any means—graphic, electronic, or mechanical, including photocopying, recording, taping, Web distribution, or information storage retrieval systems—without the written permission of the publisher.

For permission to use material from this product, submit your request via Web at http://www.gale-edit.com/permissions, or you may download our Permissions Request form and submit your request by fax or mail to:

Permissions Department
Thomson Gale
27500 Drake Rd.
Farmington Hills, MI 48331-3535
Permissions Hotline:
248-699-8006 or 800-877-4253, ext. 8006
Fax: 248-699-8074 or 800-762-4058

Cover photograph of Frederick Douglass reproduced courtesy of the National Archives and Records Administration.

While every effort has been made to ensure the reliability of the information presented in this publication, Thomson Gale, does not guarantee the accuracy of data contained herein. Thomson Gale accepts no payment for listing; and inclusion in the publication of any organization, agency, institution, publication, service, or individual does not imply endorsement by the editors or publisher. Errors brought to the attention of the publisher and verified to the satisfaction of the publisher will be corrected in future editions.

LIBRARY OF CONGRESS CATALOGING-IN-PUBLICATION DATA

Grumet, Bridget Hall.
   Reconstruction era : primary sources / Bridget Hall Grumet ; Lawrence W. Baker, project editor.
      p. cm
Includes bibliographical references and index.
   ISBN 0-7876-9219-0 (hardcover : alk. paper)
   1. Reconstruction (U.S. history, 1865–1877)—Sources—Juvenile literature. I. Baker, Lawrence W. II. Title.

E668.G85 2004
973.8—dc22

2004017309

This title is also available as an e-book.
ISBN 1-4144-0454-9
Contact your Thomson Gale sales representative for ordering information.

Printed in the United States of America
10 9 8 7 6 5 4 3

Contents

Reader's Guide

Reconstruction Era: Primary Sources tells the story of the Reconstruction era in the words of the people who lived and shaped it and the laws that contributed to it. The Reconstruction era was the period stretching roughly from the end of the American Civil War in April 1865 to the inauguration of President Rutherford B. Hayes in 1877. Reconstruction was a federal policy intended to restore the relationship between the former Confederate states and the federal Union, to oversee the transition of the newly freed slaves into citizens, and to help convert the Southern economy from one based on slave labor to one based on paid labor. Reconstruction officially ended following the resolution to the controversial presidential election of 1876 in which an electoral commission declared Hayes the victor, just days before he was inaugurated in March 1877. The new president had federal troops removed from the former Confederate region in the South to bring an end to the Reconstruction era.

Coverage and features

Reconstruction Era: Primary Sources's nineteen complete or excerpted documents provide a wide range of perspectives on this period of history. Included are excerpts from abolitionist Frederick Douglass's famous article about Reconstruction, Frances Butler Leigh's account of life after slavery as the daughter of a plantation owner, former slave John Paterson Green's experiences with the Ku Klux Klan, and U.S. senator Charles Sumner's argument in favor of the impeachment of President Andrew Johnson. Document-specific glossaries provide context to unfamiliar terms on the pages on which they appear.

Each document presented in *Reconstruction Era: Primary Sources* includes the following additional material:

- An **introduction** places the document and its author in a historical context.

- **"Things to remember while reading ..."** offers readers important background information and directs them to central ideas in the text.

- **"What happened next ..."** provides an account of subsequent events, both in Reconstruction and in the life of the author.

- **"Did you know ..."** provides significant and interesting facts about the document, the author, or the events discussed.

- **"Consider the following ..."** gives students and teachers research and activity ideas that pertain to the subject of the document.

- **"For more information"** lists sources for further reading on the author, the topic, or the document.

Reconstruction Era: Primary Sources also features sidebars containing interesting facts about people and events related to immigration and migration, nearly sixty black-and-white photographs, a "Reconstruction Era Timeline" that lists significant dates and events associated with Reconstruction, and an index.

U•X•L Reconstruction Era Reference Library

Reconstruction Era: Primary Sources is only one component of the three-part U•X•L Reconstruction Era Reference Library. The other two titles in this set are:

- *Reconstruction Era: Almanac:* This volume presents a comprehensive overview of the Reconstruction era. Its nine chapters are arranged chronologically and explore such topics as the effects of freedom on black family life, Radical Republicans, carpetbaggers and scalawags, amnesty for white Southerners, Black Codes, the impeachment of President Andrew Johnson, the rise of the Ku Klux Klan, attempts to restore the old order in the South, the disputed presidential election of 1876, and the Compromise of 1877. The *Almanac* also contains nearly sixty black-and-white photographs and maps, "Words to Know" boxes, a timeline, research and activity ideas, and an index.

- *Reconstruction Era: Biographies:* This volume presents twenty-five entries covering twenty-eight people who lived during the Reconstruction era. Profiled are well-known figures such as embattled president Andrew Johnson, his political enemies Thaddeus Stevens and Charles Sumner, and African American pioneers Frederick Douglass and Hiram Revels, as well as lesser-known individuals such as chemist and home economics founder Ellen Richards, 1876 presidential election loser Samuel J. Tilden; and early baseball star Harry Wright. *Biographies* includes nearly eighty photographs and illustrations, a timeline, and an index.

Acknowledgments

Thanks to copyeditor Rebecca Valentine; caption writer Theresa Murray; proofreader Amy Marcaccio Keyzer; the indexers from Synapse, the Knowledge Link Corporation; and typesetter Marco Di Vita of the Graphix Group for their fine work.

Comments and suggestions

We welcome your comments on *Reconstruction Era: Primary Sources* and suggestions for other topics to consider. Please write: Editors, *Reconstruction Era: Primary Sources,* U•X•L, 27500 Drake Rd., Farmington Hills, Michigan 48331-3535; call toll free: (800) 877-4253; fax to (248) 699-8097; or send e-mail via http://www.gale.com.

Reconstruction Era Timeline

1622   The first African slaves are brought to the British colonies in North America, which will eventually become the United States of America.

1803   The Louisiana Purchase adds about 800,000 square miles of new territory to the United States.

1820   The Missouri Compromise allows Missouri to be admitted to the Union as a slave state, while Maine is admitted as a free state, thus maintaining the balance between states where slavery is allowed and where it is illegal. Slavery is prohibited in any of the lands of the Louisiana Purchase that are north of the Missouri border.

1848   The U.S. victory in the Mexican-American War brings a large area of new territory into the United States, including what will become the states of Texas, New Mexico, Arizona, and California.

February 28, 1854   The Republican Party is formed by politicians—most of them from the Northern states—who favor protections for business interests, public support for internal improvements (like roads and services), and social reforms, especially an end to slavery.

May 30, 1854 The Kansas-Nebraska Bill, which reverses the Missouri Compromise by allowing the status of slavery in Kansas and Nebraska to be decided by settlers, is signed into law.

May 19–20, 1856 U.S. senator Charles Sumner of Massachusetts gives his "Crime against Kansas" speech in which he insults proslavery supporters of the Kansas-Missouri bill of 1854.

August 21, 1858 Future president Abraham Lincoln and U.S. senator Stephen A. Douglas of Illinois hold the first in a series of seven debates on the issue of slavery; they take place over a period of two months.

November 6, 1860 Illinois Republican Abraham Lincoln is elected president, sending shockwaves of panic through the South, where many believe that Lincoln will immediately take steps to outlaw slavery.

February 4, 1861 Seven Southern states that have seceded (broken away) from the Federal Union form a government of their own called the Confederate States of America, or the Confederacy. They establish their capitol in Richmond, Virginia, with former U.S. senator Jefferson Davis of Mississippi as president. In April and May, four more Southern states will join the Confederacy.

April 12–13, 1861 A successful Confederate attack on the Union outpost at Fort Sumter, South Carolina, marks the beginning of the American Civil War.

May 24, 1861 Three Virginia slaves who have escaped from their plantation and fled to a Union army camp are labeled "contraband" (property confiscated during a war) by Union general Benjamin Butler.

July 21, 1861 The Confederate army defeats Union forces at the first Battle of Bull Run in Virginia, not far from Washington, D.C.

November 7, 1861 The U.S. Navy occupies the city of Port Royal in the Sea Islands off the shore of South Carolina. The white plantation owners in the area have already fled, leaving behind a large population of slaves.

February 24, 1862 The Union army takes control of Nashville, Tennessee. In early April, they will also win a victory at Shiloh, Tennessee.

March 13, 1862 Congress passes an Article of War that prohibits the Army from returning runaway slaves to their masters.

April 25, 1862 Union naval forces under Commander David Farragut capture the important southern city of New Orleans, Louisiana.

May 13, 1862 South Carolina slave Robert Smalls steals a Confederate navy ship from Charleston Harbor and turns it over to the Union forces.

July 17, 1862 President Abraham Lincoln signs the Second Confiscation Act, which declares free all slaves who escape to the Union lines.

September 17, 1862 The Union army wins a decisive victory at the Battle of Antietam near Sharpsburg, Maryland.

September 27, 1862 The First Louisiana Native Guard, made up of African Americans from New Orleans's free black community, becomes the first official black regiment to join the Union army.

1863 The Militia Act, passed on July 17, 1862, allows former slaves to enroll in the U.S. Army.

January 1, 1863 President Abraham Lincoln signs the Emancipation Proclamation, which declares forever free most of the four million slaves living in the Confederate states. Excluded are approximately 450,000 slaves in the loyal border states, the 275,000 in Union-held Tennessee, and those in the parts of Virginia and Louisiana that are under Union control.

January 25, 1863 The Fifty-fourth Massachusetts Infantry becomes the first African American regiment in the North to join the Union army.

March 1863 The group of idealistic northern missionaries and teachers known as Gideon's Band arrives in Port

Royal, South Carolina, intending to assist the large population of former slaves living there.

May 1863 The all-black Fifty-fourth Massachusetts Regiment departs from Boston for South Carolina, where the soldiers will win acclaim for their bravery during a battle at Fort Wagner.

July 1–3, 1863 At Gettysburg, Pennsylvania, the Union army wins an important victory, forcing the Confederate army to retreat into Virginia.

July 4, 1863 After an eight-week siege, Union forces under General Ulysses S. Grant defeat Confederate troops in Vicksburg, Mississippi.

July 13–16, 1863 Nearly a thousand people are killed or wounded in a bloody race riot in New York City that highlights northern opposition to the war and white hostility toward African Americans.

November 1863 At Beaufort, South Carolina, the First South Carolina Volunteers become the first Union regiments of black soldiers to be formed in the Confederate states.

December 8, 1863 President Abraham Lincoln issues his Proclamation of Amnesty and Reconstruction, also known as the Ten Per Cent Plan. The plan allows almost any Southerner who will take an oath of loyalty to the United States to receive a full pardon and all rights of a U.S. citizen. Once 10 percent of a Southern state's population have signed the oath, the state may form a new government. Lincoln's plan is criticized by several members of Congress as too lenient toward the Confederacy.

March 1864 Davis Bend, Mississippi, is the site of an experiment in which about 5,000 blacks are given control over their own land and labor. The freed people not only establish their own government but, by 1865, raise almost 2,000 bales of cotton, earning a profit of $160,000.

July 4, 1864 President Abraham Lincoln pocket-vetoes the Wade-Davis Bill, which would have allowed a Southern state to be readmitted to the Union only after 50 percent of those who voted in 1860 signed a loyalty oath.

September 2, 1864 The Southern city of Atlanta, Georgia, falls to Union forces under General William T. Sherman.

November 8, 1864 Abraham Lincoln is reelected president.

November 16, 1864 Union general William T. Sherman leaves Atlanta, Georgia, and begins his "March to the Sea," which ends on December 21 when he takes control of the coastal city of Savannah without a fight.

January 16, 1865 Union general William T. Sherman issues his Special Field Order #15, which sets aside land along the Georgia coast for settlement by African Americans.

January 31, 1865 Congress passes the Thirteenth Amendment, officially abolishing slavery in the United States.

March 3, 1865 The U.S. Department of War establishes the Freedmen's Bureau, a federal agency authorized to assist the former slaves in their transition to freedom by distributing clothing, food, fuel, and medical care and to help coordinate the establishment of black schools. Later, the agency's powers will be expanded to set up black schools and handle legal cases brought by blacks.

April 3, 1865 Union forces capture Richmond, Virginia, the Confederate capitol. The next day, President Abraham Lincoln travels down from Washington, D.C., to stroll through the city.

April 9, 1865 Confederate general Robert E. Lee formally surrenders to the Union army at Appomattox Courthouse, Virginia.

April 14, 1865 Southern actor John Wilkes Booth shoots Abraham Lincoln while the president is attending a play at Ford's Theatre in Washington, D.C. Lincoln dies the next day, and Vice President Andrew Johnson is sworn in as president.

May 29, 1865 Choosing not to wait until Congress is in session, President Andrew Johnson announces his plan for the Reconstruction of the South. His program is so lenient toward the Confederacy that it will allow most of those who dominated Southern politics before the war to return to power.

Summer 1865 The Southern states hold conventions to form state governments under President Andrew Johnson's plan. They put in place new laws called Black Codes that are meant to restrict the employment options and personal freedom of African Americans. At the same time, Southern blacks hold Freedmen's Conventions throughout the South, at which they discuss and record their views.

Fall 1865 Noted orator and writer Frederick Douglass undertakes a speaking tour in support of voting and civil rights for freedmen. The following year, Douglass speaks and writes against the policies of President Andrew Johnson, who refused to use his federal powers to pursue voting rights for freedmen or to interfere with states on civil rights issues.

December 1865 Politician and former Union general Carl Schurz reports on conditions in the South, warning that blacks need the federal government's protection from hostile white Southerners. Although President Andrew Johnson ignores the report, many Northerners are horrified by its contents.

December 6, 1865 In an address to the Thirty-ninth Congress, President Andrew Johnson announces that the Reconstruction of the South has been completed. Congress disagrees, and refuses to seat the new Southern representatives and senators.

December 18, 1865 After being named House chairman of a joint congressional committee on Reconstruction, U.S. representative Thaddeus Stevens of Pennsylvania declares that it is the duty of Congress to supervise Reconstruction and demand tough terms of the former Confederate states, rejecting President Andrew Johnson's authority to define the terms of Reconstruction.

January 1866 Alexander Stephens, former vice president of the Confederate States of America, is elected to the U.S. Senate in Georgia under the Reconstruction Plan initiated by President Andrew Johnson. Congress, however, rejects the plan and does not allow Stephens to serve.

March 27, 1866 President Andrew Johnson vetoes the Civil Rights Bill of 1866.

April 9, 1866 A Congress dominated by a group called the Radical Republicans passes the Civil Rights Bill over President Andrew Johnson's veto. This legislation guarantees that all persons born in the United States (except for Native Americans) are to be considered U.S. citizens with full protection of "person and property" under the law.

April 11, 1866 In testimony before U.S. Congress, former Confederate vice president Alexander Stephens speaks out against Reconstruction.

May 1, 1866 A three-day race riot begins in Memphis, Tennessee. When it is over, forty-six blacks will have died.

June 13, 1866 Congress approves the Fourteenth Amendment to the U.S. Constitution, which makes it illegal for any state to deny equality before the law to any male citizen; it is ratified on July 28.

July 16, 1866 Over President Andrew Johnson's veto, Congress passes a bill extending the life and expanding the powers of the Freedmen's Bureau.

July 30, 1866 Thirty-four blacks and three whites die in a race riot in New Orleans, Louisiana.

August 28, 1866 President Andrew Johnson embarks on what will prove to be a disastrous "swing around the circle" speaking tour.

November 1866 The Republicans win a landslide victory in the midterm elections. They are now in control of every Northern state legislature and government, and the Radicals Republicans in the U.S. Congress are at their peak of power.

March 2, 1867 Over President Andrew Johnson's veto, Congress passes the first in a series of Reconstruction Acts. This one divides the South into five military districts, to be run by military commanders until the states meet the federal requirements for forming new governments. Seeking to prevent Johnson from overriding the Republicans' Reconstruction efforts, Congress also passes the Tenure of Office Act, which limits the president from dismissing government officials who have been approved by Congress.

May 1867 Former Confederate general Nathan Bedford Forrest becomes the first Grand Wizard of the Ku Klux Klan, a white terrorist group formed a year earlier.

Fall 1867 In accordance with the Reconstruction Act, the former states of the Confederacy hold constitutional conventions. Nearly a million and a half voters are registered, including about seven hundred thousand African Americans.

February 1868 After President Andrew Johnson dismisses Secretary of War Edwin Stanton, whose political views differ from his own, Congress impeaches him on the grounds that he has violated the Tenure of Office Act and other charges.

May 1868 U.S. senator Charles Sumner of Massachusetts offers a fierce argument in favor of removing President Andrew Johnson from office.

May 16, 1868 President Andrew Johnson is acquitted of violating the Tenure of Office Act. He escapes being dismissed from office by one vote.

June 1868 The states of Alabama, Arkansas, Florida, Georgia, Louisiana, North Carolina, and South Carolina are readmitted to the Union under the Reconstruction plan developed by the Republicans in Congress.

August 11, 1868 The death of U.S. representive Thaddeus Stevens of Pennsylvania a longtime advocate for black equality, represents waning congressional advocacy concern for African American civil rights.

November 3, 1868 Civil War hero Ulysses S. Grant is elected president. The votes cast by newly enfranchised African Americans play a key role in his win.

1869 The newly formed Reconstruction governments are established.

February 26, 1869 Jefferson Davis, former president of the Confederate States of America, is released from prison following delays in his trial and a general amnesty proclamation for ex-Confederates by President Andrew Johnson.

May 1869 The National Woman Suffrage Association (NWSA) is founded by Susan B. Anthony and Elizabeth Cady Stanton.

February 25, 1870 Hiram Revels of Mississippi, the first African American to serve in the U.S. Senate, takes over the seat once occupied by former Confederate president Jefferson Davis.

February 25, 1870 U.S. representative Hiram Revels of Mississippi speaks up about the readmission to the union of Georgia.

March 30, 1870 The Fifteenth Amendment, which bars state governments from denying or abridging voting rights "on account of race, color, or previous condition of servitude," becomes part of the U.S. Constitution.

May 21, 1870 Georgia governor Rufus B. Bullock writes a letter to Congress describing what it is like to be a supporter of Reconstruction in the South.

May 31, 1870 In response to the widespread violence that had terrorized Southern blacks, Congress passes the first of three Enforcement Acts designed to protect the civil and political rights of African Americans.

1871 Congress declares that the Indian nations are no longer sovereign, an act that will lead to the gradual relocation of all Native Americans onto reservations.

April 20, 1871 The second Enforcement Act, known as the Ku Klux Klan Act, is passed by Congress.

May 1, 1872 The Liberal Republican Party nominates New York newspaper editor Horace Greeley for president. Two months later, the Democratic Party also nominates Greeley.

November 5, 1872 President Ulysses S. Grant wins reelection.

December 11, 1872 African American P. B. S. Pinchback becomes acting governor of Louisiana, serving for a little less than one month.

1873 Author Edward Winslow Martin writes about the Crédit Mobilier scandal in his book *Behind the Scenes in Washington.*

September 18, 1873 The period of serious economic decline known as the Panic of 1873 begins, set off by the bankruptcy of Jay Cooke, one of the most powerful bankers in the country. More than a million people lose their jobs, thousands of businesses close, and agricultural prices and land values fall. Miners and factory workers react to wage cuts with violent strikes.

1874 Journalist James Shepherd Pike publishes *The Prostrate State,* an inaccurate account of a typical African American politician.

March 11, 1874 With the death of U.S. senator Charles Sumner of Massachusetts, the waning influence of the Radical Republicans of Congress effectively ends. The Radical Republicans had controlled Reconstruction policy.

June 8, 1874 U.S. representative James Rapier of Alabama gives a speech in which he describes the discrimination he faces as an African American.

Fall 1874 To keep blacks away from the polls in the November elections in Mississippi, a program of terrorism called the "Mississippi Plan" is put into effect. Widespread violence and intimidation are successfully employed as weapons to prevent blacks from exercising their voting rights. Similar effects will be achieved by the same means in other states during the 1876 elections, leading to victories by white supremacists across the South.

November 1874 Blanche K. Bruce of Mississippi becomes the first African American to be elected to a full term to the U.S. Senate.

March 1, 1875 Congress passes the Civil Rights Act, which is meant to reinforce the government's commitment to protecting black rights. Key provisions of the act will be found unconstitutional in the Slaughterhouse Cases, which will come before the Supreme Court in the 1880s.

December 9, 1875 The Whiskey Ring corruption scandal erupts when President Ulysses S. Grant's private secretary, Orville E. Babcock, is charged with participating in fraud involving tax revenues.

November 7, 1876 The results of the presidential election in which Republican Rutherford B. Hayes narrowly beats Democrat Samuel J. Tilden are disputed. Four months later, in a compromise that will allow the Redemption movement to overthrow the southern Reconstruction governments, Democrats agree to accept Hayes's election if the government will leave the South to manage its own affairs.

March 5, 1877 Rutherford B. Hayes gives his Inaugural Address as the new president of the United States.

April 1877 Federal troops are withdrawn from the state capitols of South Carolina and Louisiana, allowing white supremacists known as "Redeemers" to take control of these states' governments. Soon the Redemption movement will have overthrown all of the Reconstruction governments.

Summer 1877 President Rutherford B. Hayes tours the South and makes speeches announcing the end of Reconstruction.

Spring 1879 Discouraged by the overthrow of the multiracial Reconstruction governments by white supremacists, some Southern blacks migrate to the new western state of Kansas. Members of the Exoduster movement, as it is called, seek wider employment opportunities, protection of civil rights, and an escape from the anti-black violence that plagues the South.

1880 Poverty is widespread in the South, where the per capita income is only 40 percent of that of the North.

1880 Former slave John Paterson Green recounts his encounters with the Ku Klux Klan, a white supremacist group.

1881 Influential black leader Booker T. Washington is named principal of the Tuskegee Institute, which will soon become the leading black educational institution in the nation.

1883 Frances Butler Leigh, the daughter of a Southern plantation owner, publishes *Ten Years on a Georgia Plantation Since the War.*

1887 The first Jim Crow law is enacted in Florida. This system of legalized segregation mandates separate schools and public facilities (such as hospitals, prisons, hotels, restaurants, parks, waiting rooms, elevators, cemeteries, and drinking fountains) for blacks and whites.

1894 W. E. B. Du Bois, who will become the leading black intellectual and founder of the Niagara Movement, earns a Ph.D. from Harvard University.

September 18, 1895 African American activist Booker T. Washington delivers his famous Atlanta Compromise Speech, in which he tells a white audience that blacks are more interested in economic advancement than political and social equality.

1896 In the *Plessy v. Ferguson* case, the Supreme Court validates the concept of "separate but equal," asserting that the Fourteenth Amendment was never intended to prevent social segregation.

1897 Ex-slave Louis Hughes publishes *Thirty Years as a Slave.*

1903 Southern general John Brown Gordon publishes *Reminiscences of the Civil War.*

January 1, 1913 African American communities across the nation hold Jubilee celebrations to commemorate the fiftieth anniversary of the signing of the Emancipation Proclamation.

1929 The stock market crash marks the onset of the Great Depression, a period of economic hardship that will last until the entrance of the United States into World War II.

1955–56 Civil rights advocates take part in the Montgomery Bus Boycott, refusing to ride on the city buses of Montgomery, Alabama, until they are integrated. Many believe that this event inaugurates the Civil Rights Movement.

1965 The passage of the Voting Rights Act marks a new era in public and government commitment to the guarantee of black civil and political rights.

Reconstruction Era
Primary Sources

John Brown Gordon

Excerpt from Reminiscences of the Civil War

Covering events from April 1865; published in 1903; reprinted on
***Documenting the American South* (Web site)**

An ex-Confederate general remembers the end of the Civil War

The American Civil War (1861–65)—a bloody struggle described by Northerners as a rebellion, and by Southerners as a fight for independence—drew to a close April 9, 1865, with the surrender of Confederate general Robert E. Lee (1807–1870) and his troops in Appomattox Courthouse, Virginia. The Southern troops were surrounded and outnumbered, and in many ways they were too weak to continue fighting. About twenty-five thousand Confederates were gathered at Appomattox, and Southern general John Brown Gordon (1832–1904) later wrote in his memoirs, "but two thirds of them were so enfeebled [weakened] by hunger, so wasted by sickness, and so foot-sore from constant marching that it was difficult for them to keep up with the army."

Union general Ulysses S. Grant (1822–1885) allowed generous terms of surrender. He permitted the Southern soldiers to keep their horses, for example, because he realized many of them had a long journey home and a farm that would need to be tilled (plowed) when they got there. The soldiers on both sides saluted each other as the Confederates stacked their guns on the ground. While the surrender ended

"They knew that burnt homes and fenceless farms, poverty and ashes, would greet them on their return from the war."

Confederate soldiers returned home to find the cities of the eastern theater of war in ruins, such as these remains in a burned district of Richmond, Virginia. *The Library of Congress.*

the military conflict, however, a larger political question remained: Under what terms would the North bring the Southern states back into the Union?

Both sides also wondered how they would recover from a war that had taken such a devastating toll. The North lost about 110,100 soldiers in battle and 224,580 more to disease. The South lost 94,000 in combat and 164,000 more to

Reconstruction Era: Primary Sources

disease. Another 277,401 Union soldiers and 194,026 Confederates came home wounded. Particularly in the South, many soldiers came home to scorched fields and cities left in ruins. The famed "march to the sea" by Union general William T. Sherman (1820–1891) cut a 60-mile-wide path of destruction through Georgia, as troops took whatever food and supplies they could carry and demolished everything else. When Confederate troops evacuated cities such as Atlanta, Georgia, and Richmond, Virginia, they set fire to arsenals and destroyed railroad lines to keep those assets from falling into the hands of Northern troops. Sometimes the flames spread to factories, flour mills, and other shops before Union forces arrived.

Perhaps most jarring to the Southern soldiers heading home, the war had freed about four million African Americans from slavery. Whites had lost the forced labor pool that had made the South so prosperous. They would have to find a new way to run their large farming operations. They would also have to accept a new social order with African Americans as freed men, not slaves. This would prove to be a challenge for whites who clung to ignorant, racist views of African Americans as inferior people.

Faced with a destroyed homeland and an uncertain future, the ex-Confederates had several choices. Some fled to Mexico, British Honduras, or Brazil. There they "tried to preserve their Southern agricultural society," as noted in *Out of the Storm*, "but it was not long before internal squabbling, coupled with the harsh external realities of Mexican [and other foreign] politics, put an end to the experiment." Most soldiers made the tough trek home, stopping at strangers' houses to beg for food, even stealing from warehouses. Arthur Peronneau Ford, a Confederate soldier from South Carolina, joined a pack of soldiers who stormed a military supply house in Salisbury, North Carolina, just ten days after Lee's surrender at Appomattox. He described the scene in his memoirs, *Life in the Confederate Army:*

> The warehouse was guarded by about a dozen boys of the home guard, who protested violently; but they were just swept [to] one side, and the door was broken open, and every man helped himself to what he wanted or needed. I got a handful of Confederate money, a pair of shoes, some

flour and bacon, a pair of socks, and a small roll of jeans. This roll of cloth I carried clear home across my shoulders, and when I reached Aiken, in May, exchanged it with the baker for one hundred bread tickets, which provided our family with bread for the rest of the summer.

For a few months after the war, the South was in a state of near lawlessness. Some of the discharged soldiers, deserters (soldiers who abandoned their units), and newly freed slaves turned into vandals and thieves, taking what little remained to the Southerners after the war. George Cary Eggleston (1839–1911), a Confederate soldier from Virginia, described the robbers in his memoirs, *A Rebel's Recollections.* "They moved about in bands, from two to ten strong, cutting horses out of plows, plundering helpless people, and wantonly destroying valuables which they could not carry away," Eggleston wrote. He described one group that descended on a mansion "where only ladies lived" and demanded dinner. After they were fed, the men poured molasses over the carpets and furniture, and left. Eggleston continued:

> Outrages were of every-day enactment, and there was no remedy. There was no State, county, or municipal government in existence among us. We had no courts, no justices of the peace, no sheriffs, no officers of any kind invested with a shadow of authority, and there were not men enough in the community, at first, to resist the marauders [robbers], comparatively few of the surrendered soldiers having found their way home as yet.

As the details of surrender were negotiated at Appomattox, General Gordon saw the sadness, anxiety, and dread among his troops. They did not know what they would find when they got home, or what the coming years of Reconstruction would hold. As he later recounted in his 1904 memoirs, Gordon told his men their duties did not end with the war. They would have to show their strength and courage in rebuilding the South and forging new ties with the North.

Things to remember while reading an excerpt from *Reminiscences of the Civil War:*

- The Civil War had freed the slaves, leaving whites to wonder how they would interact with freed African

Americans and how they would run their plantations without forced labor.

- The destruction was not limited to the battlefield. Sherman's march through Georgia brought the war to the people by destroying their homes and farmlands. As Confederate troops fled certain cities, they burned their own armories and railroad lines (with flames sometimes spreading to neighboring buildings) to leave nothing to the Union troops.

- Faced with a home front in ruins and an uncertain political future, some war-weary soldiers thought about moving to Mexico or South America, where they believed they could set up their own slave-holding civilizations.

Excerpt from Reminiscences of the Civil War

*During these last scenes at Appomattox some of the Confederates were so depressed in spirit, so filled with **apprehensions** as to the policy to be adopted by the **civil authorities** at Washington, that the future seemed to them shrouded in gloom. They knew that burnt homes and fenceless farms, poverty and ashes, would greet them on their return from the war. Even if the administration at Washington should be friendly, they did not believe that the Southern States could recover in half a century from the **chaotic** condition in which the war had left them. The situation was enough to **daunt** the most hopeful and **appall** the **stoutest** hearts. "What are we to do? How are we to begin life again?" they asked. "Every dollar of our **circulating medium** has been **rendered** worthless. Our banks and rich men have no money. The **commodities** and personal property which formerly gave us credit have been destroyed. The Northern banks and money-lenders will not take as **security** our lands, **denuded** of houses and without animals and **implements** for their **cultivation**. The railroads are torn up or the tracks are worn out. The negroes are freed and may refuse to work. Besides, what **assurance** can we have of law and order and the safety of our families with four million slaves suddenly **emancipated** in the midst of us and the restraints to which they have been accustomed entirely removed?"*

*To many intelligent soldiers and some of the officers the conditions were so discouraging, the gloom so **impenetrable**, that they*

Apprehensions: Fears.

Civil authorities: Political officials.

Chaotic: Extremely disorganized.

Daunt: Frighten.

Appall: Horrify.

Stoutest: Most courageous.

Circulating medium: Currency.

Rendered: Made.

Commodities: Belongings.

Security: A pledge for repayment.

Denuded: Stripped.

Implements: Tools.

Cultivation: Use as farm land.

Assurance: Guarantee.

Emancipated: Freed.

Impenetrable: Impossible to understand.

seriously discussed the **advisability** of leaving the country and beginning life anew in some other land.

While recognizing the **dire extremity** which confronted us, I was inclined to take a more hopeful view of the future. I therefore spoke to the Southern soldiers on the field at Appomattox, in order to **check** as best I could their **disposition** to leave the country, and to **counteract**, if possible, the paralyzing effect of the overwhelming discouragements which met them on every side.

As we reached the designated point, the **arms** were stacked and the battle-flags were folded. Those sad and suffering men, many of them weeping as they saw the old banners laid upon the stacked guns like **trappings** on the coffin of their dead hopes, at once gathered in compact mass around me. Sitting on my horse in the midst of them, I spoke to them for the last time as their commander. In all my past life I had never **undertaken** to speak where my own emotions were so literally overwhelming. I **counselled** such course of action as I believed most **conducive** to the welfare of the South and of the whole country. I told them of my own grief, which almost **stifled utterance**, and that I realized most **keenly** the sorrow that was breaking their hearts, and appreciated fully the countless and **stupendous** barriers across the paths they were to tread.

Reminding them of the **benign** Southern climate, of the **fertility** of their lands, of the vastly increased demand for the South's great **staple** and the high prices paid for it, I offered these facts as **legitimate** bases of hope and encouragement. I said to them that through the **rifts** in the clouds then above us I could see the hand of Almighty God stretched out to help us in the **impending** battle with **adversity**; that He would guide us in the gloom, and bless every manly effort to bring back to desolated homes the sunshine and comforts of former years. I told them the principles for which they had so grandly fought and uncomplainingly suffered were not lost,—could not be lost,—for they were the principles on which the Fathers had built the Republic, and that the very throne of **Jehovah** was pledged that truth should triumph and liberty live. As to the thought of their leaving the country, that must be abandoned. It was their duty as patriots to remain and work for the **recuperation** of our stricken section with the same courage, energy, and devotion with which they had fought for her in war. I urged them to enter cheerfully and hopefully upon the tasks imposed by the fortunes of war, obeying the laws, and giving, as I knew they would, the same loyal support to the general Government which they had yielded to

Advisability: Wisdom.

Dire extremity: Most terrible situation.

Check: Block.

Disposition: Inclination.

Counteract: Act against.

Arms: Guns.

Trappings: Decorative coverings.

Undertaken: Tried.

Counselled: Advised.

Conducive: Likely to lead.

Stifled utterance: Left me speechless.

Keenly: Deeply, strongly.

Stupendous: Astonishing.

Benign: Favorable.

Fertility: Ability to produce.

Staple: Main crop, such as cotton.

Legitimate: Reasonable.

Rifts: Openings.

Impending: Imminent.

Adversity: Difficulty.

Jehovah: God.

Recuperation: Recovery.

the Confederacy. I closed with a prophecy that **passion** would speedily die, and that the brave and **magnanimous** soldiers of the Union army, when disbanded and scattered among the people, would become promoters of sectional peace and **fraternity**....

As the Confederates were taking leave of Appomattox, and about to begin their long and dreary **tramp** homeward, many of the Union men **bade** them **cordial** farewell. One of Grant's men said good-naturedly to one of Lee's veterans:

"Well, **Johnny**, I guess you fellows will go home now to stay."

The tired and **tried** Confederate, who did not clearly understand the spirit in which these playful words were spoken, and who was not at the moment in the best mood for **badinage,** replied:

"Look here, Yank; you guess, do you, that we fellows are going home to stay? Maybe we are. But don't be giving us any of your **impudence.** If you do, we'll come back and **lick** you again."

Passion: Intense emotions.

Magnanimous: Generous.

Fraternity: Brotherhood.

Tramp: Hike.

Bade: Expressed.

Cordial: Friendly.

Johnny: Generic name for a soldier.

Tried: Tested.

Badinage: Teasing.

Impudence: Rudeness.

Lick: Whip.

What happened next ...

Most of the soldiers returned to their homes. Unless they had a horse or caught a ride on one of the few still-running trains, they had to make the trip on foot. Some were lucky enough to return to areas untouched by fighting or looting. Some found their former slaves would still work for them, this time as paid employees.

The memoirs of several Southern soldiers say the Reconstruction period that followed was, in many ways, more difficult than the war. Resentment grew among many ex-Confederates as they watched the freed slaves vote, hold elected office, and even go to school as part of the North's plan to rebuild the South. Most Southerners had to take a "loyalty oath" in order to be pardoned, or forgiven, for participating in the "rebellion." They had to pay higher taxes to rebuild the roads and cities ruined by the war. Many soured at the thought of their taxes paying for African American schools or going to African American legislators whom, they believed, were incompetent or corrupt.

Jefferson Davis in a Dress?

In the weeks after Southern troops surrendered to the North, Confederate president Jefferson Davis (1808–1889) became a fugitive—a man on the run. Many Northerners wanted to see him charged with treason, the crime of betraying one's country. Davis fled the Confederate capital of Richmond, Virginia, and headed west, possibly to join the effort to recreate the Confederacy in Texas. Union troops followed him, and a $100,000 reward was offered for Davis's capture, as President Andrew Johnson (1808–1875; served 1865–69) suspected Davis was involved in the assassination of Abraham Lincoln (1809–1865), a charge that later turned out to be untrue.

Union troops surrounded Davis's camp near Irwinsville, Georgia, early on the morning of May 10, 1865. In his book, *The Capture of Jefferson Davis,* Colonel Henry Harnden (1823–1900), commander of the First Wisconsin Cavalry, described Davis as a "tall, elderly, and rather dignified-looking gentleman" who surrendered without a fight. Davis's wife, four children, and several other Confederate officials were also taken into custody.

Harnden wrote that Davis had been awakened by the approaching soldiers, quickly threw on his wife's shawl, and stepped outside his tent to see what was happening. A couple of soldiers saw

Davis wearing the women's garment. The description of Davis's clothing quickly became exaggerated as the story of his capture spread through the North. Political cartoons showed Davis wearing a dress and a bonnet. Some soldiers told wild stories about Davis trying to escape while dressed as an old lady. In the transcript of a speech given to the Loyal Legion of Connecticut (now published on the Web site of the 7th Pennsylvania Cavalry Descendents Association), Colonel C. L. Greeno described how "the cloak of the old lady caught on a bush, which lifted it just enough to disclose a pair of cavalry boots and spurs.... Davis threw off his disguise" and surrendered.

The descriptions of Davis fleeing in women's clothing became a powerful image of the desperate, defeated South. But the story was not true, according to Harnden. "When I saw him, (Davis) wore a common slouched hat, fine boots, no spurs, coat and trousers of light-blue English broadcloth," Harnden wrote in his book. Davis was eventually taken to Fort Monroe, Virginia, and charged with treason in 1866, but the case never went to trial. Shortly before the end of his term, Johnson pardoned Davis and other ex-Confederates through the Christmas Day presidential proclamation of 1868.

The bitterness of many Southerners was summed up in the lyrics to the song "O, I'm a Good Old Rebel," reprinted in *The Confederate War:*

Three hundred thousand Yankees is
stiff in Southern dust

We got three hundred thousand before they conquered us.

They died of Southern fever and
Southern steel and shot

I wish they was three million instead
of what we got.

I can't take up my musket and fight
them now no more,

But I ain't gonna love them, now
that is certain sure.

And I don't want no pardon for
what I was and am

I won't be reconstructed, and I don't
care a damn.

Did you know ...

- The Confederacy created its own form of paper money, but as that government crumbled, the money became almost worthless. At one point, it took $60 or $70 in Confederate money to equal one gold dollar.

John Brown Gordon. *The Library of Congress.*

- In the South alone, half of the white men of military age were killed or maimed (disfigured or handicapped) by the war.

- Gordon became a prominent Georgia politician after the war. He served as U.S. senator (1873–80, 1891–97) and governor (1886–90). He was shot in the face at the Battle of Antietam in 1862, the bloodiest day of the Civil War, and collapsed face-first into his cap. He later claimed the only thing that kept him from drowning in his blood was another bullet hole in the cap from earlier that day, which allowed the blood to flow out.

- Determined to preserve the memory of the Confederacy's so-called "Lost Cause," many Southern white women formed groups to maintain soldiers' graves, build monuments, and organize events honoring their war heroes. In many Southern states, the birthdays of Lee and

The capture of Jefferson Davis, May 10, 1865, at Irwinsville, Georgia. Davis was misreported as wearing a woman's dress when captured. *The Library of Congress.*

Jefferson Davis (1808–1889), the first and only president of the Confederacy, became official holidays.

Consider the following ...

- What did the freedom for African Americans mean for Southern whites?

- Why did some Confederates consider moving to Mexico or South America at the end of the war? Why did General Gordon think it was better for the soldiers to stay?

- What caused the looting after the war ended?

For More Information

Eggleston, George Cary. *A Rebel's Recollections.* New York: Hurd and Houghton; Cambridge: Riverside Press, 1875. Reprint, Baton Rouge: Louisiana State University Press, 1996.

Ford, Arthur Peronneau, and Marion Johnstone Ford. "Life in the Confederate Army." *Documenting the American South: University of North Carolina at Chapel Hill Libraries.* http://docsouth.unc.edu/ford/ford.html (accessed on September 14, 2004).

Gallagher, Gary W. *The Confederate War.* Cambridge, MA: Harvard University Press, 1997.

Gordon, John Brown. *Reminiscences of the Civil War.* New York: Charles Scribner's Sons, 1903. Reprint, Baton Rouge: Louisiana State University Press, 1993. Also available at *Documenting the American South: University of North Carolina at Chapel Hill Libraries.* http://docsouth.unc.edu/gordon/gordon.html (accessed on September 14, 2004).

Greeno, Col. C. L. "The Capture of Jefferson Davis." *The Sabre Regiment: 7th Pennsylvania Cavalry.* http://personal.lig.bellsouth.net/7/t/7th-pa-cavalry/davis.htm (accessed on September 14, 2004).

Harnden, Henry. *The Capture of Jefferson Davis.* Madison, WI: Tracy, Gibbs & Co., 1898.

Trudeau, Noah Andre. *Out of the Storm: The End of the Civil War, April–June 1865.* Boston: Little, Brown and Company, 1994.

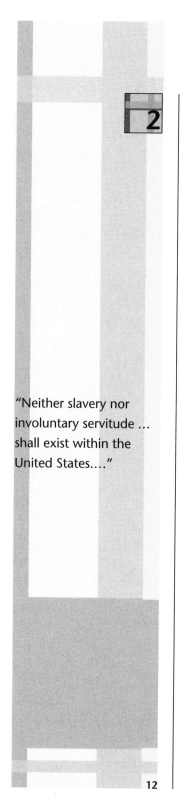

2 Thirteenth Amendment to the U.S. Constitution

Ratified by the required three-fourths of states on December 18, 1865

Reprinted on *GPO Access: Constitution of the United States* (Web site)

Slavery is outlawed in the United States

"Neither slavery nor involuntary servitude ... shall exist within the United States...."

The most obvious result of the American Civil War (1861–65) was the elimination of slavery. But that was not the original goal of President Abraham Lincoln (1809–1865; served 1861–65) and it was not achieved all at once. The end to forced labor came in phases, as Lincoln and Congress adopted measures to take slaves away from the Confederacy and enlist African Americans in the Northern effort to win the war.

Lincoln had always hated slavery, but at first he did not think the federal government could eliminate a form of servitude that had been preserved in the Constitution, the document establishing the country's legal framework. In creating the congressional districts based on population, the authors of the Constitution decided in 1787 that each slave should count as three-fifths of a person, a concept known as the "three-fifths compromise." This deal pleased Southerners, who wanted slaves counted because they would boost the number of congressional seats in the South; and it satisfied Northerners, who did not think slaves should count as full people because they did not vote or pay taxes. The compro-

The Emancipation Proclamation, as depicted by painter A. A. Lamb.
© Francis G. Mayer/Corbis.

mise was firmly fixed in the Constitution—proof that slavery was not only legal when the country was founded, but that early leaders had created a legal concept of African Americans as inferior people.

When the intensifying debate over slavery prompted the Southern states to pull out of the Union in 1861 and form the Confederate States of America, Lincoln clearly stated that his goal was to unify the country. At first he did not talk of freeing the slaves, as he feared it would make the South less likely to rejoin the Union. But as the war dragged on, Lincoln realized most Southerners were unlikely to surrender. In the meantime, the Confederacy had the strength of millions of slaves digging trenches, building forts, and tilling the fields (working the soil), freeing the hands of more white men to serve as soldiers. As noted in *African Americans and Civil Rights,* Northerners increasingly believed "that Southerners should pay the price of secession [leaving the Union] by losing their slaves" and "that ex-slaves then should share the burden of battle."

After the Emancipation Proclamation, newly freed African American slaves headed toward Union lines during the Civil War. *The Library of Congress.*

Congress passed the First Confiscation Act in 1861, allowing Union troops to take any property (including slaves) helping the Confederate cause. Although the act still treated slaves as property, it gave African Americans the hope of freedom if they were taken by Union troops. Congress passed the Second Confiscation Act in 1862, freeing the slaves belonging to anyone supporting the Southern "rebellion" against the North. Lincoln followed with the Emancipation Proclamation on January 1, 1863, which freed all three million slaves in the Confederacy—but not in Maryland, Delaware, Kentucky, Missouri, and West Virginia, the border states that had stayed in the Union. Lincoln did not want to alienate those loyal states by including their one million slaves in the Emancipation Proclamation.

The North had little power to enforce the Emancipation Proclamation, as it applied to the Southern states that considered themselves a separate country. But the promise of freedom inspired thousands of slaves to escape to the North

Reconstruction Era: Primary Sources

to help the Union win the war. At this time the North opened its military ranks to African Americans, a historic move. According to *African Americans and Civil Rights,* of the 108,000 African Americans who served in the Union army during the war, about three-fourths came from slave states. Other ex-slaves built roads, bridges, and forts for the North. Fugitives such as William A. Jackson, the carriage driver for Confederate president Jefferson Davis (1808–1889), provided valuable information to the North about the South's military plans and assets.

A year before the war ended, Congress drafted the Thirteenth Amendment to the Constitution to permanently outlaw slavery. Adding a new rule, or amendment, to the Constitution is a two-step process. At least two-thirds of the Senate and the House of Representatives must vote in favor of the amendment. Then it must be ratified, or approved, by at least three-fourths of the state governments. The Thirteenth Amendment passed in the Senate on April 8, 1864, but the House of Representatives could not gather a two-thirds majority to approve it. Republican members of Congress spent months trying to convince their Democratic opponents that the public supported an end to slavery. When the House of Representatives took another vote on January 31, 1865, the amendment passed 199 to 56—with just two votes over the two-thirds majority needed to pass. African Americans gathered at the Capitol for this historic vote hugged each other and cried tears of joy, as noted in *Ordeal by Fire.* Republicans cheered and congratulated each other. The members of the House voted to take the rest of the day off in honor of the important event.

Things to remember while reading the Thirteenth Amendment:

- The end to slavery came in several steps. Congress passed laws during the Civil War allowing the North to take slaves used by Southern troops. In 1863, Lincoln announced the Emancipation Proclamation, which freed slaves in the Confederacy, but not in the states that stayed in the Union. The Thirteenth Amendment to the Constitution finally outlawed slavery completely.

Legislators and visitors celebrate in the House of Representatives after Congress passes the Thirteenth Amendment, which outlawed slavery, on January 31, 1865. *Getty Images.*

• While it was nearly impossible for Union troops to enforce the Emancipation Proclamation in Confederate territory, the promise of freedom inspired thousands of slaves to flee to the North, where they played an important role in winning the war. African Americans joined the Army, built forts and roads for the North, and provided information about the South to military leaders, all with the hope that a Union victory would mean an end to slavery.

• The Constitution is the legal framework for the U.S. government. Until the passage of the Thirteenth Amendment, reprinted here from the *GPO Access: Constitution of the United States* Web site, the Constitution legally recognized slavery under the "three-fifths compromise," a provision that counted each slave as three-fifths of a person when creating congressional districts based on population.

Thirteenth Amendment to the U.S. Constitution

*Section 1. Neither slavery nor **involuntary servitude**, except as punishment for crime whereof the party shall have been **duly convicted**, shall exist within the United States, or any place subject to their **jurisdiction**.*

*Section 2. Congress shall have the power to enforce this **article** by appropriate legislation.*

Involuntary servitude: Forced labor.

Duly convicted: Found guilty after a trial.

Jurisdiction: Authority.

Article: Provision of the Constitution.

What happened next ...

Every Northern state but New Jersey approved the Thirteenth Amendment in the spring of 1865. The border states of Maryland, Missouri, and West Virginia ratified it; but Kentucky and Delaware did not. Other Southern states approved the amendment before the end of the year as part of the requirements to return to the Union as set forth by President Andrew Johnson (1808–1875; served 1865–69). But they did so grudgingly: Alabama amended its state constitution to say it would not give Congress "the power to legislate upon the political status [rights] of freedmen [freed slaves] in this state," according to *Black Voices from Reconstruction*. Mississippi outlawed slavery in its state constitution, but rejected the Thirteenth Amendment on the grounds that it could give Congress an excuse to interfere with state decisions on African Americans' rights. Even with such protests, the measure ending slavery officially became part of the Constitution on December 18, 1865.

In the meantime, the surrender of the Confederate troops in April 1865 also signaled an end of slavery, as the Union would now enforce Lincoln's Emancipation Proclamation. Congress created the Freedmen's Bureau (see Chapter 4) to help African Americans make the transition to freedom. Former slaves left plantations by the thousands to search for

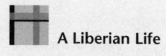

A Liberian Life

For decades before and after the Civil War, some of the freed slaves left America for a land of their own: Liberia. The small country on Africa's west coast started as a colony in the 1820s where ex-slaves could set up their own society. The theory, shared by the U.S. whites who founded the colony, was that African Americans would succeed faster in their own country than in a white America (although many African Americans preferred to stay in the states). In reality, however, Liberia would travel down a similar racist path as the United States.

The colony, named for the liberty it offered African Americans, passed a constitution and other laws in 1825 prohibiting slavery or any participation in the slave trade. Its early ties to America were strong. It modeled its declaration of independence and its flag after those of the United States. The capital city of Monrovia was named after the fifth U.S. president, James Monroe (1758–1831; served 1817–25). Virginia, Maryland, and Mississippi established settlements in Liberia for some former slaves. In some cases prior to the Civil War, slaves were only freed if they agreed to move to Liberia.

Over time, two distinct groups emerged: the Americo-Liberians, who were the freed slaves from America, and native Africans from neighboring areas. The Americo-Liberians forced the natives to work on their plantations and sometimes sold those workers to other countries. They also drafted discriminatory laws, much like the ones the ex-slaves faced in America: The natives could not vote or attend school, and they were restricted to inferior hospitals and less-desirable jobs.

Many of those restrictions were lifted by the mid-1900s, but decades of tension between different factions led to a bloody coup (overthrow of the government) in 1980, followed by a civil war from 1989 to 1996. After the war, much of the country lacked decent roads, jobs, or medical care, and various groups struggled for control of the government. Even then, many Liberians pointed to slavery as the heart of their problems. "We cannot blame the Americans for teaching us slavery," Liberian community leader Mary Brunell told the *Christian Science Monitor*. "As for America," she said, "we could have taken the best from them. We took the worst. We could have risen above slavery, but we didn't, and that is the crux [source] of our problems."

lost relatives, visit new places, or find better jobs in the cities. But they were not entirely free. Union major-general Francis J. Herron (1837–1902) feared this mass departure of African Americans from the plantations would leave the season's crops to die, creating starvation for thousands and financial ruin for an already-devastated South. In a June 11, 1865, proclamation for the Northern Division of Louisiana, Herron required all ex-slaves to stay with their former masters through the end of the crop season. "If found wandering about the country or gathering at military posts they will be arrested and punished," read Herron's order, which was reprinted in *Out of the Storm*.

African Americans would face a tough road toward equality. As soon as the war freed the slaves, communities throughout the South limited African Americans' rights through a series of local rules called "Black Codes." The rules allowed African Americans to marry, to buy and sell property, and to bring lawsuits against each other. In many communities, however, the laws also required African Americans to get their employers' permission before going into town or receiving guests at the plantation. African Americans could be arrested for being out too late, or even for being unemployed. No longer able to control African Americans as slaves, Southern whites tried to restrict their activities through laws.

Antislavery advocates such as U.S. representative Thaddeus Stevens (1792–1868) of Pennsylvania, as well as African American community leaders, realized former slaves needed economic independence in order to be truly free. Without their own land, many African Americans were still dependent for work and shelter on the plantation owners who once enslaved them. Baptist preacher Garrison Frazier led a group of twenty ex-slaves who met in 1865 with Secretary of War Edwin Stanton (1814–1869) in Savannah, Georgia, to discuss this concern. "The way we can best take care of ourselves is to have land, and turn it and till it by our own labor ... and we can soon maintain ourselves and have something to spare," Frazier said, as noted in *Black Voices from Reconstruction*. "We want to be placed on land until we are able to buy it and make it our own."

Did you know ...

- Lincoln sent a proposal to the Delaware legislature in November 1861 to gradually free that state's slaves over a period of thirty years. Under this plan, the federal government would have paid slave owners for part of the value of their slaves. The plan was one of Lincoln's early efforts to end slavery without alienating the slaveholding states. But the idea fizzled as the ongoing Civil War required a more immediate answer to the slavery issue.

- Historians estimate about twelve million Africans were placed on slave ships bound for the Americas from the late 1400s to the early 1800s, but only 5 percent of those slaves came to the United States. The vast majority went to Brazil and the Caribbean, where the hot climate and back-breaking work conditions on sugar and rice plantations led to shorter life spans. By comparison, the U.S. plantations produced less labor-intensive crops, such as cotton and tobacco, in a cooler climate. This allowed American slaves to live longer lives and have families— and by 1825, one-third of all slaves in the Western Hemisphere were in the United States.

- The North drew African Americans into the Army as part of its strategy to win the Civil War, but it did not give them the same pay as white soldiers until 1864. Prior to that, white soldiers received $13 a month plus clothing, while African American soldiers received $10 a month, from which $3 was deducted to pay for their clothing.

- Recognizing that African Americans helped turn the tide for the North, the Confederate Congress voted in March 1865 to bring slaves into its Southern army. But the plan came too late. The war ended a month later, before any of the soldier slaves could be used.

Consider the following ...

- Why did it take several years—and several gradual measures from Lincoln and Congress—before slavery was outlawed?

- Do you think the outcome of the Civil War would have been different if the North had not used African American soldiers, or if the South had tried to use them sooner?

- Once they were freed from slavery, what obstacles did African Americans face on the road to equality?

For More Information

Harman, Danna. "Liberia: From Oasis of Freedom to Ongoing Civil War." *Christian Science Monitor* (June 12, 2002): p. 7.

Levine, Michael L. *African Americans and Civil Rights: From 1619 to the Present.* Phoenix: Oryx Press, 1996.

McPherson, James M. *Ordeal by Fire: The Civil War and Reconstruction.* New York: Alfred A. Knopf, 1982.

Smith, John David. *Black Voices from Reconstruction.* Gainesville: University Press of Florida, 1997.

Trudeau, Noah Andre. *Out of the Storm: The End of the Civil War, April–June 1865.* Boston: Little, Brown and Company, 1994.

United States Government Printing Office. "Thirteenth Amendment— Slavery and Involuntary Servitude." *GPO Access: Constitution of the United States.* http://www.gpoaccess.gov/constitution/html/amdt13.html (accessed on September 20, 2004).

Louis Hughes

Excerpt from Thirty Years a Slave

Describing events in 1865; published in 1897; reprinted on
Documenting the American South **(Web site)**

Reminiscences from a long-time slave

"We knew it was our right to be free ... yet they still held us...."

Four million slaves were freed by the American Civil War (1861–65), but their bondage did not end the instant Confederate troops surrendered in April 1865. In some pockets of the rural South, white men continued to keep African Americans as slaves for months after the war until Union troops liberated, or freed, them. Other plantation owners simply hired their former slaves to do their old jobs for meager pay, until the Freedmen's Bureau, a federal agency created to help exslaves, stepped in and required better terms of employment. Still other landowners created "sharecropping" arrangements with ex-slaves: The whites provided the land and farming equipment, the African Americans provided the labor, and the two split the value of the crop at the end of the year. While the deal sounded attractive at first, some African Americans ended up financially trapped. Sometimes the landowner would tell his sharecroppers that they owed him money at the end of the season—for food, clothing, medical care, and other supplies—so they would have to stay the next season to work off the debt. For the unlucky ones, the debt became a deeper hole from which they struggled to emerge.

The lucky ones found themselves in Union-controlled territory, where ex-slaves were given land to build homes and raise their own crops. Union general William T. Sherman (1820–1891) issued an order January 16, 1865, seizing all land within 30 miles of the coast of the Carolinas and northern Florida, then dividing it among African Americans, up to 40 acres per family. The Army also provided leftover mules to help African Americans plow their new farmlands. This promise of "40 acres and a mule" spread quickly through the South, as former slaves dreamed of starting their new life.

But the deal would not last. After the war ended, the white landowners returned to those lands. Many received pardons from President Andrew Johnson (1808–1875; served 1865–69), entitling them to take their property back. Johnson also gave a series of orders in August 1865 that required the military to return the confiscated Confederate land to its previous owners. In his 1866 book, *The South: A Tour of Its Battlefields and Ruined Cities,* Northern journalist John Townsend

Slaves working on the James Hopkins plantation, Edisto, South Carolina. *Getty Images.*

The Sea Islands Experiment

The war brought freedom to some slaves sooner than others—in some cases, years sooner. Slaves on the Sea Islands of South Carolina gained their freedom in November 1861, as their masters fled before a Union attack. Most of the ten thousand African Americans remained on the islands, protected by Northern troops, and created their own communities. In his book *After the War: A Southern Tour,* Northerner Whitelaw Reid observed:

> On [the island of] St. Helena, and wherever else they have had the opportunity, the negroes have bought the titles to their little farms—or "plantations," as they still ambitiously [hopefully] style them. They have erected their own cabins, secured whatever cheap furniture they contain, and clothed themselves far better than their masters ever clothed them. All who have been established [working] more than a year, have paid back to the Government the rations [supplies] drawn in their first destitution [state of poverty]....

> In the houses, chairs have made their appearance; dishes and knives and forks are no longer the rarities they were when our troops arrived.

The Sea Islands provided a unique freedom experiment, and everyone from reporters to government officials visited the communities to see how African Americans would fare. As noted in *Reconstruction: America's Unfinished Revolution,* many preferred to plant food instead of cotton, a cash crop that had made their masters rich but never fed them. By 1866, however, many of the crops had failed and African Americans could not feed their families. In the meantime, U.S. government officials seized much of the islands for unpaid taxes, and the land fell into the hands of Army officers, other officials, and sometimes the previous plantation owners. As in much of the South, African Americans would struggle to get by.

Trowbridge described an African American man in Hampton, Virginia, who built his home and blacksmith shop on a half-acre seized from its Confederate owner during the war.

> He [the African American man] was doing very well until the owner of the soil appeared, with the President's pardon, and orders to have his property restored to him. The land was worth twenty dollars an acre. He [the previous owner] told the blacksmith that he could remain where he was, by paying twenty-four dollars a year rent for his half acre. "I am going to leave," said the poor man, quietly, and without uttering a complaint.

As noted in *The Struggle for Equality,* a different African American man who made his home on the South Carolina

Sea Islands said: "To turn us off from the land that the Government has allowed us to occupy, is nothing less than returning us to involuntary [forced] servitude" (see box).

Hundreds of thousands of African Americans fled the plantations and flooded the Union military bases and occupied cities. They looked for jobs. Some headed to the North in search of better opportunities. Many looked for lost family members who had been sold off years ago. Newspapers filled with ads like this one from the *Nashville Colored Tennesseean*, reprinted in *Black Voices from Reconstruction*:

> $200 Reward. During the year 1849, Thomas Sample carried away from this city, as his slaves, our daughter, Polly, and son, Geo. Washington, to the state of Mississippi, and subsequently [afterward], to Texas, and when last heard from they were in Lagrange, Texas. We will give $100 each for them to any person who will assist them, or either of them, to get to Nashville, or get word to us of their whereabouts, if they are alive. Ben & Flora East.

African Americans harvesting cotton at Port Royal, South Carolina. After the war, ex-slaves often preferred working on crops other than cotton, since cotton was such a fierce symbol of slavery. *© Corbis.*

Like scores of other ex-slaves, Louis Hughes would spend the years after the war searching for long-lost relatives, such as his brother, Billy, and the mother of his wife, Matilda. But first he faced a larger obstacle: escaping from the owner who still held him as a slave, months after the war had supposedly freed him. A house servant born in Virginia, Hughes had tried to escape Edmund McGee's Memphis home and Mississippi plantations four previous times, only to get caught and beaten by his master. But now the war was over. He knew he was entitled to freedom, and he was determined this time to get it.

Things to remember while reading an excerpt from *Thirty Years a Slave:*

- The North declared the slaves free when the Civil War ended, but some whites stubbornly held onto their slaves for months after the war, until Union troops came to their area.

- Former slaves left plantations by the thousands and flocked to Union military bases and cities, where they felt safer. They wanted to distance themselves from the farmlands where they had been mistreated. Many started to search for long-lost relatives.

- The rural South held several options for freed slaves. They could work for their former owners for a small wage. They could enter into a "sharecropping" agreement that could place them further in debt, if the landowner charged high prices for food, clothing, farming equipment, and other necessities. Or they could set up their own farm on land confiscated from the Confederates—until the white landowners came back and reclaimed their property. Faced with those options, some African Americans headed instead for the cities, particularly in the North, where they hoped to find better opportunities.

Excerpt from Thirty Years a Slave

Ever since the beginning of the war, and the slaves had heard that possibly they might some time be free, they seemed unspeakably *happy. They were afraid to let the masters know that they ever thought of such a thing, and they never dreamed of speaking about it except among themselves. They were a happy race, poor souls! notwithstanding their **downtrodden** condition. They would laugh and chat about freedom in their cabins; and many a little rhyme about it originated among them, and was softly sung over their work....*

*We had remained at old Jack's [plantation in Panola, Mississippi, belonging to their master's father] until June, 1865, and had tried to be **content**. The Union soldiers were still **raiding** all through that section. Every day some town would be taken, and the slaves would [secretly] rejoice. After we came back from Alabama we were held with a tighter **rein** than ever. We were not allowed to go outside of the premises. George Washington, a fellow servant, and Kitty, his wife, and I had talked considerably about the Yankees, and how we might get away. We knew it was our right to be free, for the [Emancipation] proclamation had long been issued—yet they still held us. I did not talk much to my wife about going away, as she was always so afraid I would be killed, and did not want me to try any more to escape. But George, his wife and I continued to discuss the matter, whenever we had a chance. We knew that Memphis was headquarters for the Union troops, but how to reach it was the great question....*

*It was Sunday afternoon, June 26th, 1865, when George and I, having made ready for the start for the **Union lines,** went to bid our wives good-bye. I told my wife to cheer up, as I was coming again to get her. I said to Kitty, George's wife: "We are going, but look for us again. It will not be with us as with so many others, who have gone away, leaving their families and never returning for them. We will be here again." She looked up at me, smiling, and with a look of **resolution,** said: "I'll be ready." She was of a firm, daring nature—I did not fear to tell her all my plans. As my wife was so **timid,** I said as little as possible to her. George and I hurriedly said our farewells to our wives. The parting was **heart-rending,** for we knew the dangers were great, and the chances were almost even that we should not meet again....*

We crept through the orchard, passing through farm after farm until we struck the railroad, about seven miles from home. We followed this road until we reached Senatobia, about half past seven in the evening. We felt good, and, stopping all night, we started the next morning for Hernando, Miss., another small town, and reached there at two o'clock in the afternoon. The most of the bridges had

Downtrodden: Oppressed.

Content: Satisfied.

Raiding: Attacking or invading.

Rein: Restraint.

Union lines: Area controlled by Northern troops.

Resolution: Determination.

Timid: Fearful.

Heart-rending: Causing much grief.

A barge carrying African American refugees and their belongings passes through the ruins of Richmond shortly after the end of the Civil War in April 1865. *The Library of Congress.*

Flat cars: Railroad cars without walls or a roof.

Scarcely: Hardly.

Making inquiries: Asking for information.

Thence: Then.

been burned, by the troops, and there were no regular railroad trains. Fortunately, however, **flat cars**, drawn by horses were run over the road; and on a train of this kind we took passage....

We at last reached Memphis, arriving about seven o'clock Monday evening. The city was filled with slaves, from all over the south, who cheered and gave us a welcome. I could **scarcely** recognize Memphis, things were so changed. We met numbers of our fellow servants who had run away before us, when the war began. Tuesday and Wednesday we spent in **making inquiries**.... Thursday we went to see Col. Walker, a Union officer, who looked after the colored folks, and saw that they had their rights. When we reached his office we found it so filled with people, waiting to see him, that we were delayed about two hours, before we had an opportunity of speaking with him. When our turn came, we went in, and told him that we were citizens of Memphis until the fall of Fort Pillow and Donelson, when our master had run us off, with a hundred other slaves, into Mississippi, and **thence** to the salt works in Alabama.... After a few minutes, I said: "Colonel, we want protection to go back to Mississippi after our wives, who are still held as slaves." He replied: "You are both free men to go and come as you please." "Why," said I, "Colonel, if we go back to Mississippi they will shoot the **gizzards** out of us." "Well," said he, "I can not grant your request. I would be overrun with similar applications; but I will tell you what you can do. There are hundreds of just such men as you want, who would be glad of such a **scout**." We thanked him and left....

[In exchange for a bottle of whiskey, a Union soldier tells Louis about two soldiers who might take him and George back to the plantation to get their wives. Louis and George find the two soldiers, who agree to the trip, although it must be keep secret from their commanding officer.] We gave them each ten dollars; and promised, if they brought us out safely, to give each ten dollars more. It was now about half-past eleven o'clock. They had to go to camp, and slip their horses out cautiously, so as not to be seen by the captain. In half an hour we were on our way.... After a long and weary ride we reached old Master Jack's a little after sundown [the following day]. The soldiers rode into the yard ahead of us, and the first person they met was a servant (Frank) at the woodpile. They said to him: "Go in and tell your master, Mr. McGee, to come out, we want to see him," at the same time asking for Louis' and George's wives. Young William McGee [the son of owner Edmund McGee] came out and the soldiers said to him: "We want **feed** for seventy-five **head** of horses." McGee said: "We have not got it." .... [While the soldiers distracted McGee, Louis and George drove their wagon to their wives' cabin.] Kitty met us at the door and said: "I am all ready." She was looking for us. We **commenced** loading our wagon with our few things.... My wife, Aunt Kitty and nine other servants followed the wagon. I waited for a few moments for Mary Ellen, sister of my wife; and as she came running out of the white folks' house, she said to her **mistress**, Mrs. Farrington: "Good-bye; I wish you good luck." "I wish you all the bad luck," said she [Mrs. Farrington, Edmund McGee's sister-in-law] in a rage....

We arrived in Memphis on the Fourth of July, 1865. My first effort as a freeman was to get something to do to sustain myself and wife and a babe of a few months, that was born at the salt works. I succeeded in getting a room for us, and went to work the second day driving a public carriage. I made enough to keep us and pay our room rent. By our **economy** we managed to get on very well. I worked on, hoping to go further north, feeling somehow that it would be better for us there; when, one day I ran across a man who knew my wife's mother. He said to me: "Why, your wife's mother

Gizzards: Guts.

Scout: Spy.

Feed: Food.

Head: Individual units.

Commenced: Started.

Mistress: Female master.

Economy: Thriftiness.

*went back up the river to Cincinnati. I knew her well and the people to whom she belonged." This information made us eager to take steps to find her. My wife was naturally anxious to follow the clue thus obtained, in hopes of finding her mother, whom she had not seen since the separation at Memphis years before.... On arriving at Cincinnati, our first inquiry was about her, my wife giving her name and description; and, fortunately, we came upon a colored man who said he knew of a woman answering to the name and description which my wife gave of her mother, and he directed us to the house where she was stopping. When we reached the place to which we had been directed, my wife not only found her mother but one of her sisters. The meeting was a joyful one to us all. No mortal who has not experienced it can imagine the feeling of those who meet again after long years of enforced separation and hardship and utter ignorance of one another's condition and place of **habitation**....*

Habitation: Living.

What happened next ...

Louis Hughes and his family continued north to Canada, a country he considered "the safest place for refugees from slavery." Over the next decade, he worked in hotels in Windsor, Ontario, Canada; Chicago, Illinois; and Milwaukee, Wisconsin. While in Chicago, Hughes attended a night school for African Americans, finally learning to read and write. After settling in Milwaukee, Hughes got a job working for a doctor, and eventually became a nurse. By word of mouth, Hughes learned his brother, Billy, was working at a hotel in Cleveland, Ohio. The two brothers, who had been auctioned off to different owners as young boys, had a joyful reunion. "As we related our varied experiences—the hardships, the wrongs, and sorrows which we endured and at last the coming of brighter days, we were sad, then happy," Hughes wrote.

Some African Americans had happier endings than others in the years after the Civil War. Some would scrape together their savings (money saved from selling garden vegetables, chickens, and livestock they raised on the side as slaves) to buy land and become independent farmers. Some

African Americans working near their home over a decade after the end of the Civil War. *Valentine Richmond History Center. Reproduced by permission.*

would run for political office and help shape the new laws providing free education and better opportunities for African Americans. Some would find family members after decades of separation. But others would struggle to make a living for their former masters, or suffer attacks at the hands of racist whites. Former slave Norvel Blair wrote *Book for the People!* in 1880, which described how dishonest whites in Illinois—including his own attorney—tried to trick him out of his life's savings through a series of unfair contracts. "I have gone from the lower courts to the higher courts.... I am going to go on til I see if a colored man has any rights before the law," a frustrated Blair wrote.

Did you know ...

- Sherman's order dividing property among former slaves put about 40,000 African American families on about 485,000 acres. But those families were kicked off the land under President Johnson's orders when the previous owners returned.

• A Confederate colonel from Tennessee, P. H. Anderson, wrote to one of his escaped slaves in 1865 asking him to return as a paid employee. The ex-slave, Jourdon Anderson, replied that he would consider the offer if the colonel would pay him and his wife, Mandy, for their years of service as slaves. "At $25 a month for me, and $2 a week for Mandy, our earnings would amount to $11,680," Anderson wrote in a letter reprinted in *Black Voices from Reconstruction*. "Add to this the interest for the time our wages has been kept and deduct what you paid for our clothing and three doctors visits to me, and pulling a tooth for Mandy, and the balance will show what we are in justice entitled to...." The colonel refused the offer.

Consider the following ...

• Why were some African Americans not free the moment the Civil War ended?

• How did some African Americans search for lost relatives after the war? How do those methods compare with ways of looking for people today?

• What do you think the government should have done with the land that belonged to Confederates before the war: Return it to the former slaveholders, or divide it among the former slaves? Why?

For More Information

Blair, Norvel. "Book for the People!" *Documenting the American South: University of North Carolina at Chapel Hill Libraries.* http://doc south.unc.edu/neh/blair/frontis.html (accessed on September 15, 2004).

Foner, Eric. *Reconstruction: America's Unfinished Revolution.* New York: HarperCollins, 1988.

Hughes, Louis. *Thirty Years a Slave: From Bondage to Freedom.* Milwaukee: South Side Printing Company, 1897. Reprint, Montgomery, AL: NewSouth Books, 2002. Also available at *Documenting the American South: University of North Carolina at Chapel Hill Libraries.* http://doc

south.unc.edu/hughes/menu.html (accessed on September 21, 2004).

McPherson, James M. *The Struggle for Equality.* Princeton, NJ: Princeton University Press, 1974.

Reid, Whitelaw. *After the War: A Southern Tour.* New York: Harper & Row, 1965. Also available at *Making of America Books.* http://www.hti.umich.edu/cgi/t/text/text-idx?c=moa;idno=AFJ8942 (accessed on September 15, 2004).

Smith, John David. *Black Voices from Reconstruction.* Gainesville: University Press of Florida, 1997.

Trowbridge, John Townsend. *The South: A Tour of Its Battle-fields and Ruined Cities.* New York: Arno Press, 1969. Also available at *Making of America Books.* http://www.hti.umich.edu/cgi/t/text/text-idx?c=moa;idno=AFJ8852 (accessed on September 15, 2004).

Freedmen's Bureau Act

Enacted by U.S. Congress, approved March 3, 1865
Reprinted on *Freedmen's Bureau Online* (Web site)

A government agency assists the recently freed African Americans

"The Secretary of War may direct such issues of provisions, clothing, and fuel ... for the immediate and temporary shelter and supply of destitute and suffering refugees and freedmen...."

The end of the Civil War (1861–65) brought sudden freedom—and a new kind of hardship—to four million African Americans in the South. The war had ended slavery, but most African Americans faced the overwhelming prospect of starting over without money, the ability to read, or their own plot of farmland. Their former masters had no reason to give them shelter or food, unless they continued to work their old slave jobs. Thousands of African Americans fled the plantations (large estates on which basic crops like cotton, rice, and tobacco were grown) for the cities in search of work. In August 1865, according to *Black Voices from Reconstruction,* a partly literate African American man described the freed slaves in Kansas and Missouri as "all most Thread less & Shoeless without food & no home to go [to.] sevral of there Masters Run them off & as fur as I can see the hole Race will fall back if the U.S. Government dont pervid [provide] for them Some way or ruther."

During the war, Union troops provided food, supplies, and land to African Americans as they gained control of various pockets of the South. Colonel John Eaton

(1829–1906) provided food for about ten thousand poor African Americans in Tennessee and Arkansas, and leased about seven thousand acres of abandoned farmland to some of the one hundred thousand African Americans in his region, African American civil rights leader W. E. B. Du Bois (1868–1963) wrote in *Black Reconstruction in America*. General Nathaniel Banks (1816–1894) compiled records on ninety thousand African Americans in Louisiana, handled complaints, collected taxes, and created a system of free schools for ex-slaves, Du Bois wrote. Northern groups called "Freedmen's Aid Societies" pitched in by sending money, clothing, books, and teachers to the South.

Some of those groups sent petitions to President Abraham Lincoln (1809–1865; served 1861–65) urging him to create a plan, and perhaps an agency, to help African Americans adjust to their new lives. Often they suggested dividing the Confederate-owned plantations into smaller tracts, then leasing the land to former slaves. After a couple

Freed slaves leaving the South. *The Library of Congress.*

of years, African Americans could raise enough money to buy the land. The freed African Americans, or freedmen, would have the land needed to make their own living, and the government would raise money to administer the transitional programs for African Americans.

That idea became the heart of the "Freedmen's Bureau Bill," a measure passed by Congress in March 1865. The act created a new agency in the War Department (now known as the Department of Defense) to handle "all abandoned lands" and "all subjects relating to [white] refugees and freedmen." That included the ability to provide food, clothing, fuel, and even "temporary shelter" to "destitute [needy] and suffering refugees and freedmen and their wives and children." The agency would also help African Americans negotiate fair contracts with their new employers (often their former masters), and it would handle disputes over wages and working conditions. As noted in *Black Voices from Reconstruction,* "Never before had a branch of the U.S. government taken on such a social and humanitarian function."

Congress hoped the leasing and sale of land to African Americans would provide the money for the agency's relief efforts. President Andrew Johnson (1808–1875; served 1865–69), the man who inherited the White House after Lincoln's assassination, had other ideas.

Things to remember while reading the Freedmen's Bureau Act:

- The Civil War freed four million slaves, but many of them had no money, little education, and no land from which to make a living on their own. As soon as they left their former masters, they lost their source of food and shelter.

- As they took control of some parts of the South, Union troops provided food, supplies, and land to African Americans in the area. In some cases, they started schools and settled disputes involving African Americans, functions that would later be handled by the Freedmen's Bureau.

- Congress created the Freedmen's Bureau in March 1865, a month before the war ended, to provide emergency food and shelter to freed slaves. The bureau would lease, and eventually sell, former Confederate land to African Americans. That would give African Americans a way to make their own living, and the money raised from selling the land would pay for running the bureau.

An Act to Establish a Bureau for the Relief of Freedmen and Refugees

*Be it **enacted** by the Senate and House of Representatives of the United States of America in Congress assembled, That there is hereby established in the War Department, to continue during the present war of rebellion, and for one year thereafter, a bureau of refugees, freedmen, and abandoned lands, to which shall be committed, as **hereinafter** provided, the supervision and management of all abandoned lands, and the control of all subjects relating to refugees and freedmen from rebel states, or from any district of country within the territory **embraced** in the operations of the army, under such rules and regulations as may be **prescribed** by the head of the bureau and approved by the President. The said bureau shall be under the management and control of a commissioner to be appointed by the President, by and with the advice and consent of the Senate, whose **compensation** shall be three thousand dollars per **annum**, and such number of clerks as may be assigned to him by the Secretary of War, not exceeding one chief clerk, two of the fourth class, two of the third class, and five of the first class. And the commissioner and all persons appointed under this act, shall, before entering upon their duties, take the oath of office prescribed in an act entitled "An act to prescribe an oath of office, and for other purposes," approved July second, eighteen hundred and sixty-two, and the commissioner and the chief clerk shall, before entering upon their duties, give bonds to the treasurer of the United States, the former in the sum of fifty thousand dollars, and the latter in the sum of ten thousand dollars, **conditioned for** the faithful **discharge** of their duties respectively, with **securities** to be approved as sufficient by the Attorney-General, which bonds shall be filed in the office of the first **comptroller** of the treasury, to be by him put in suit for the benefit of any **injured** party upon any **breach** of the conditions thereof.*

Enacted: Put into law.

Hereinafter: The following.

Embraced: Included.

Prescribed: Ordered.

Compensation: Pay.

Annum: Year.

Conditioned for: Depending on.

Discharge: Performance.

Securities: Money pledged as a guarantee.

Comptroller: Financial chief.

Injured: Wronged.

Breach: Violation.

*Sec. 2. And be it further enacted, That the Secretary of War may direct such issues of **provisions,** clothing, and fuel, as he may **deem** needful for the immediate and temporary shelter and supply of **destitute** and suffering refugees and freedmen and their wives and children, under such rules and regulations as he may direct.*

*Sec. 3. And be it further enacted, That the President may, by and with the advice and consent of the Senate, appoint an assistant commissioner for each of the states declared to be in **insurrection,** not exceeding ten in number, who shall, under the direction of the commissioner, aid in the **execution** of the provisions of this act; and he shall give a bond to the Treasurer of the United States, in the sum of twenty thousand dollars, in the form and manner prescribed in the first section of this act. Each of said commissioners shall receive an annual salary of two thousand five hundred dollars in full compensation for all his services. And any military officer may be **detailed** and assigned to duty under this act without increase of pay or allowances. The commissioner shall, before the **commencement** of each regular session of congress, make full report of his proceedings with exhibits of the state of his accounts to the President, who shall communicate the same to congress, and shall also make special reports whenever required to do so by the President or either house of congress; and the assistant commissioners shall make quarterly reports of their proceedings to the commissioner, and also such other special reports as from time to time may be required.*

*Sec. 4. And be it further enacted, That the commissioner, under the direction of the President, shall have authority to set apart, for the use of loyal refugees and freedmen, such tracts of land within the insurrectionary states as shall have been abandoned, or to which the United States shall have acquired **title** by **confiscation** or sale, or otherwise, and to every male citizen, whether refugee or freedman, as **aforesaid,** there shall be assigned not more than forty acres of such land, and the person to whom it was so assigned shall be protected in the use and enjoyment of the land for the term of three years at an annual rent not exceeding six **per centum** upon the value of such land, as it was **appraised** by the state authorities in the year eighteen hundred and sixty, for the purpose of taxation, and in case no such appraisal can be found, then the rental shall be based upon the estimated value of the land in said year, to be **ascertained** in such manner as the commissioner may by regulation prescribe. At the end of said term, or at any time during said term, the occupants of any parcels so assigned may purchase the land and receive such title thereto as the United States can convey, upon*

Provisions: Supplies.

Deem: Determine.

Destitute: Needy.

Insurrection: Rebellion.

Execution: Carrying out.

Detailed: Placed on special duty.

Commencement: Beginning.

Title: Ownership rights.

Confiscation: Taking.

Aforesaid: Previously mentioned.

Per centum: Percent.

Appraised: Valued.

Ascertained: Determined.

Reconstruction Era: Primary Sources

paying therefor the value of the land, as ascertained and fixed for the purpose of determining the annual rent aforesaid.

*Sec. 5. And be it further enacted, That all acts and parts of acts **inconsistent with** the provisions of this act, are hereby **repealed.***

Approved, March 3, 1865.

What happened next ...

Major General Oliver O. Howard (1830–1909), a Union officer from Maine who fought in Gettysburg and joined in the famed march to the sea led by General William T. Sherman (1820–1891), was appointed head of the Freedmen's Bureau. His agents, mostly former soldiers, distributed food, supplies, and land. From 1865 to 1869, the agents distributed about twenty-one million rations worth more than four million dollars to black and white refugees alike, according to *Black Reconstruction in America.* The agents also drafted hundreds of thousands of contracts between black workers and white employers, setting the hours, wages, and working conditions. When a dispute arose between two African Americans, or an African American and a white, the Freedmen's Bureau usually intervened.

The promise of land for African Americans quickly melted away, however. President Johnson announced that ex-Confederates who took a loyalty oath and received a pardon could reclaim the land they owned before the war. The land that had been set aside for African Americans—some 800,000 acres under the Freedmen's Bureau—was returned to whites. Once again landless, many African Americans returned to plantations as employees who had few more rights than slaves. Under their contracts through the Freedmen's Bureau, African Americans had to be paid and could not be beaten, but they still worked from dawn-to-dusk, six days a week, with only a handful of holidays. Many could not leave the plantation or bring a guest home without their employer's permission.

Some Freedmen's Bureau agents worked hard to help African Americans. For example, when a white farmer fired

Inconsistent with: In opposition to.

Repealed: Overturned.

Oliver Otis Howard, head of the Freedmen's Bureau.

his African American workers to avoid paying them for the season, the bureau would force the farmer to pay what he owed. Oscar J. Dunn (1820–1871), African American lieutenant governor of Louisiana, quoted in *Black Voices from Reconstruction,* told Congress, "The Freedmen's Bureau is a great eyesore to the planters; they do not like it at all."

But other agents used their position to fill their own pockets or further their own goals. Some took the meats and other supplies set aside for African Americans and sold them for profit instead. Others grew sympathetic with the white plantation owners who invited them to dinner and showered them with gifts. Such agents allowed their judgment to be clouded by "the aristocratic Rebel's flattering attentions and the smiles of his fair daughters," Northern journalist John Townsend Trowbridge wrote in his 1866 book, *The South: A Tour of Its Battle-fields and Ruined Cities.* Sidney Andrews, author of the 1866 book *The South Since the War,* was even less impressed with the Freedmen's Bureau commissioner he met in South Carolina:

> He doesn't really intend to outrage the rights of the negroes, but he has very little idea that they have any rights except such as the planters choose to give them. His position, of course, is a difficult one; and he brings to it a head more or less muddled with liquor, a rough and coarse [crude] manner, a dictatorial [bossy] and impatient temper, a most remarkable ability for cursing, and a hearty contempt for [African Americans].

The bureau was unpopular among many whites, in the North and South alike. Southerners saw the bureau as another arm of the Union occupation. Many resented the bureau's efforts to help African Americans, particularly as the agency set up schools to educate African Americans—a step

A Freedman's Education

The Freedmen's Bureau's greatest legacy may be the one thing it was not originally designed to do: Create a public school system for Southern African Americans. Congress was thinking of the ex-slaves' basic needs when it created the bureau in 1865 to supply food, clothing, land, fuel, and other provisions. But it quickly became clear that African Americans also needed an education for successful lives as freedmen. As later acts of Congress expanded the bureau's powers, the agency provided funding, teachers, and even old government buildings for freedmen's schools.

With the help of teachers sent by Northern freedmen's aid societies and Christian groups, these schools sprung up wherever there was space: churches, sheds, even former slave auction houses. In his 1866 book *The South: A Tour of Its Battle-fields and Ruined Cities*, Northern journalist John Townsend Trowbridge wrote, "For my own part, I could never enter one of those schools without emotion." He went on to describe what he saw:

> Six years and sixty may be seen, side by side, learning to read from the same chart or book. Perhaps a bright little negro boy or girl is teaching a white-haired old man, or bent old woman in spectacles [glasses], their letters [alphabet]. There are few more affecting [moving] sights than these aged people beginning the child's task so late in life, often after their eyesight has failed. Said a very old man to a teacher who asked him his age, "I'm jammed on to a hundred, and dis is my fust chance to git a start."

African Americans of all ages were hungry for literacy. Younger African Americans wanted the better job opportunities that education could bring. Adults needed reading skills to review their new labor contracts, and to make sure they voted as they intended on election day. Elderly African Americans wanted to learn to read their Bibles before they died.

From 1865 to 1870, the Freedmen's Bureau spent more than $5 million on schools, African American civil rights leader W. E. B. Du Bois (1868–1963) wrote in *Black Reconstruction in America*. In July 1870, Du Bois wrote, the bureau oversaw 4,239 schools in the South with 247,333 students. Some whites resented that those schools represented a chance for African Americans to move up in society. In some communities, the teachers were treated as social outcasts, and the school buildings were vandalized or burned. "The opposition to Negro education was bitter in the South," Du Bois wrote, "for the South believed an educated Negro to be a dangerous Negro."

toward racial equality (see box). Teachers and bureau agents were treated as outcasts—or worse, they were attacked. Three bureau agents in Texas were killed.

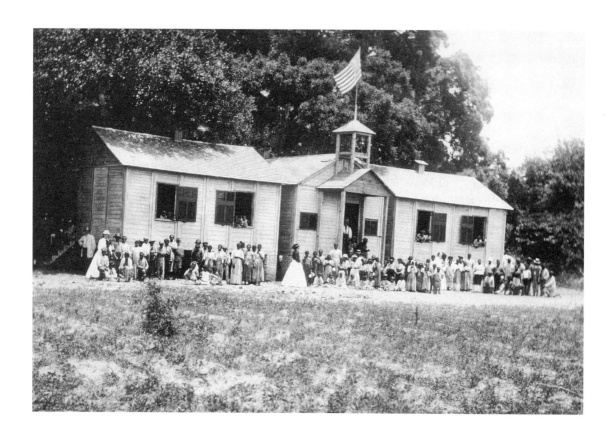

Students and teachers at a Freedmen's Bureau school in Beaufort, South Carolina. © *Corbis.*

Some Northerners resented the Freedmen's Bureau as well. They supported ending slavery. But they thought the bureau was simply providing handouts to African Americans instead of expecting them to work. And because the bureau could not be funded through the sale of abandoned Confederate lands—which had been reclaimed by their pre-war owners—people had to pay higher taxes on everyday items to fund the agency. A flier circulated in Pennsylvania, on file at the Library of Congress, described how Congress set aside $7 million in 1866 for the Freedmen's Bureau, a cost of $1.50 per Pennsylvania voter. The flier read: "You are MADE TO PAY to keep up the FREEDMAN'S BUREAU, by your Coffee, Tea and Sugar … and your children must go barefooted, and your wife have fewer dresses, so that THE NEGRO MAY BE KEPT IN HIS IDLENESS."

Congress created the bureau to last for a year after the Civil War, but to many members, it became clear the agency needed more time and broader powers. For one thing,

African Americans were not treated equally in courts: They could not sit on juries, and they could only be witnesses in cases involving African Americans. U.S. senator Lyman Trumbull (1813–1896) of Illinois drafted a bill in 1866 extending the bureau's life and allowing agents to take over court cases in which African Americans were being treated unfairly. The president vetoed the bill (although Congress eventually overturned Johnson's veto), arguing African Americans could fare just fine without such an agency:

> His [the African American man's] condition is not so exposed [vulnerable] as may at first be imagined. He is in a portion of the country where his labor cannot well be spared. Competition for his services from planters, from those who are constructing or repairing railroads, and from capitalists [investors] in his vicinage [area] or from other states will enable him to command almost his own terms. He also possesses a perfect right to change his place of abode [home], and if, therefore, he does not find in one community or state a mode of life suited to his desires or proper remuneration [payment] for his labor, he can move to another where that labor is more esteemed [valued] and better rewarded.

Political support for the Freedmen's Bureau faded within a couple of years after the war. Without lands to lease and sell to ex-slaves, the bureau was left without one of its main functions. Congress began decreasing the bureau's funding in 1868, and in June 1872, the agency was officially disbanded.

Did you know ...

- Except in a few regions, the South did not have a public school system before the Civil War. The Freedmen's Bureau helped create more than forty-two hundred schools for ex-slaves, and the Southern states included plans for public school systems in their new state constitutions written after the war.

- Howard University, a college founded in 1866 in Washington, D.C., for African American students, was named for Oliver O. Howard, the first and only director of the Freedmen's Bureau. The college also received funding from the Freedmen's Bureau.

- At the same time Congress passed the Freedmen's Bureau Act, it created the Freedman's Savings Bank so that ex-slaves could save their earnings. As noted in *Reconstruction: America's Unfinished Revolution,* "African Americans by the thousands came to the bank with tiny deposits—the majority of accounts were under fifty dollars and some amounted only to a few pennies." But the people who managed the bank made some poor investments, and the bank closed in 1874 with only $31,000 to repay its 61,000 account holders, Foner wrote.

Consider the following …

- Why did Congress create the Freedmen's Bureau?

- How was the Freedmen's Bureau supposed to provide land to ex-slaves? Why didn't this happen?

- Why was the bureau unpopular with some people in the North and South alike?

For More Information

Andrews, Sidney. *The South Since the War.* Boston: Ticknor and Fields, 1866. Reprint, Baton Rouge: Louisiana State University Press, 2004. Also available at *Making of America Books.* http://www.hti.umich.edu/cgi/t/text/text-idx?c=moa;idno=AAW0193.0001.001 (accessed on September 16, 2004).

Bergeron, Paul H., ed. "Freedmen's Bureau Veto Message." *The Papers of Andrew Johnson, vol. 10.* Knoxville: University of Tennessee Press, 1992. Available online at *Instructional Technology Workshop at the University of the South.* http://itw.sewanee.edu/reconstruction/html/docs/freedveto.htm (accessed on September 16, 2004).

Du Bois, W. E. B. *Black Reconstruction in America.* New York: Harcourt, Brace and Co., 1935. Multiple reprints.

"Economise and Pay Your Debt! Restore the South and Increase Your Resources." 1866. *Library of Congress: American Memory.* http://hdl.loc.gov/loc.rbc/rbpe.1590090b (accessed on September 16, 2004).

Foner, Eric. *Reconstruction: America's Unfinished Revolution.* New York: HarperCollins Publishers, 1988.

"The Freedmen's Bureau Act: Chapter XC: An Act to Establish a Bureau for the Relief of Freedmen and Refugees." *University of Maryland College of Arts and Humanities.* http://www.history.umd.edu/Freedmen/fbact.htm (accessed on September 16, 2004).

Freedmen's Bureau Online. http://www.freedmensbureau.com (accessed on September 16, 2004).

Smith, John David. *Black Voices from Reconstruction.* Gainesville: University Press of Florida, 1997.

Trowbridge, John Townsend. *The South: A Tour of Its Battle-fields and Ruined Cities.* Hartford, CT: L. Stebbins, 1866. Also available at *Making of America Books.* http://www.hti.umich.edu/cgi/t/text/text-idx?c= moa;idno=AFJ8852 (accessed on September 16, 2004).

Wallace, John. *Carpet-Bag Rule in Florida.* Gainesville: University of Florida Press, 1964 [a facsimile reproduction of the 1888 edition].

5

Frederick Douglass

Excerpt from "Reconstruction"
Published in *Atlantic Monthly*, 1866; reprinted on *About.com* (Web site)

A leading African American abolitionist fights for intervention from the federal government and Union military to gain equal rights for blacks

"If with the negro was success in war, and without him failure, so in peace it will be found that the nation must fall or flourish with the negro...."

In many ways, the end of the American Civil War (1861–65) raised more questions than it answered. The North won the bloody struggle to end slavery and keep the South from seceding, or forming its own country. But how would these Southern states rejoin the Union? What changes would be made to their governments and their ways of life? What rights would African Americans have? And what would be their role in shaping a new South? The answers to these questions would define the process known as Reconstruction.

President Andrew Johnson (1808–1875; served 1865–69) developed the first Reconstruction policy during the summer of 1865, without any input from Congress. He appointed governors in each of the Southern states and required them to hold conventions to draft new state constitutions. The conventions were only open to men who were eligible to vote in 1860, effectively barring African Americans from participating in the process. (Johnson later argued that giving African American men the ballot would spark a racial war.) But most whites involved in the "rebellion" against the North could participate, as long as they had taken an oath of allegiance to the Union. The only exceptions were the highest ranking Confederates and Southerners with property worth more than $20,000 who had to apply to the president directly for a pardon.

Not surprisingly, these new Southern governments put prominent Confederates back in power without giving African American men the right to vote. Many Southern towns and states passed "Black Codes," discriminatory laws designed to keep African Americans under the control of whites. The laws in some areas barred African Americans from owning land or meeting after dark. Unemployed African Americans could be arrested and put to work for the white men who bailed them out. In South Carolina, African Americans had to get a special license to do any work besides farming. As noted in *Frederick Douglass and the Fight for Freedom,* "These so called 'Black Codes' virtually reconstituted [recreated] slavery in everything but name."

It was a devastating outcome for African Americans, particularly the 180,000 African American men who joined the Union army during the war to fight for their freedom. A group of African Americans met in Virginia in August 1865 to draft a message to Congress, reprinted on the "From Revolution to Reconstruction" Web site. They reminded Congress of the African Americans who helped in the war effort, only to see this sad result:

> Four fifths of our enemies are paroled or amnestied [freed], and the other fifth are being pardoned, and the President has, in his efforts at the reconstruction of the civil government of these States ... left us entirely at the mercy of these subjugated [defeated] but unconverted [unchanged] rebels, in everything save [except] the privilege of bringing us, our wives and little ones, to the auction block....

Recognizing that Johnson's Reconstruction plan would leave the South largely unchanged, Congress responded with its own plan. The assembly refused to seat the ex-Confederates and other Southerners sent to Congress in December 1865. Instead, Congress created the Joint Committee on Reconstruction to hold hearings on Southern attitudes and offer a plan for rebuilding the region (see Chapter 7). Congress already created the Freedmen's Bureau (see Chapter

Frederick Douglass. *The Library of Congress.*

4) shortly before the war ended to provide food, lease land, and negotiate labor contracts for the newly freed slaves. It also officially ended slavery with the Thirteenth Amendment to the U.S. Constitution (see Chapter 2), which was ratified by the states in 1865. In response to the Black Codes, Congress passed the Civil Rights Act of 1866 (see Chapter 8) and proposed the Fourteenth Amendment to the U.S. Constitution (see Chapter 9). Both measures (which passed over Johnson's objections) granted citizenship to African Americans and required they receive the same legal treatment as whites.

But it would take more than a couple of laws to change the way Southern whites treated African Americans. Visiting the South shortly after the war, Union general Carl Schurz (1829–1906) made the following observations, reprinted in *A History of Affirmative Action, 1619–2000:*

> Wherever I go ... I hear the people talk in such a way as to indicate that they are yet unable to conceive of the Negro as possessing any rights at all. Men who are honorable in their dealings with white neighbors, will cheat a Negro without feeling a single twinge of their honor.... The reason for all this is simple and manifest [obvious]. The whites esteem [consider] blacks their property by natural right ... they still have an ingrained feeling that the blacks at large belong to the whites at large.

Frederick Douglass (1817–1895), a former slave who became a leader in the abolitionist (antislavery) movement, was well aware of the obstacles facing African Americans. Raised on a Maryland farm, Douglass escaped to New York at age twenty after experiencing first-hand the tragedies of slavery: brutal whippings, separation from family members, and the humiliation of belonging to another person. He contributed to antislavery newspapers before writing his life's story, *Narrative of the Life of Frederick Douglass, an American Slave,* in 1845. A couple of years later he created his own antislavery newspaper, *North Star,* named for the star used by slaves escaping to freedom in the North.

Douglass knew that ending slavery was only half the battle. African Americans needed to be able to rent or buy land so they could work for themselves. They also needed the right to vote and run for office, so they could support officials who would protect their rights. The passage of the Black Codes throughout the South showed how African Americans would be treated as long as Southern whites were in control. Any push for equal rights for blacks must come from the federal government, backed up by Union soldiers, Douglass argued in the following article from *Atlantic Monthly* magazine.

Things to remember while reading an excerpt from "Reconstruction":

- President Johnson drafted the first Reconstruction plan to bring the South back into the Union after the Civil War. Under his plan, Southern whites drafted new state constitutions and elected new officials, including many former Confederates. African Americans could not vote, however, and new laws called Black Codes restricted every aspect of their lives. These local laws barred African Americans from owning land, required them to get special permits for certain jobs, and allowed them to be arrested and put to work if they were unemployed.

- Congress rejected Johnson's Reconstruction plan and passed some measures of its own. It created the Freedmen's Bureau to provide supplies to African Americans and help them negotiate their labor contracts. Congress also passed the Civil Rights Act of 1866 and proposed the Fourteenth Amendment to the Constitution to outlaw the Black Codes and ensure equal legal treatment for African Americans.

- Douglass, a former slave who became a leading abolitionist, believed ending slavery was only half the battle. African Americans needed the right to vote and the ability to work for themselves in order to be free, he said. Knowing many Southern whites would not give African

Americans these opportunities, Douglass called for Congress to lead the push for African Americans' rights and use Union troops to enforce those rights.

Excerpt from "Reconstruction"

*The assembling of the Second Session of the Thirty-ninth Congress may very properly be made the occasion of a few **earnest** words on the already much-worn topic of reconstruction.*

*Seldom has any legislative body been the subject of a **solicitude** more intense, or of **aspirations** more sincere and **ardent**. There are the best of reasons for this **profound** interest. Questions of vast moment, left undecided by the last session of Congress, must be **manfully grappled** with by this. No political **skirmishing** will **avail**. The occasion demands **statesmanship**.*

*Whether the tremendous war so heroically fought and so victoriously ended shall pass into history a miserable failure, **barren** of permanent results,—a scandalous and shocking waste of blood and **treasure**,—a strife for **empire**, … of no value to liberty or civilization,—an attempt to re-establish a Union by force, which must be the **merest mockery** of a Union,—an effort to bring under Federal authority States into which no loyal man from the North may safely enter, and to bring men into the national councils who **deliberate** with daggers and vote with revolvers, and who do not even conceal their deadly hate of the country that conquered them; or whether, on the other hand, we shall, as the rightful reward of victory over **treason**, have a solid nation, entirely delivered from all contradictions and social **antagonisms**, based upon loyalty, liberty, and equality, must be determined one way or the other by the present session of Congress. The last session really did nothing which can be considered final as to these questions. The Civil Rights Bill and the Freedmen's Bureau Bill and the proposed constitutional amendments, with the amendment already adopted and recognized as the law of the land, do not reach the **difficulty**, and cannot, unless the whole structure of the government is changed from a government by States to something like a **despotic** central government, with power to control even the **municipal** regulations of States, and to make them conform to its own despotic will. While there remains*

Earnest: Serious.

Solicitude: Concern.

Aspirations: Hopes.

Ardent: Passionate.

Profound: Very deep.

Manfully grappled: Forcefully addressed.

Skirmishing: Minor battling.

Avail: Be of use.

Statesmanship: Wise leadership.

Barren: Empty.

Treasure: Money.

Empire: Territory.

Merest mockery: Smallest joke.

Deliberate: Consider.

Treason: Betrayal of country.

Antagonisms: Hostilities.

Difficulty: Problem.

Despotic: Oppressive.

Municipal: Local.

such an idea as the right of each State to control its own local affairs,—an idea, by the way, more deeply rooted in the minds of men of all sections of the country than perhaps any one other political idea,—no general **assertion** of human rights can be of any practical value. To change the character of the government at this point is neither possible nor desirable. All that is necessary to be done is to make the government consistent with itself, and **render** the rights of the States compatible with the sacred rights of human nature.

The arm of the Federal government is long, but it is far too short to protect the rights of individuals in the **interior** of distant States. They must have the power to protect themselves, or they will go unprotected, **spite** of all the laws the Federal government can put upon the national **statute-book.…**

If time was at first needed, Congress has now had time. All the **requisite** materials from which to form an intelligent judgment are now before it. Whether its members look at the origin, the progress, the **termination** of the war, or at the mockery of a peace now existing, they will find only one unbroken chain of argument in favor of a radical policy of reconstruction. For the **omissions** of the last session, some excuses may be allowed. A **treacherous** President stood in the way; and it can be easily seen how **reluctant** good men might be to admit an **apostasy** which involved so much of **baseness** and **ingratitude.** It was natural that they should seek to save him by bending to him even when he leaned to the side of error. But all is changed now. Congress knows now that it must go on without his aid, and even against his **machinations.** The advantage of the present session over the last is immense. Where that investigated, this has the facts. Where that walked by faith, this may walk by sight. Where that **halted,** this must go forward, and where that failed, this must succeed, giving the country whole measures where that gave us half-measures.… In every **considerable** public meeting, and in almost every **conceivable** way, whether at court-house, school-house, or cross-roads, in doors and out, the subject has been discussed, and the people have **emphatically** pronounced in favor of a **radical** policy. Listening to the **doctrines** of **expediency** and compromise with pity, impatience, and disgust, they have everywhere broken into demonstrations of the wildest enthusiasm when a brave word has been spoken in favor of equal rights and **impartial suffrage.** Radicalism, so far from being **odious,** is not the popular passport to power. The men most bitterly charged with it go to Congress with the largest majorities, while the timid and doubtful are sent by lean majorities, or else left at home. The strange controversy be-

Assertion: Statement.

Render: Make.

Interior: Inner area.

Spite: Regardless.

Statute-book: Law book.

Requisite: Necessary.

Termination: Ending.

Omissions: Failures.

Treacherous: Untrustworthy.

Reluctant: Hesitant.

Apostasy: Abandoning of belief.

Baseness: Meanness.

Ingratitude: Thanklessness.

Machinations: Schemes.

Halted: Stopped.

Considerable: Important.

Conceivable: Thinkable.

Emphatically: Strongly.

Radical: Drastically different (in this case, for African American rights).

Doctrines: Ideas being preached.

Expediency: Convenience.

Impartial suffrage: Unbiased voting rights.

Odious: Offensive.

tween the President and the Congress, at one time so threatening, is **disposed of** by the people. The high reconstructive powers which he so confidently, **ostentatiously,** and **haughtily** claimed, have been disallowed, **denounced**, and utterly **repudiated;** while those claimed by Congress have been confirmed....

Without attempting to settle here the **metaphysical** and somewhat **theological** question (about which so much has already been said and written), whether once in the Union means always in the Union ... it is obvious to common sense that the rebellious States stand to-day, in point of law, precisely where they stood when, exhausted, beaten, conquered, they fell powerless at the feet of Federal authority. Their State governments were overthrown, and the lives and property of the leaders of the Rebellion were **forfeited.** In reconstructing the institutions of these shattered and overthrown States, Congress should begin with a clean slate, and make clean work of it. Let there be no hesitation. It would be a cowardly **deference** to a defeated and treacherous President, if any account were made of the **illegitimate**, one-sided, **sham** governments hurried into existence for a **malign** purpose in the absence of Congress. These pretended governments, which were never submitted to the people, and from participation in which four millions of the loyal [African American] people were excluded by Presidential order, should now be treated according to their true character, as shams and **impositions**, and **supplanted** by true and **legitimate** governments, in the formation of which loyal men, black and white, shall participate....

The plain, common-sense way of doing this work, as **intimated** at the beginning, is simply to establish in the South one law, one government, one administration of justice, one **condition** to the exercise of the elective franchise, for men of all races and colors alike. This great measure is sought as earnestly by loyal white men as by loyal African Americans, and is needed alike by both. Let sound political **prescience** but take the place of an unreasoning prejudice, and this will be done....

The policy that **emancipated** and armed the negro—now seen to have been wise and proper by the **dullest**—was not certainly more **sternly** demanded than is now the policy of **enfranchisement**. If with the negro was success in war, and without him failure, so in peace it will be found that the nation must fall or flourish with the negro....

Disposed of: Settled.

Ostentatiously: Grandly.

Haughtily: Arrogantly.

Denounced: Condemned.

Repudiated: Rejected.

Metaphysical: Abstract.

Theological: Religious.

Forfeited: Taken away.

Deference: Yielding.

Illegitimate: Unlawful.

Sham: Fake.

Malign: Evil.

Impositions: Forced frauds.

Supplanted: Replaced.

Legitimate: Lawful.

Intimated: Implied.

Condition: Requirement.

Prescience: Foresight.

Emancipated: Freed.

Dullest: Stupidest.

Sternly: Firmly.

Enfranchisement: Voting rights (for African Americans).

What happened next ...

Congress passed the Reconstruction Act in 1867 setting a drastic new policy for bringing the Southern states back into the Union (see Chapter 10). The act divided the South into five military districts, each one headed by a Union general. Each state was required to draft a new state constitution at a convention open to African American *and* white delegates alike—except high-ranking ex-Confederates. African American and white men alike would get to vote on the constitution. Once the states approved new constitutions and ratified (formally confirm) the Fourteenth Amendment, they could be readmitted to the Union.

For the first time, these new state constitutions gave Southern African American men the ballot. About 703,400 African American men registered to vote that year, and about 2,000 African American men were elected to various offices during the next decade (see Chapter 12). To further protect

Three African American men discuss politics, as shown in the November 20, 1869, issue of *Harper's Weekly. The Library of Congress.*

A man speaks to children in the segregated Zion School for Colored Children. *The Library of Congress.*

the right of African American men to vote, Congress passed the Fifteenth Amendment to the Constitution, ratified by the states in 1870, guaranteeing African American men the ballot (see Chapter 16). "We certainly hope that the time will come when the colored man in America shall cease to require special efforts to guard their rights and advance their interests as a class," Douglass wrote in an 1870 article supporting the Fifteenth Amendment, reprinted in *A History of Affirmative Action, 1619–2000.* "But that time has not yet come, and is not even at the door."

Indeed, that time would be decades away. When Reconstruction ended in 1877 with the withdrawal of federal troops (see Chapter 19), the Southern states started chipping away at the hard-won rights for African Americans. They imposed literacy tests (to test for ability to read and write) or poll taxes to discourage African Americans from voting. They created separate schools, railroad cars, and other facilities for African Americans and whites, a practice upheld by the

Supreme Court in the 1896 *Plessy v. Ferguson* ruling. Nearly a century passed after Reconstruction before the civil rights movement of the 1950s and 1960s resumed the push for racial equality.

Did you know …

- Two of Douglass's sons, Lewis and Charles, served in the Fifty-fourth Massachusetts Regiment, the first African American Union regiment to fight in the Civil War. The regiment was later made famous by the 1989 movie *Glory* starring Matthew Broderick (1962–) and Denzel Washington (1954–).

- After the death of his first wife, a former slave named Anna, Douglass caused a stir by marrying a white woman. The new Mrs. Douglass was Helen Pitts, a college-educated woman who had been Douglass's secretary. Interracial marriage was socially forbidden in that era, and even Douglass's children opposed the union. But for a man who spent his life preaching racial equality, the pairing was only natural. "I could never have been at peace with my own soul or held up my head among men had I allowed the fear of popular clamor [uproar] to deter [discourage] me from following my convictions as to this marriage," Douglass wrote in a letter reprinted in *Frederick Douglass and the Fight for Freedom*.

- Douglass was a strong supporter of women's rights, including the suffrage movement to grant women the right to vote. He participated in the Seneca Falls convention of 1848, a gathering in New York that started the women's rights movement.

Consider the following …

- Why did Douglass think Congress needed to create a stronger Reconstruction policy?

- Why did Douglass describe the Southern state governments formed after the Civil War, under President Johnson's Reconstruction plan, as "shams?"

• What was life like for African Americans right after the Civil War? How would that change by allowing African Americans the right to vote and own land?

For More Information

"An Address to the Loyal Citizens and Congress of the United States of America Adopted by a Convention of Negroes Held in Alexandria, Virginia, from August 2 to 5, 1865." *From Revolution to Reconstruction.* http://odur.let.rug.nl/~usa/D/1851-1875/slavery/addres.htm (accessed on September 15, 2004).

Cashman, Sean Dennis. *America in the Gilded Age.* New York: New York University Press, 1984.

Douglass, Frederick. *Narrative of the Life of Frederick Douglass, an American Slave.* Boston: Anti-slavery Office, 1845. Reprint, 150th anniversary ed., New York: Laurel, 1997.

Douglass, Frederick. "Reconstruction." *Atlantic Monthly* (1866): pp. 761–65. Also available at http://afroamhistory.about.com/library/bldouglass_reconstruction.htm (accessed on September 15, 2004).

Miller, Douglas T. *Frederick Douglass and the Fight for Freedom.* New York: Facts on File, 1988.

Rubio, Philip F. *A History of Affirmative Action, 1619–2000.* Jackson: University Press of Mississippi, 2001.

Frances Butler Leigh

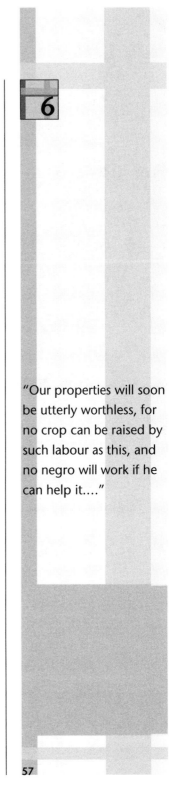

6

Excerpt from Ten Years on a Georgia Plantation Since the War
**Covering events from 1866 to 1868; published in 1883; reprinted
on *Documenting the American South* (Web site)**

A plantation owner writes about life after slavery

After the Civil War ended, the South had to start over in many ways. Homes, hospitals, and businesses needed to be rebuilt. Neglected fields needed to be sown (planted) with new seeds. Families that lost a husband or father in battle had to rebuild on their own. African Americans and whites alike had to learn how to make a living in a new economy— one in which African Americans were no longer slaves, but wage-earning employees.

Major stretches of the South were in ruins. In the opening account of *The South Since the War,* Charleston, South Carolina, was described as "a city of ruins, of desolation, of vacant houses, of widowed women, of rotting wharves [docks], of deserted warehouses, of weed-wild gardens, of miles of grass-grown streets, of acres of pitiful and voiceful barrenness...." The destruction had not been limited to the battlefield. It spread to the cities and homes that had been occupied by soldiers during the war. A Northern journalist, John Townsend Trowbridge, wrote about a man from Columbia, South Carolina, who said Union troops burned his house after using it as their headquarters. "I owned my own house, my own servants, my own garden, and in one

"Our properties will soon be utterly worthless, for no crop can be raised by such labour as this, and no negro will work if he can help it...."

Northern journalist John Townsend Trowbridge.
© Corbis.

night they reduced me to poverty," the man told Trowbridge, who included the story in his 1866 book, *The South: A Tour of Its Battle-fields and Ruined Cities.*

Southern whites faced the intimidating task of rebuilding without their most important prewar asset: the cheap labor of four million slaves. The war freed the slaves, and Union troops threatened to seize the land of anybody who continued using the African Americans as slaves. The whites who needed workers would have to hire them. Northern visitor Whitelaw Reid believed many Southerners would end up selling their land, as they did not know how to work the fields without slaves. "I have found no Georgian who, now that his slaves can no longer be made to work for him, expects to work for himself," Reid wrote in his 1866 book, *After the War: A Southern Tour.*

But many whites clung to their land—often the only asset that had survived the war. They negotiated contracts with their former slaves through the Freedmen's Bureau, a federal agency created in March 1865 to help African Americans start their new lives after the war (see Chapter 4). Sometimes whites would split the crop with their workers. Other times they would pay them in cash and other supplies. Kate Stone (1842–1907), whose family owned a cotton plantation in northeastern Louisiana, complained that her family could only buy "bare necessities [food] for the table and plainest clothes for the family" because the rest of the profits went to pay their African American workers. "The Negroes demand high wages, from $20 to $25 for men, in addition to the old rations of sugar, rice, tobacco, molasses, and sometimes hams," Stone wrote in her journal in 1867.

Frances Butler Leigh (1838–1910) found the same problems when she and her father, Pierce Butler (1806–1867), returned to their rice and cotton plantations on the Georgia Sea Islands after the war. The fields had not been cultivated in four years. Her house had no furniture. The former slaves

An example of a house on a Southern plantation.
© Medford Historical Society Collection/Corbis. Reproduced by permission of Corbis.

agreed to work, but they would have to be paid. Leigh was born in Philadelphia, Pennsylvania, and stayed in the North during the war, but she was intensely loyal to the South and she supported slavery. (As she refurnished the plantation house, she hung a portrait of Confederate general Robert E. Lee [1807–1870] over the fireplace.) Her book describes her father's kindness to his slaves, and the slaves' loyalty to her father. At the same time, Leigh believed some free African Americans would not work—or work as hard—as they did as slaves. She wondered how she would make the plantation successful again without forced labor.

Things to remember while reading an excerpt from *Ten Years on a Georgia Plantation Since the War:*

- Butler's rice and cotton plantations, among the largest in Georgia, used more than one thousand slaves before the

Slaves picking cotton during the Civil War. *The Library of Congress.*

war. After the African Americans were freed, many stayed or returned to Butler's plantation to work—but this time they would have to be treated as paid employees. Leigh feared the African Americans would work just enough to get paid, but not enough to keep her father's plantation running.

• Leigh spent the war years in Philadelphia, so this trip to Georgia was her first glimpse of the devastation from the war. She came home to an empty house with no furniture and little food. This was a common scene in the South, as Union troops took whatever food they could find and chopped up the furniture for their campfires. Looters took anything else of value.

• The war threw women into new roles. Some took charge of the household and even the family business while their husbands or fathers were away at war (duties they kept if the men did not return). Some took jobs in factories or other businesses in order to feed their families.

Wealthy women, such as Leigh, had to learn to cook and perform other chores once done by slaves. Former debutantes (girls making their first formal appearances in society) found themselves running plantations.

Excerpt from Ten Years on a Georgia Plantation Since the War

The year after the war between the North and the South, I went to the South with my father to look after our property in Georgia to see what could be done with it.

*The whole country had of course undergone a complete revolution. The changes that a four years' war must bring about in any country would alone have been enough to give a different **aspect** to everything; but at the South, besides the changes brought about by the war, our slaves had been freed; the white population was conquered, ruined, and disheartened, unable for the moment to see anything but the ruin before as well as behind, too **wedded** to the **fancied prosperity** of the old system to believe in any possible success under the new. And even had the people desired to begin at once to rebuild their fortunes, it would have been in most cases impossible, for in many families the young men had perished in the war, and the old men, if not too old for the **labour** and effort it required to set the machinery of peace going again, were **beggared**, and had not even the money enough to buy food for themselves and their families, let alone their negroes, to whom they now had to pay wages as well as feed them....*

*On Wednesday, when my father returned [to the plantation], he reported that he had found the negroes all on the place, not only those who were there five years ago, but many who were sold three years before that. Seven had worked their way back from the up country. They received him very affectionately, and made an agreement with him to work for one half the crop, which agreement it remained to be seen if they would keep. Owing to our coming so late, only a small crop could be planted, enough to **make seed** for another year and clear expenses. I was sorry we could do no more, but too thankful that things were as promising as they were. Most of*

Aspect: Appearance.

Wedded: Tied.

Fancied prosperity: Image of success.

Labour: Work.

Beggared: Made poor.

Make seed: Produce the seeds that will be used to plant the following year's crop.

the finest plantations were lying *idle* for *want* of hands to work them, so many of the negroes had died; seventeen thousand deaths were recorded by the Freedmen's Bureau alone. Many had been taken to the South-west, and others preferred hanging about the towns, making a few dollars now and then, to working regularly on the plantations; so most people found it impossible to get any labourers, but we had as many as we wanted, and nothing could *induce* our people to go anywhere else. My father also reported that the house was bare, not a bed nor chair left, and that he had been sleeping on the floor, with a piece of wood for a pillow and a few *negro blankets* for his covering. This I could hardly do, and as he could attend to nothing but the planting, we agreed that he should devote himself to that, while I looked [for] some furniture. So the day after, armed with five hundred bushels of seed rice, corn, bacon, a straw mattress, and a tub, he started off again for the plantation, leaving me to buy tables and chairs, pots and pans....

The *prospect* of getting in the crop did not grow more promising as time went on. The negroes talked a great deal about their desire and intention to work for us, but their idea of work, unaided by the *stern* law of necessity, is very vague, some of them working only half a day and some even less. I don't think one does a really honest full day's work, and so of course not half the necessary amount is done and I am afraid never will be again, and so our properties will soon be *utterly* worthless, for no crop can be raised by such labour as this, and no negro will work if he can help it, and is quite satisfied just to scrape along doing an odd job here and there to earn money enough to buy a little food. They are affectionate and often trustworthy and honest, but so hopelessly lazy as to be almost worthless as labourers.

My father was quite encouraged at first, the people seemed so willing to work and said so much about their intention of doing so; but not many days after they started he came in quite *disheartened*, saying that half the *hands* had left the fields at one o'clock and the rest by three o'clock, and this just at our busiest time. Half a day's work will keep them from starving, but won't raise a crop. Our contract with them is for half the crop; that is, one half to be divided among them, according to each man's rate of work, we letting them have in the meantime necessary food, clothing, and money for their present *wants* (as they have not a penny) which is to be *deducted* from whatever is due to them at the end of the year.

This we found the best arrangement to make with them, for if we paid them wages, the first five dollars they made would have

Idle: Unused.

Want: Lack.

Induce: Force.

Negro blankets: Poorer quality blankets provided for slaves.

Prospect: Possibility.

Stern: Strict.

Utterly: Totally.

Disheartened: Discouraged.

Hands: Workers.

Wants: Needs.

Deducted: Subtracted.

seemed like so large a sum to them, that they would have imagined their fortunes made and refused to work any more. But even this arrangement had its objections, for they told us, when they missed working two or three days a week, that they were losers by it as well as ourselves, half the crop being theirs. But they could not see that this sort of work would not raise any crop at all, and that such should be the result was quite beyond their **comprehension**. They were quite convinced that if six days' work would raise a whole crop, three days' work would raise half a one, with which they as partners were satisfied, and so it seemed as if we should have to be too....

I had a pretty hard time of it that first year, owing to my **wretched** servants, and to the **scarcity** of **provisions** of all sorts. The country was absolutely swept; not a chicken, not an egg was left, and for weeks I lived on **hominy**, rice, and fish, with an occasional bit of **venison**. The negroes said the Yankees had eaten up everything, and one old woman told me they had refused to pay her for the eggs, but after they had eaten them said they were **addled**; but I think the people generally had not much to complain of. The only two good servants we had remained with my father at Butler's Island, and mine were all raw field hands, to whom everything was new and strange, and who were really **savages**. My white maid, watching my **sable** housemaid one morning through the door, saw her dip my toothbrush in the tub in which I had just bathed, and with my small hand-glass in the other hand, in which she was attentively regarding the operation, proceed to scrub her teeth with the brush. It is needless to say I presented her with that one, and locked my new one up as soon as I had finished using it.

My cook made all the flour and sugar I gave him (my own **allowance** of which was very small) into sweet cakes, most of which he ate himself, and when I scolded him, cried. The young man who was with us, dying of **consumption**, was my chief **anxiety**, for he was terribly ill, and could not eat the **fare** I did, and to get anything else was an impossibility. I **scoured** the island one day in search of chickens, but only succeeded in getting one old **cock**, of which my wretched cook made such a mess that Mr. J— could not touch it after it was done. I tried my own hand at cooking, but without much success, not knowing really how to cook a potato, besides which the roof of the kitchen leaked badly, and as we had frequent showers, I often had to cook, holding up an umbrella in one hand and stirring with the other....

This part of the country has suffered more heavily than any other from the war. Hundreds of acres of rice land, which yielded

Comprehension: Understanding.

Wretched: Unworthy.

Scarcity: Lack.

Provisions: Supplies.

Hominy: Dried, ground corn boiled for food.

Venison: Deer meat.

Addled: Rotten.

Savages: Uncivilized people.

Sable: Black.

Allowance: Regularly received amount.

Consumption: A disease, such as tuberculosis, in which the person wastes away.

Anxiety: Worry.

Fare: Food.

Scoured: Searched.

Cock: Rooster.

Reclaimed: Recovered.

Infinite: Endless.

Adrift: Directionless.

Shop: Factory.

Paddles: Rows in a canoe.

Underclothes: Underwear.

*millions before the war, are fast returning to the original swamp from which they were **reclaimed** with **infinite** pains and expense, simply because their owners are ruined, their houses burnt to the ground, and their negroes made worthless as labourers. It is very sad to see such wide-spread ruin, and to hear of girls well-educated, and brought up with every luxury, turned **adrift** as dressmakers, schoolteachers, and even **shop** girls, in order to keep themselves and their families from starvation. One of Mrs. F—s' nieces **paddles** her old father over to the plantation every morning herself, and while he is giving his orders in the fields, [she] sits on a heap of straw, making **underclothes** to sell in Charleston. It is wonderful to see how bravely and cheerfully they do work, knowing as I do how they lived before the war.*

What happened next …

Leigh continued to help her father run the plantations until his death in 1867. Then she took over. She grew increasingly frustrated at her inability to control hundreds of African American workers. For example, with the 1868 elections approaching, Leigh told the workers they must finish their duties on the plantation before going to the polls. But her workers took the entire day off—an act Leigh partly blamed on the political organizers who falsely told African Americans they could be fined or sent out of the country if they failed to vote. In another passage, Leigh described how one African American worker burned down the mill and other plantation buildings after a dollar had been taken from his pay "for some neglect in his work." The fire caused $15,000 in damage.

Contrary to Leigh's descriptions of African Americans, Northern visitors such as Whitelaw Reid and Sidney Andrews found ex-slaves hard-working and eager to make a living. Many simply preferred to work for themselves, or under different conditions than the foreman-supervised, gang-labor system they knew as slaves. In his 1866 book *The South Since the War*, Andrews wrote that he had interviewed hundreds of African Americans but "have yet to find the first one [who] wanted to go back and live with their old masters as slaves."

Like many Southern whites struggling to maintain their plantations after the war, Leigh looked for alternatives to African American labor. She hired Irish immigrants to dig and maintain the irrigation ditches, and described them as "faithful" workers. She brought over a group of workers from England, but fired them after two years because they were "troublesome … constantly drunk, and shirked [avoided] their work so abominably [horribly]." With the spread of railroad lines to the West, Leigh even considered bringing over Chinese workers from California. She also watched for any technological advances, such as more sophisticated plowing equipment, that could reduce her reliance on human labor.

Leigh married an English minister in 1871 and began spending more time in Great Britain, her mother's homeland. She kept the plantation but gave greater responsibilities to her managers to run it in her absence. By 1876, England became her permanent home. She died in 1910 at age 72.

Frances Butler Leigh. *Courtesy of the Historical Society of Pennsylvania Collection, Atwater Kent Museum of Philadelphia.*

Did you know …

- Once African Americans began getting paid for their work, some dishonest whites opened stores near the plantations to sell goods at inflated (greatly raised) prices. Such store owners took advantage of African Americans who did not know the value of their money. Leigh described several stores in the nearby town of Darien, Georgia, where African Americans were charged three times the actual price of the goods. To offer the African Americans an alternative, Leigh's father opened a store at the plantation that sold goods to African Americans at actual cost.

- Leigh's mother was a famous British actress named Fanny Kemble (1809–1893). She held strong antislavery views and became outraged when she saw how the slaves were treated on Pierce Butler's plantations. The couple divorced in 1849.

- After her father died, Leigh spent weeks going through the plantation ledgers to figure out how much money her father owed each worker. Altogether she paid the workers $6,000, with some of them getting $200 or $300 apiece. Some of the workers used the money to buy 5 or 10 acres of land where they could build their own house and raise their own crops.

Consider the following ...

- What would be a fair working agreement between a plantation owner and the freed African Americans working for him after the war? What kind of benefits could he offer to attract good workers and encourage them to work hard?

- What kind of effect did the war have on areas *beyond* the battlefields, such as cities and plantations?

- How did the war place women in new roles?

For More Information

Anderson, John Q., ed. *Brokenburn: The Journal of Kate Stone, 1861–1868.* Baton Rouge: Louisiana State University Press, 1995.

Andrews, Sidney. *The South Since the War.* Boston: Ticknor and Fields, 1866. Reprint, Baton Rouge: Louisiana State University Press, 2004. Also available at *Making of America Books.* http://www.hti.umich.edu/cgi/t/text/text-idx?c=moa;idno=AAW0193.0001.001 (accessed on September 16, 2004).

Leigh, Frances Butler. *Ten Years on a Georgia Plantation Since the War.* London: Richard Bentley & Son, New Burlington Street, 1883. Reprint, Savannah: Library of Georgia, Beehive Foundation, 1992. Also available at *Documenting the American South: University of North Carolina at Chapel Hill Libraries.* http://docsouth.unc.edu/leigh/leigh.html (accessed on August 7, 2004).

Reid, Whitelaw. *After the War: A Southern Tour.* New York: Harper & Row, 1965. Also available at *Making of America Books.* http://www.hti.umich.edu/cgi/t/text/text-idx?c=moa;idno=AFJ8942 (accessed on September 16, 2004).

Trowbridge, John Townsend. *The South: A Tour of Its Battle-fields and Ruined Cities.* New York: Arno Press, 1969. Also available at *Making of America Books.* http://www.hti.umich.edu/cgi/t/text/text-idx?c=moa;idno=AFJ8852 (accessed on September 16, 2004).

Alexander Stephens

7

Excerpt from "On Reconstruction"

Testimony before Congress April 11, 1866; published in the
Report of the Joint Committee on Reconstruction of the First Session
Thirty-Ninth Congress, 1866

*The former Confederate vice president speaks
out on Reconstruction*

The end of the American Civil War (1861–65) raised a thorny question: How would the former Confederate states be brought back into the Union? Many Southerners believed they simply needed to pledge their loyalty to the Union and send their congressmen back to Washington, D.C.—almost as if the war never happened. Some Northerners supported that idea at first, eager for a quick reconciliation that would allow the country to move forward. But others found the idea tough to swallow after four years of bloody conflict. They believed the North's victory would be meaningless if it did not bring equal rights to African Americans. As time went on, a growing number of Northerners wanted the Southern states to grant equal rights to African Americans before returning to the Union.

Eager to reunite the country above all else, President Abraham Lincoln (1809–1865; served 1861–65) outlined generous terms in his "Proclamation of Amnesty and Reconstruction" on December 8, 1863, about a year and a half before the war ended. Lincoln said a Southern state could return to the Union if at least 10 percent of the residents who

> "It would be best for the peace, harmony, and prosperity of the whole country that there should be an immediate restoration, an immediate bringing back of the States into their original practical relations...."

voted in the 1860 presidential election took a loyalty oath and established a new state government. In time, Louisiana, Arkansas, Tennessee, and Virginia would accept Lincoln's offer. But the plan was roundly criticized by congressmen who thought *they* should decide the terms for readmitting the Southern states. Antislavery advocates, or abolitionists, also objected that African Americans would have no say in the new state governments under this plan, as they could not vote in 1860, or any previous year for that matter.

Congress outlined a stricter plan for readmitting the Southern states under the Wade-Davis bill of 1864. This plan required a majority of a Southern state's voters, not Lincoln's 10 percent, to pledge to uphold the U.S. Constitution. Then a group of delegates would create a new state government. In order to qualify as delegates, they would have to take an "iron-clad oath" that they never served as a soldier or an official in the Confederacy, and that they never supported "the rebellion" against the Union. Lincoln objected to the plan, however, because it required men to swear that they had not done anything wrong, as noted in *Reconstruction: After the Civil War*. Lincoln said, "It rejects the Christian principle of forgiveness on terms of repentance. I think it is enough if the man does no wrong hereafter." Lincoln defeated the bill by "pocket veto," meaning it did not become law because he did not sign it within ten days after Congress ended its session.

Lincoln's assassination on April 14, 1865, came less than a week after the surrender of Confederate general Robert E. Lee (1807–1870) ended the war. The fate of the Southern states was now in the hands of the new president, Andrew Johnson (1808–1875; served 1865–69), a Tennesseean who wanted to punish individual "traitors" but spare the South. In May 1865, Johnson announced a plan to grant pardons and restore property rights to anyone who would take an oath of allegiance to the Union. Once they were pardoned, the Southerners could draft new state constitutions and return to the Union.

But there was a catch: High-ranking Confederate officials and anyone with property worth more than $20,000 would have to personally apply to the president for a pardon. Johnson singled out the rich because he blamed the wealthy plantation owners for bringing the South to war. Eager to reclaim their land, Southerners lined up for the pardons, and Johnson created a special office to handle the requests. The office was granting more than one hundred pardons per day by September 1865. About fourteen thousand prominent or wealthy Confederates received their pardons by February 1866.

Johnson believed that once the war was over, the Southern states were entitled to return with the same rights they once had under the Constitution, such as the right to send senators and representatives to Congress. Whitelaw Reid, a Northern visitor who wrote *After the War: A Southern Tour* in 1866, came across many ex-Confederates who shared that view. In Florida, he met former U.S. senator David Yulee (1810–1886) of Florida, who fully expected to "help the Governor engineer the State back into the Union, and ... patch up some policy for 'taking care of the negroes,' and then prepare to resume his seat in the United States Senate at the beginning of the next session." In Savannah, Georgia, Reid debated a couple of men who believed they still enjoyed all of the rights outlined in the Constitution. Reid asked them: "You do not regard any of your rights, then, as destroyed or imperiled by your rebellion?" To Reid's surprise, one of the men answered: "Why should they be? The right to hold slaves has been destroyed by the military authorities; but, unless the Constitution is destroyed, we have all the powers under it we ever had."

That idea horrified some Northerners. The abolitionists feared Johnson's plan would bring an unchanged South back into the Union, with the same ex-Confederate leaders holding office and whites still mistreating African Americans. Abolitionist Theodore Tilton (1835–1907), as quoted in *The Struggle for Equality,* summed up the fear: "If the whip-using gentry [upper-class] who formerly held sway (had influence) in those regions are to return to their former crown and kingdom, the North will have won only half a victory over the rebellion."

The fears of abolitionists like Tilton were confirmed by the end of 1865. Newspapers routinely ran stories about Southern whites attacking African Americans and Union soldiers. Southern state legislatures and local governments passed "Black Codes" that restricted the rights of the recently freed slaves (see Chapter 8). In Tennessee, for example, African Americans could be given stiffer penalties than

Former Confederate vice president Alexander Stephens. *The Library of Congress.*

whites for the same crime, and they could be sold into temporary slavery if they lacked a job or permanent home. When it came time for Southern voters to pick their new congressmen, they sent a slate of ex-Confederate leaders to Washington, D.C.

Northerners were outraged at the list of new Southern congressmen, which included former Confederate vice president Alexander Stephens (1812–1883), as well as six ex-Confederate Cabinet members, nine men who had been high-ranking officers in the Confederate military, and fifty-eight former members of the Confederate Congress. Once sworn in as congressmen, these men could provide the votes for a lenient (merciful) Reconstruction policy that would preserve the Southern status quo.

Ironically, the North's victory in the war would increase the South's political power in Congress. As long as African Americans remained slaves, they counted as only three-fifths of a person for the purpose of drawing congressional districts based on population. Now that the Civil War had freed the slaves, each African American would count as a full person—providing a population boost that would give the South twelve new seats in the House of Representatives.

The Northern congressmen refused to put that much power in the hands of unchanged Southerners. They refused to seat, or swear into office, the Southern congressmen in December 1865. Instead, they created the Joint Committee on Reconstruction to gather testimony on the political atmosphere in the South. The committee would make recommendations on whether the Southern congressmen should be seated, whether the Freedmen's Bureau should be expanded to help ex-slaves start their new lives, and whether Congress should draft laws protecting African Americans' rights.

Slavery had been abolished (outlawed) by the end of 1865 under the Thirteenth Amendment to the Constitution

In this tobacco label depicting Reconstruction, the North and the South symbolically shake hands. *The Library of Congress.*

(see Chapter 2). The debate now centered on civil rights and voting rights for African Americans. Southerners believed the states should decide what rights to grant to African Americans, and President Johnson shared that view. But the newspaper accounts of racial violence and the Black Codes gave Northerners little hope that the Southern states would grant those rights to African Americans on their own. More and more, Northerners argued that the Southern states must provide those rights to African Americans before returning to the Union.

While the Joint Committee on Reconstruction was conducting its hearings in the spring of 1866, Congress was also considering a Fourteenth Amendment to the Constitution that would require states to give African Americans the right to vote—or lose the right to include African Americans in the population counts that determine how many congressmen each state gets (see Chapter 9). The committee asked Stephens: Would his native Georgia approve such an amendment in order to return to the Union? In reply, Stephens responded with his famous Reconstruction speech.

Things to remember while reading an excerpt from "On Reconstruction:"

- After the Civil War, Southerners believed they should be allowed to instantly return to the Union, with all of the rights they enjoyed before the war (including the right, under the Constitution, to send senators and representatives to Washington, D.C.). They did not think any other conditions could be placed on their ability to rejoin the Union.

- Some Northerners feared the Union victory would be a hollow one if the South was not forced to change. They did not want to see ex-Confederate leaders return to power or African Americans remain oppressed.

- The end of the war and the passage of the Thirteenth Amendment put an end to slavery. But other questions remained: Would African Americans be allowed to vote? Would they be granted other rights? Southerners believed each state should answer those questions for itself. But many Northerners did not trust the former slave owners to do right by African Americans.

Excerpt from "On Reconstruction"

*I think the people of the State [of Georgia] would be unwilling [to] do more than they have done for restoration [into the Union]. Restricted to **limited suffrage** would not be so objectionable as **general or universal**. But it is a matter that belongs to the State to regulate. The question of suffrage, whether universal or restricted, is one of State policy exclusively, as they believe. Individually I should not be opposed to a propose[d] system of restricted or limited suffrage to this class [of] our population.... The only view in their opinion that could possibly justify the war that was carried on by the federal government against them was the idea of the **indissolubleness** of the Union; that those who held the administration for the time were*

Limited suffrage: Voting rights for some African Americans, such as those who served in the military or knew how to read.

General or universal: Voting rights for all.

Indissolubleness: Unbreakable nature.

bound to enforce the execution of the laws and the maintenance of the integrity of the country under the Constitution.... They expected as soon as the confederate cause was abandoned that immediately the States would be brought back into their **practical relations** with the government as previously **constituted.** That is what they looked to. They expected that the States would immediately have their representatives in the Senate and in the House; and they expected in good faith, as loyal men, as the term is frequently used—loyal to law, order, and the Constitution—to support the government under the Constitution.... Towards the Constitution of the United States the great mass of our people were always as much **devoted** in their feelings as any people ever were towards any laws or people. They resorted to **secession** with a view of more securely maintaining these principles. And when they found they were not successful in their **object** in perfect good faith, as far as I can judge from meeting with them and **conversing** with them, looking to the future development of their country ... their **earnest** desire and expectation was to allow the past struggle ... to pass by and to co-operate with ... those of all **sections** who earnestly desire the preservation of constitutional liberty and the **perpetuation** of the government in its **purity.** They have been ... disappointed in this, and are ... patiently waiting, however, and believing that when the **passions** of the hour have passed away this delay in representation will cease....

My own opinion is, that these terms ought not to be offered as **conditions precedent.**... It would be best for the peace, harmony, and **prosperity** of the whole country that there should be an immediate restoration, an immediate bringing back of the States into their original practical relations; and let all these questions then be discussed in common council. Then the representatives from the south could be heard, and you and all could judge much better of the tone and **temper** of the people than you could from the opinions given by any individuals....

My judgment, therefore, is very **decided,** that it would have been better as soon as the **lamentable** conflict was over, when the people of the south abandoned their cause and agreed to accept the issue, desiring as they do to resume their places for the future in the Union, and to look to the arena of reason and justice for the protection of their rights in the Union—it would have been better to have allowed that result to take place, to follow under the policy adopted by the [Johnson] administration, than to delay or **hinder** it by **propositions** to **amend** the Constitution in respect to suffrage.... I think the people of all the southern States would in the halls of

Practical relations: Previous relationship.

Constituted: Established.

Devoted: Dedicated.

Secession: Leaving the Union.

Object: Goal.

Conversing: Talking.

Earnest: Serious.

Sections: Areas.

Perpetuation: Continuation.

Purity: Unspoiled nature.

Passions: Strong emotions.

Conditions precedent: Requirements.

Prosperity: Success.

Temper: State of mind.

Decided: Certain.

Lamentable: Sorrowful.

Hinder: Block.

Propositions: Plans.

Amend: Change.

*Congress discuss these questions calmly and **deliberately**. And if they did not show that the views they **entertained** were **just** and proper, such as to control the judgment of the people of the other sections and States, they would quietly yield to whatever should be constitutionally determined in common council. But I think they feel very sensitively the offer to them of propositions to accept while they are denied all voice ... in the discussion of these propositions. I think they feel very sensitively that they are denied the right to be heard.*

What happened next ...

The committee heard from 144 witnesses before concluding that many Southerners had a "vindictive and malicious hatred" of African Americans and feelings of "bitterness and defiance" toward the U.S. government, according to the *Report of the Joint Committee on Reconstruction.* The South's rebellion "is paraded as a virtue" in those states, the report said, while the North's efforts to preserve the country through war "are denounced as unjust and oppressive."

Congress responded with a bill expanding the powers and funding for the Freedmen's Bureau, the agency charged with getting African Americans on their feet. It also passed a series of Reconstruction Acts in 1867 (see Chapter 10) that would reorder the South's political system. New state governments would be formed under the watch of federal troops, and this time, African Americans would be invited to participate, and high-ranking ex-Confederates would be excluded. Some African Americans would hold elected offices in these new governments, and some whites would angrily lash back as members of the Ku Klux Klan and other white supremacists (those who believe that whites are superior and should be in charge; see Chapter 15).

But before that happened, Georgia got to vote on the Fourteenth Amendment. Just as Stephens predicted, his state rejected the measure. The amendment later became law anyway.

Did you know ...

- Stephens was a frail, often sick man who never weighed more than 100 pounds. An attorney who served in Congress before the war, Stephens was reelected to the House of Representatives in 1872. He served for a decade, then resigned and won the governor's election in Georgia. He died a few months after inauguration (being sworn in).

- Stephens was arrested at the end of the Civil War on charges of treason, or betraying one's country. He was released after spending five months at Fort Warren in Boston Harbor. Johnson eventually pardoned him and other top Confederates.

- Johnson's plan for granting pardons to Southerners created a small industry: For fees ranging from $150 to $500, lawyers and brokers promised to line up presidential pardons for their clients. As noted in *Reconstruction: After the Civil War,* "this was an ideal climate for corruption, and the enormous pressures applied by those who wanted pardons in order to participate in political activities or to regain their property made graft [the use of bribes or political influence] inevitable."

- Johnson and Congress continued to fight over the Reconstruction plans for the South. They later disagreed over the role of the Freedmen's Bureau and the need for civil rights legislation. Ultimately Congress tried—and narrowly failed—to remove Johnson from office by impeachment.

Consider the following ...

- Why did Congress refuse to admit the newly elected senators and representatives from the South?

- Under what conditions would you allow the Southern states to return to the Union after the war? Who would be allowed to create the new state governments and hold elected offices?

- Presidents Lincoln and Johnson drafted Reconstruction policies. So did Congress (a couple of times). Who should be responsible for creating such a policy: the president or Congress?

For More Information

Franklin, John Hope. *Reconstruction: After the Civil War.* 2nd ed. Chicago: University of Chicago Press, 1994.

McPherson, James M. *The Struggle for Equality.* Princeton: Princeton University Press, 1964.

Reid, Whitelaw. *After the War: A Southern Tour.* New York: Harper & Row, 1965. Also available at *Making of America Books.* http://www.hti.umich.edu/cgi/t/text/text-idx?c=moa;idno=AFJ8942 (accessed on September 17, 2004).

Report of the Joint Committee on Reconstruction of the First Session Thirty-Ninth Congress. Washington, DC: Government Printing Office, 1866.

Schott, Thomas Edwin. *Alexander H. Stephens of Georgia: A Biography.* Baton Rouge: Louisiana State University Press, 1988.

Andrew Johnson

8

Excerpt from his veto of the Civil Rights Bill of 1866
Carried forth on March 27, 1866

The president angers many by vetoing a bill designed to assist African Americans

S even months after the slaves were freed by the North's victory in the American Civil War (1861–65), the state of Mississippi passed new laws affecting African American residents. For the first time, African Americans were given rights to buy land, sue and be sued, even marry in state-recognized ceremonies. But the laws did not stop there. Every African American person had to provide written proof of having a "lawful home or employment." Any African Americans caught wandering the streets at night, neglecting their jobs, or even "misspend[ing] what they earn" could be arrested as vagrants (jobless or homeless people) and jailed for up to ten days. African American children whose parents could not provide for them, at least in a judge's determination, could be sent to white families to serve as apprentices (or assistants).

Mississippi was the first state to pass such discriminatory "Black Codes," but other Southern communities would quickly follow suit. The Louisiana towns of Opelousas and Saint Landry Parish required African Americans to get permission from town leaders before preaching to congregations, and barred African Americans from carrying guns or

"The distinction of race and color is by the bill made to operate in favor of the colored and against the white race."

Civil Rights Act of 1866

The Civil Rights Act of 1866 provided equal rights for African Americans:

An Act to protect all Persons in the United States in their Civil Rights, and furnish the Means [methods] of their Vindication [defense].

Be it enacted … That all persons born in the United States and not subject to any foreign power, excluding Indians not taxed, are hereby declared to be citizens of the United States; and such citizens, of every race and color, without regard to any previous condition of slavery or involuntary [forced] servitude, except as a punishment for crime whereof the party shall have been duly convicted, shall have the same right in every State and Territory in the United States, to make and enforce contracts, to sue, be parties, and give evidence, to inherit, purchase, lease, sell, hold, and convey real and personal property, and to full and equal benefit of all laws and proceedings for the security of person and property, as is enjoyed by white citizens, and shall be sub-ject to like punishment, pains, and penalties, and to none other, any law, statute, ordinance, regulation, or custom, to the contrary notwithstanding.

Section 2. And be it further enacted, That any person who, under color [appearance] or any law, statute, ordinance, regulation, or custom, shall subject, or cause to be subjected, any inhabitant [resident] of any State or Territory to the deprivation [withholding] of any right secured or protected by this act, or to different punishment, pains, or penalties on account of such person having at any time been held in a condition of slavery or involuntary servitude, except as a punishment for crime whereof the party shall have been duly convicted, or by reason of his color or race, than is prescribed for the punishment of white persons, shall be deemed guilty of a misdemeanor, and, on conviction, shall be punished by fine not exceeding one thousand dollars, or imprisonment not exceeding one year, or both, in the discretion of the court....

other weapons unless they belonged to the military. In South Carolina, African Americans working as anything other than farmers or servants had to pay an annual tax ranging from $10 to $100, as noted in *Reconstruction: America's Unfinished Revolution*. In Florida, disobedience or "disrespect" to an employer was a crime. Local militias, often filled with former Confederate soldiers still in uniform, "frequently terrorized the African American population, ransacking their homes to seize shotguns and other property and abusing those who refused to sign plantation labor contracts."

This was not the outcome the North envisioned at the end of the Civil War. Slavery may have ended, but a new series of Black Codes kept the South's four million African Americans as second-class citizens. Making matters worse, blacks found little justice in the local courts. They could only testify as witnesses in cases involving an African American person, and they were barred from sitting on juries. Leading abolitionist (slavery opponent) James Miller McKim (1810–1874) asked Congress to create a separate military court system for African Americans through the Freedmen's Bureau, the federal agency created to help former slaves start their new lives (see Chapter 4). U.S. senator Lyman Trumbull (1813–1896) of Illinois responded with a bill expanding the Freedmen's Bureau to provide such courts. He also offered a bill outlining equal rights for African Americans.

The latter bill became known as the Civil Rights Act of 1866. The bill declared that everyone born in the United States, with the exception of Native Americans, was a citizen. This would extend citizenship to the African Americans—a response to the infamous 1857 *Dred Scott* decision, in which the U.S. Supreme Court said African Americans could not file lawsuits because they were not U.S. citizens. The bill also gave citizens "of every race and color" the right to enter into contracts, buy and sell property, and enjoy "full and equal benefit of all laws … enjoyed by white citizens" (see box). Any person depriving an ex-slave of these rights could be tried in the federal courts (separate from the local court system), and sentenced to up to a year in prison and fined up to $1,000.

Congress passed the bill March 13, 1866, but no one was sure President Andrew Johnson (1808–1875; served 1865–69), a former slave owner with Southern sympathies, would sign it. A month earlier, Johnson vetoed the expanded Freedmen's Bureau bill, which he thought trampled on local communities' rights by establishing a military court system for African Americans during peacetime. He argued that African Americans already had the ability to take care of themselves and use the existing local courts. He also objected that the bill was passed without input from the newly elected Southern congressmen, whom the Northerners refused to seat until a new Reconstruction policy was created for the South (see Chapter 7). As noted in *The Struggle for Equality*, Johnson's veto surprised many, including Speaker of the House Schuyler Colfax (1823–1885), who bet a friend a box of Cuban cigars that the president would sign the bill.

Johnson started getting criticism from the supporters and opponents of the Civil Rights Bill. Longtime political fig-

Political cartoon from about 1866, referring to President Andrew Johnson's veto of the Freedmen's Bureau Bill.
© Corbis-Bettmann. Reproduced by permission.

ure Francis P. Blair Sr. (1791–1876) wrote Johnson a four-page letter complaining that the bill would leave the states unable to "discriminate between *Whites* & Black," a result he considered "disastrous," according to *Politics, Principle, and Prejudice, 1865–1866.* Ohio governor Jacob Cox (1828–1900) urged Johnson to sign the bill because the public supported granting the freedmen "the same rights of property and persons, the same remedies for injuries received and the same penalties for wrongs committed, as other men...."

But Johnson's advisors knew he was leaning against the bill, which he viewed as another federal intrusion on issues belonging to the states. His advisors also knew another unpopular veto could undermine his efforts to bring the Southern states back into the Union as quickly as possible, by allowing his opponents to paint him as unsympathetic to the problems facing African Americans. According to *Politics, Principle, and Prejudice*, Secretary of State William Seward (1801–1872) sent a note to Johnson the night before the veto was announced: "If you can find a way to intimate [imply] that *you are not opposed to the policy of the bill,* but *only to its detailed* provisions, it will be a great improvement and make the support of the veto easier for our friends in Congress." Instead, Johnson sent a strongly worded veto message that even his most loyal supporters would struggle to defend.

Things to remember while reading an excerpt from Johnson's veto of the Civil Rights Bill of 1866:

- The end of the Civil War had freed the slaves, but Southern states responded by passing Black Codes that required African Americans to have jobs, prevented them from being out at night, and allowed their children to be apprenticed to white families.

- Johnson was a strong supporter of states' rights, and believed local governments should decide for themselves what rights to grant their citizens. After seeing the discriminatory Black Codes adopted in most Southern states after the war, however, Northerners believed the federal government should pass laws to protect African Americans from being mistreated.

- Johnson objected to a previous bill that had been passed without input from the Southern congressmen, whom the Northerners refused to seat until a new Reconstruction plan was approved for the South. The president thought it was unfair for Congress to pass laws affecting the South without hearing from those states.

President Andrew Johnson.
The Library of Congress.

- A Southerner and former slave owner himself, Johnson did not believe African Americans were entitled to the same rights as whites. Johnson made his case in this passage with an example about interracial marriage, a socially forbidden subject that struck at the heart of whites' worst fears about racial equality.

Excerpt from Johnson's veto of the Civil Rights Bill of 1866

*By the first section of the bill all persons born in the United States and not subject to any foreign power, excluding **Indians not taxed**,*

Indians not taxed: Native Americans were not taxed and regulated as U.S. citizens.

Comprehends: Includes.

Gypsies: Wandering people.

Grave: Serious.

Sound: Wise.

Supposed: Assumed.

Requisite: Necessary.

Immunities: Legal exemptions.

Conviction: Strong belief.

Institutions: Customs.

Probation: Test period.

Attaining: Getting.

Coveted: Greatly desired.

Fixed: Firmly placed.

Vast: Large.

Jurisdiction: Authority.

Enumerated: Listed.

Exclusively: Only.

Expedient: Useful.

Statutes: Laws.

Enacted: Passed as law.

Intermarry: Wed across racial lines.

Mulatto: Person who is half–African American, half–white.

Repeals: Overrides.

Abrogate: Nullify.

Embraced: Included.

Enumeration: Listing.

---

are declared to be citizens of the United States. This provision **comprehends** the Chinese of the Pacific States, Indians subject to taxation, the people called **gypsies**, as well as the entire race designated as blacks.... Every individual of these races born in the United States is by the bill made a citizen....

The **grave** question presents itself whether, when eleven of the thirty-six States are unrepresented in Congress at the present time, it is **sound** policy to make our entire colored population and all other excepted classes citizens of the United States. Four millions of them have just emerged from slavery into freedom. Can it be reasonably **supposed** that they possess the **requisite** qualifications to entitle them to all the privileges and **immunities** of citizens of the United States? Have the people of the several States expressed such a **conviction**....? The policy of the Government from its origin to the present time seems to have been that persons who are strangers to and unfamiliar with our **institutions** and our laws should pass through a certain **probation,** at the end of which, before **attaining** the **coveted** prize, they must give evidence of their fitness to receive and to exercise the rights of citizens as contemplated by the Constitution of the United States. The bill in effect proposes a discrimination against large numbers of intelligent, worthy, and patriotic foreigners [who must wait five years for citizenship], and in favor of the negro [who would automatically get it]....

A perfect equality of the white and colored races is attempted to be **fixed** by Federal law in every State of the Union over the **vast** field of State **jurisdiction** covered by these **enumerated** rights. In no one of these can any State ever exercise any power of discrimination between the different races. In the exercise of State policy over matters **exclusively** affecting the people of each State it has frequently been thought **expedient** to discriminate between the two races. By the **statutes** of some of the States, Northern as well as Southern, it is **enacted**, for instance, that no white person shall **intermarry** with a negro or **mulatto**....

I do not say that this bill **repeals** State laws on the subject of marriage between the two races.... I cite this discrimination, however, as an instance of the State policy as to discrimination, and to inquire whether if Congress can **abrogate** all State laws of discrimination between the two races in the matter of real estate, of suits, and of contracts generally Congress may not also repeal the State laws as to the contract of marriage between the two races. Hitherto every subject **embraced** in the **enumeration** of rights contained in this bill has been considered as exclusively belonging to the States. They all relate to the internal *police* and economy of the *respective* States. They are matters which in each State concern the *domestic* condition of its people, varying in each according to its own *peculiar* circumstances and the safety and well-being of its own citizens....

If, in any State which denies to a colored person any one of all those rights, that person should commit a crime against the laws of a State—murder, *arson,* rape, or any other crime—all protection and punishment through the courts of the State are taken away, and he can only be tried and punished in the Federal courts.... So that over this vast domain of criminal *jurisprudence* provided by each State for the protection of its own citizens and for the punishment of all persons who violate its criminal laws, Federal law, whenever it can be made to apply, displaces State law.... This section of the bill undoubtedly comprehends cases and *authorizes* the exercise of powers that are not, by the Constitution, within the jurisdiction of the courts of the United States....

I do not propose to consider the policy of this bill. To me the details of the bill seem *fraught* with evil. The white race and the black race of the South have *hitherto* lived together under the relation of master and slave—*capital* owning labor. Now, suddenly, that relation is changed, and as to ownership capital and labor are *divorced.* They stand now each master of itself. In this new relation, one being necessary to the other, there will be a new adjustment, which both are deeply interested in making *harmonious*....

This bill *frustrates* this adjustment. It intervenes between capital and labor and attempts to settle questions of political economy through the *agency* of numerous officials whose interest it will be to *foment discord* between the two races, for as the *breach* widens their employment will continue, and when it is closed their occupation will *terminate.*

In all our history, in all our experience as a people living under Federal and State law, no such system as that contemplated by the details of this bill has ever before been proposed or adopted. They establish for the security of the colored race *safeguards* which go *infinitely* beyond any that the General Government has ever provided for the white race. In fact, the distinction of race and color is by the bill made to operate in favor of the colored and against the white race. They interfere with the *municipal* legislation of the States, with the relations existing exclusively between a State and its citizens, or between *inhabitants* of the same State—an absorption and as-

Police: Control of order.

Respective: Individual.

Domestic: Of one's home.

Peculiar: Special.

Arson: Crime of setting fires.

Jurisprudence: Division of law.

Authorizes: Allows.

Fraught: Filled.

Hitherto: Up until now.

Capital: Wealth.

Divorced: Separated.

Harmonious: In agreement.

Frustrates: Prevents.

Agency: Action.

Foment: Stir up.

Discord: Disagreement.

Breach: Gap (between the races).

Terminate: End.

Safeguards: Protections.

Infinitely: Endlessly.

Municipal: Local.

Inhabitants: Residents.

Acquiesced: Accepted.

Sap: Weaken.

Federative: Central government.

Tendency: Course.

Resuscitate: Revive.

Arrest: Stop.

*sumption of power by the General Government which, if **acquiesced** in, must **sap** and destroy our **federative** system of limited powers and break down the barriers which preserve the rights of the States. It is another step, or rather stride, toward centralization and the concentration of all legislative powers in the National Government. The **tendency** of the bill must be to **resuscitate** the spirit of rebellion and to **arrest** the progress of those influences which are more closely drawing around the States the bonds of union and peace.*

What happened next ...

Johnson's veto angered most members of Congress. Moderate Republicans who had tried to compromise with the president decided he was a lost cause. U.S. representative Henry L. Dawes (1816–1903) of Massachusetts wrote that Johnson's veto message deprived "every friend he has of the least ground upon which to stand and defend him," according to *Politics, Principle, and Prejudice, 1865–1866*. Dawes and the other moderates teamed up with the Radical Republicans—the members of Congress who opposed slavery and supported equal rights for African Americans—to create the two-thirds majority needed to overturn Johnson's veto. They succeeded, and the bill became law April 6, 1866.

This newly formed super-majority would remain a powerful force for the rest of Johnson's embattled term. Congress revived Trumbull's expanded Freedmen's Bureau Bill and passed it over Johnson's veto. Congress also pushed the Reconstruction Acts of 1867 (see Chapter 10) over the president's veto, carving the South into five military-controlled districts where whites and African Americans would have to work together to build their new state governments. Ultimately a frustrated Congress would impeach (charge with wrongdoing) Johnson for interfering with those Reconstruction plans, although the Senate would come one vote short of removing him from office (see Chapter 11).

In the meantime, Congress would look to make permanent the new safeguards for African Americans. The same protections outlined in the Civil Rights Bill would become part of the Fourteenth Amendment to the U.S. Constitution (see Chapter 9) in 1868. Both measures would lay the groundwork for the Fifteenth Amendment (see Chapter 16) in 1870 granting African American men the right to vote.

Did you know …

- Under many Black Codes, the sheriff could "hire out" arrested African Americans who were unable to pay their fines. The African Americans would have to work for whoever paid off their fines until the debt was repaid. This measure ensured whites would still have a source of cheap labor in the postslavery era.

- Some Northern states during this era excluded African Americans from juries, banned marriages between African Americans and whites, or required separate school facilities for the races—not unlike their neighbors to the South. But Northerners grew concerned over the Southern Black Codes that forced African Americans to work and place their children in apprenticeships. They feared those rules were a step toward recreating the institution of slavery, which the North had fought to end through the Civil War.

- The Civil Rights Bill of 1866 outlawed government-based discrimination, such as different laws or stricter penalties for African Americans. Another Civil Rights Bill in 1875 (see Chapter 18) would go a step further: It banned discrimination in the private sector, requiring hotels, restaurants, theaters, and public transportation systems to treat African Americans the same as whites. The U.S. Supreme Court would later overturn that bill.

Consider the following …

- Why did the Southern states and local governments pass Black Codes after the Civil War?

- Why did Johnson include an example about interracial marriage in his veto message? What was his point?

• Johnson argued that the states should be allowed to decide which rights to grant their residents. Can you think of other rights or privileges today that vary from state to state?

For More Information

Cox, LaWanda, and John H. Cox. *Politics, Principle, and Prejudice, 1865–1866: Dilemma of Reconstruction America.* New York: Atheneum, 1969.

Foner, Eric. *Reconstruction: America's Unfinished Revolution.* New York: Harper & Row, 1988.

McPherson, James M. *Ordeal by Fire: The Civil War and Reconstruction.* New York: Alfred A. Knopf, 1982.

McPherson, James M. *The Struggle for Equality.* Princeton, NJ: Princeton University Press, 1964.

Fourteenth Amendment to the U.S. Constitution

Ratifieed by the required three-fourths of states on July 9, 1868
Reprinted on *GPO Access: Constitution of the United States* (Web site)

Ex-slaves are granted citizenship and afforded civil liberties

9

The rise of "Black Codes"—discriminatory local laws subjecting African Americans to harsher penalties or forced labor for certain crimes, among other restrictions—prompted the U.S. Congress to pass the Civil Rights Act of 1866 (see Chapter 8). The bill stated that all African Americans born in the United States were citizens entitled to the "full and equal benefit of all laws" enjoyed by whites. It also outlawed providing "different punishment, pains, or penalties" for ex-slaves than for whites.

Congress gathered the two-thirds majority necessary to pass the bill over the veto of President Andrew Johnson (1808–1875; served 1865–69). But the Northerners still had two problems. U.S. representative Thaddeus Stevens (1792–1868) of Pennsylvania, a leader of the antislavery Radical Republicans, feared the Civil Rights Act could be overturned by a future Congress less sympathetic to African Americans' rights. Congress also needed to establish the ground rules for Reconstruction, the process of bringing the Southern states back into the Union after the American Civil War (1861–65).

"No State shall make or enforce any law which shall abridge the privileges or immunities of citizens of the United States; nor shall any State deprive any person of life, liberty, or property, without due process of law...."

THE CONSTITUTIONAL AMENDMENT!

GEARY
Is for Negro Suffrage.

STEVENS
Advocates it.

FORNEY
Howls for it.

McCLURE
Speaks for it.

CAMERON
Wants it.

The LEAGUE
Sustains it.

They are not, and want to make

The Negro the Equal
OF THE POOR WHITE MAN,
and then rule them both.

The BLACK Roll
CANDIDATES FOR CONGRESS
WHO VOTED FOR THIS BILL.

THAD. STEVENS
WM. D. KELLEY
CHAS. O'NEILL
LEONARD MYERS
JNO. M. BROOMALL
GEORGE F. MILLER
STEPHEN F. WILSON
ULYSSES MERCUR
GEO. V. LAWRENCE
GLENNI W. SCHOFIELD
J. K. MOORHEAD
THOMAS WILLIAMS

THE RADICAL PLATFORM--"NEGRO SUFFRAGE THE ONLY ISSUE!"

Every man who votes for Geary or for a Radical Candidate for Congress, votes as surely for Negro Suffrage and Negro Equality, as if they were printed on his ballot.

A political broadside shows African Americans fighting through crowds of whites to gain entrance to a polling booth. *The Library of Congress.*

The Fourteenth Amendment to the U.S. Constitution, introduced April 30, 1866, tried to answer both concerns. The first section echoed the key points of the Civil Rights Act: The states could not "deprive any person of life, liberty, or property, without due process of law" or deny any person "equal protection of the laws." Placing those rights in the Constitution would make it much harder for a future Congress to take them away, as it would require passing a new amendment, a process that needs the approval of at least two-thirds of the members of Congress and at least three-fourths of the states.

The second section of the Fourteenth Amendment offered a compromise in the heated debate over African American suffrage (voting rights). The Radical Republicans had pushed for a measure granting African American men the right to vote, arguing that ex-slaves would not be truly free without a voice in the political process. But some moderate congressmen (many of them facing reelection in 1866) feared the idea would be unpopular even in the North, where many whites who opposed slavery still viewed African Americans as inferior. White voters in Connecticut, Minnesota, and Wisconsin had defeated proposals in 1865 to give African Americans the ballot in those states. There was also a legal question of whether the decision on African American suffrage belonged to the federal government or the individual states.

The amendment offered a compromise: Any state that denied some men the right to vote would not be able to count those men in the congressional districts, which are defined by population. Moderates hoped that measure would give Southern states an incentive to give African American men the ballot, as the South would lose up to one-third of its congressional seats if it failed to do so. But leading abolitionists (opponents of slavery) such as Frederick Douglass (1817–1895), who was African American, criticized the compromise. "To say that I am a citizen to pay taxes … obey the laws, support the government, and fight the battles of the country, but, in all that respects voting and representation [in Congress], I am but as so much inert [powerless] matter, is to insult my manhood," said Douglass, as quoted in *The Struggle for Equality*.

The third section of the Fourteenth Amendment also reflected a compromise, this time over the political rights of ex-Confederates. To prevent the former "rebels" from having a hand in building the new Southern state governments, the Radical Republicans wanted to bar all former supporters of the Confederacy from voting until 1870. But the moderates thought the measure was too extreme. After some debate, Congress changed the section to allow ex-Confederates to vote, but to exclude some of the higher-ranking officials from elected office. Specifically, anyone who had taken an oath before the war to support the Constitution (as most elected officials do), then participated in the "rebellion" against the Union, was not allowed to hold elected office again.

The fourth section rejected any responsibility for the debt accumulated by the Confederacy during the war. Finally, the fifth section gave Congress the power to enforce these measures by passing laws.

In most points, the Fourteenth Amendment reflected a compromise between the ideals of the abolitionists and the reality of what most whites were willing to accept. As quoted in *Reconstruction: America's Unfinished Revolution,* U.S. senator James W. Grimes (1816–1872) of Iowa said, "It is not exactly what any of us wanted, but we were each compelled to surrender some of our individual preferences in order to secure anything." Some abolitionists supported the amendment, hoping it would lay the groundwork for a future amendment granting African Americans the right to vote. Others opposed it for not going far enough. They particularly opposed the idea of allowing Southern states back into the Union if they approved the Fourteenth Amendment. They feared this would bring an end to Reconstruction without placing the ballot in the hands of African American men.

Congress was split along party lines—Republicans in favor of the amendment, Democrats against it—for months of passionate debate. U.S. representative Andrew J. Rogers (1828–1900), a Democrat from New Jersey, said the amendment was an attempt to legitimize (or legally justify) the Civil Rights Act, which he believed to be unconstitutional, according to a speech reprinted in *Reconstruction: Opposing Viewpoints.* The Civil Rights Act and the amendment both stepped on states' rights to determine how African Americans should be treated, Rogers said.

> Take the State of Kentucky, for instance. According to her laws, if a negro commits a rape upon a white woman he is punished by death. If a white man commits that offense, the punishment is imprisonment. Now, according to this proposed amendment, the Congress of the United States is to have the right to repeal [undo] the law of Kentucky and compel that State to inflict the same punishment upon a white man for rape as upon a black man.

But U.S. representative John A. Bingham (1815–1900), an Ohio Republican who helped draft the amendment, said the measure simply allowed Congress to enforce the rights already outlined in the Constitution. Specifically, the Fifth Amendment states no person shall be "deprived of life, liberty, or property without due process of the law." The Fourteenth Amendment would allow the federal government to step in if one of the states so deprived its citizens, Bingham argued in a speech reprinted in *Reconstruction: Opposing Viewpoints.*

The adoption of the proposed amendment will take from the States no rights that belong to the States. They elect their Legislatures; they enact their laws for the punishment of crimes against life, liberty, or property; but in the event of the adoption of this amendment, if they conspire together to enact laws refusing equal protection to life, liberty, or property, the Congress is thereby vested with power to hold them to answer before the bar of the national courts for the violation of their oaths and of the rights of their fellow-men. Why should it not be so?

Stevens, one of the leading Radical Republicans in the House, summed up the amendment this way: "Whatever law punishes a white man for a crime shall punish the black man precisely in the same way and to the same degree. Whatever law protects the white man shall afford 'equal' protection to the black man." The House of Representatives approved the amendment in May 1866; the Senate did the same the following month. Now the measure needed at least three-fourths of the states to pass it.

Things to remember while reading the Fourteenth Amendment:

- In response to the discriminatory Black Codes that popped up in the South after the Civil War, Congress passed the Civil Rights Act of 1866, which prohibited states from creating different laws or criminal penalties for African Americans and whites. But some Republicans feared a future Congress that was less sympathetic to African Americans could overturn the Civil Rights Act. So they put similar civil rights protections in the first section of the Fourteenth Amendment, knowing it would be very difficult for a future Congress to undo an amendment to the Constitution.

- Congress, like the nineteenth-century public, was divided on whether African American men should have the right to vote, and whether the federal government or the states should make the decision. The second section of the Fourteenth Amendment offered a compromise: States that refused to grant some men the ballot could lose some of their congressional seats, which are based on population. Some people hoped this would give states the incentive to provide African American men the ballot.

• After the Civil War, many Northerners were wary of seeing former Confederate leaders appear in the new Southern state governments—a possible sign that the "rebellion" against the Union had not been extinguished. The third section of the Fourteenth Amendment addresses that concern by barring certain high-ranking ex-Confederates from elected office.

Fourteenth Amendment to the U.S. Constitution

*Section 1. All persons born or **naturalized** in the United States and subject to the **jurisdiction** thereof, are citizens of the United States and of the State **wherein** they reside. No State shall make or enforce any law which shall **abridge** the privileges or **immunities** of citizens of the United States; nor shall any State deprive any person of life, liberty, or property, without **due process** of law; nor deny to any person within its jurisdiction the equal protection of the laws.*

*Section 2. Representatives shall be **apportioned** among the several States according to their **respective** numbers, counting the whole number of persons in each State, excluding **Indians not taxed**. But when the right to vote at any election for the choice of electors for President and Vice President of the United States, Representatives in Congress, the Executive and Judicial officers of a State, or the members of the Legislature thereof, is denied to any of the male **inhabitants** of such State, being twenty-one years of age, and citizens of the United States, or in any way abridged, except for participation in rebellion, or other crime, the basis of representation therein shall be reduced in the **proportion** which the number of such male citizens shall bear to the whole number of male citizens twenty-one years of age in such State.*

*Section 3. No person shall be a Senator or Representative in Congress, or elector of President and Vice President, or hold any office, civil or military, under the United States, or under any State, who, having previously taken an oath, as a member of Congress, or as an officer of the United States, or as a member of any State legislature, or as an executive or judicial officer of any State, to support the Constitution of the United States, shall have engaged in **insurrection** or rebellion against the same, or given aid or **comfort** to the*

Naturalized: Granted citizenship.

Jurisdiction: Authority.

Wherein: In which.

Abridge: Lessen.

Immunities: Exemptions.

Due process: A legal proceeding, such as a trial.

Apportioned: Distributed.

Respective: Individual.

Indians not taxed: Native Americans were not taxed or treated as U.S. citizens.

Inhabitants: Residents.

Proportion: Amount.

Insurrection: Uprising.

Comfort: Relief.

enemies thereof. But Congress may by a vote of two-thirds of each House, remove such disability.

*Section 4. The **validity** of the public debt of the United States, authorized by law, including debts **incurred** for payment of **pensions** and **bounties** for services in **suppressing** insurrection or rebellion, shall not be questioned. But neither the United States nor any State shall assume or pay any debt or obligation incurred in aid of insurrection or rebellion against the United States, or any claim for the loss or **emancipation** of any slave; but all such debts, obligations and claims shall be held illegal and **void**.*

*Section 5. The Congress shall have power to enforce, by appropriate legislation, the **provisions** of this article.*

Validity: Legal force.

Incurred: Brought about.

Pensions: Wages (often to retirees).

Bounties: Rewards for wanted men.

Suppressing: Putting down by force.

Emancipation: Freedom.

Void: Without legal force.

Provisions: Conditions.

What happened next ...

Congress discussed the possibility of requiring the Southern states to adopt the Fourteenth Amendment in order to rejoin the Union. The state of Tennessee jumped at the idea and passed the Fourteenth Amendment during the summer of 1866, then asked to be readmitted to the Union. In the spirit of cooperation, Congress agreed, but some abolitionists were upset this was done without giving African American men in Tennessee the ballot. "Tennessee is permitted to deny to her blacks a voice in the state, while she herself is permitted to resume her voice in the nation," wrote social reformer Theodore Tilton (1835–1907), as quoted in *The Struggle for Equality*. "The spectacle is a national humiliation."

The Fourteenth Amendment would face a rocky road to approval. The rest of the ex-Confederate states initially rejected it, although some of the new Southern state governments formed under the Reconstruction Acts of 1867 (see Chapter 10) later approved it. Complicating matters, two Northern states that approved it—New Jersey and Ohio—later passed resolutions withdrawing their support. On July 20, 1868, Secretary of State William Seward (1801–1872) announced that the amendment received the necessary three-fourths support from the states, but his count included the

From African Americans' Rights to Women's Rights

The antislavery movement set out to free African Americans—but along the way, the cause helped white women secure greater rights for themselves. Women were rarely allowed to make public speeches in the early 1800s, but that changed as they formed their own abolitionist societies, held meetings, and gathered petitions to outlaw slavery (even though women could not vote). Sarah Grimké (1792–1873) and Angelina Grimké (1805–1879), South Carolina sisters who opposed their family's slaveholding ways, became popular speakers at women's clubs, and soon men flocked to hear them, too. This created a stir among traditionalists who believed women belonged at home, raising their children and ignoring politics. The Council of Congregationalist Ministers of Massachusetts wrote a letter in the 1830s, reprinted in *Century of Struggle,* condemning political activism among women. "When she assumes the place and tone of man as a public reformer … her character becomes unnatural," the council wrote.

Such warnings would not silence the women who believed slavery was wrong. In fact, as noted in *Century of Struggle,* the Grimkés "began to answer their critics, linking the two issues of slavery and the position of women." Sarah Grimké wrote articles and brochures explaining that women must have a political voice in order to help men fight the evil of slavery. "To me," she wrote in 1838, "it is perfectly clear that whatsoever it is morally right for a man to do, it is morally right for a woman to do."

These early abolitionists were criticized, sometimes threatened, for straying from the role of traditional wives and mothers. This only fueled their desire to work

withdrawn states of New Jersey and Ohio. In a rare step, Congress passed a resolution declaring the Fourteenth Amendment to be part of the Constitution. In order to reach the three-fourths state approval requirement, Congress's count excluded the Southern states that had not yet been readmitted to the Union. According to *The Reconstruction of the Nation,* despite this unusual route to approval, "the amendment has been completely validated by practice and judicial decree [court decisions]."

As for the question of African American suffrage, Congress would offer a separate amendment in 1869 granting African American men the right to vote. The Fifteenth Amendment would be approved the following year (see Chapter 16). But it is worth noting: Another half-century

Women's rights advocate Sarah Grimké. *The Library of Congress.*

nize meetings, collect petitions, and circulate pamphlets—skills that would serve the women's rights movement. At the 1848 Seneca Falls (New York) Convention on women's rights, leading abolitionist Frederick Douglass even supported the resolution of Elizabeth Cady Stanton (1815–1902) calling for voting rights for women.

But the two movements parted ways over the Fourteenth Amendment to the Constitution, as noted in *Reconstruction: America's Unfinished Revolution*. Why? For the first time in the Constitution, the amendment used the term "male" to describe the people entitled to voting rights. The leaders of the women's suffrage movement felt "a deep sense of betrayal." A half-century would pass before women got the right to vote in 1920 under the Nineteenth Amendment.

harder, not only for the antislavery cause, but for their right to participate in the political process. Through the abolitionist movement, these women learned how to orga-

would pass before women of either color would get the ballot under a separate constitutional amendment.

Did you know ...

- Several leaders of the women's suffrage movement, including Susan B. Anthony (1820–1906) and Elizabeth Cady Stanton (1815–1902), also supported the abolitionist movement to end slavery and give African Americans the ballot (see box). Both causes were based on the idea that all people are equal. But the leaders of the two movements parted ways over the Fourteenth Amendment, as noted in *Reconstruction: America's Unfinished Revolution*. For the first time in the Constitution, the amendment used the word "male" to describe people entitled to voting rights. The women's suffrage leaders felt "a deep sense of betrayal."

- During the 1866 campaign, some Northern Congressmen painted the amendment as a way to keep the South from attaining too much political power—not as a measure to help African Americans.

- New Jersey, one of two Northern states that withdrew its support for the amendment, later reversed itself again. The state made a symbolic announcement on November 12, 1980, supporting the Fourteenth Amendment. Other states offered their support to the amendment years after it was ratified: Delaware in 1901, Maryland and California in 1959, and Kentucky in 1976.

Consider the following ...

- Why didn't the Fourteenth Amendment guarantee voting rights for African American men?

- What political rights, if any, do you think former Confederates should have had after the Civil War?

- Why did the majority in Congress press for the Fourteenth Amendment, after they already passed the Civil Rights Act with some of the same provisions?

For More Information

Flexner, Eleanor. *Century of Struggle: The Woman's Rights Movement in the United States*. Cambridge, MA: Harvard University Press, 1975.

Foner, Eric. *Reconstruction: America's Unfinished Revolution*. New York: Harper & Row, 1988.

McPherson, James M. *The Struggle for Equality*. Princeton, NJ: Princeton University Press, 1964.

Patrick, Rembert W. *The Reconstruction of the Nation*. New York: Oxford University Press, 1967.

Stalcup, Brenda, ed. *Reconstruction: Opposing Viewpoints*. San Diego: Greenhaven Press, 1995.

United States Government Printing Office. "Fourteenth Amendment—Rights Guaranteed: Privileges and Immunities of Citizenship, Due Process, and Equal Protection." *GPO Access: Constitution of the United States*. http://www.gpoaccess.gov/constitution/html/amdt14.html (accessed on September 20, 2004).

First Reconstruction Act of 1867

Enacted by U.S. Congress, March 2, 1867

Reprinted on *About Texas: Texas State Library and Archives Commission* (Web site)

Congress devises a plan for remaking Southern society

10

T wo horse-drawn carriages—one driven by a white man, the other by an African American man—collided May 1, 1866, on the streets of Memphis, Tennessee, a city that swelled with African American refugees and racial tensions after the American Civil War (1861–65). Police arrested the African American driver, and a nearby group of African American war veterans stepped in to ask what was happening. The scene attracted a crowd of white men, many of them resentful of the African Americans who were making a good living in the city or were wandering the streets of Memphis looking for work. Tempers began to flare. Shoves turned into punches, touching off one of the bloodiest riots of the post-war era, as noted in *Reconstruction: America's Unfinished Revolution*. By the end of the three-day Memphis riots, at least forty-six African Americans were dead, five African American women had been raped, and "hundreds of black dwellings, churches, and schools were pillaged or destroyed by fire."

A second round of riots broke out in New Orleans on July 30, 1866, outside a convention that had been called to add voting rights for African American men to the Louisiana state

> "No legal State governments or adequate protection for life or property now exists in the rebel States...."

constitution. White mobs—including some police officers—attacked any African American person in sight, firing shots at African Americans even as they fled or waved white flags of surrender, as reported in *Reconstruction: America's Unfinished Revolution.* The riot left thirty-four African Americans dead and more than a hundred injured. Union general Philip H. Sheridan (1831–1888) described the scene as "an absolute massacre."

News accounts of these riots and other attacks convinced many Northerners that President Andrew Johnson's (1808–1875; served 1865–69) plan for rebuilding the South was not working. In many Southern towns, such as New Orleans, voters elected ex-Confederate leaders as mayors and other officials. Not only did the police officers fail to protect African Americans under attack, but many of them joined in the riots. It was clear to African American abolitionist (slavery opponent) Frederick Douglass (1817–1895) that the South had replaced slavery with mob violence and discriminatory laws against African Americans. The result was the same: Whites were still able to control and, in some cases, terrorize African Americans.

Douglass wrote a passionate essay, published in January 1867 in the *Atlantic Monthly,* asking Congress to give African American men the right to vote. "There is something immeasurably mean, to say nothing of the cruelty, in placing the loyal negroes of the South under the political power of their Rebel masters," Douglass wrote, after listing the contributions of African American soldiers and informants who helped Northern troops win the Civil War. Congress "must cease to recognize the old slave-masters as the only competent persons to rule the South," Douglass added.

For months, Congress had been debating the question of how to bring the former Confederate states back into the Union (see Chapter 7). Many Southerners (including President Johnson, a Tennesseean) believed the states should immediately return to their place in the country before the war. But many Northerners rejected a Reconstruction plan that left the South unchanged, as if the Civil War had never happened. When the South sent its new representatives and senators (many of them former Confederate leaders) to Washington, D.C., in December 1865, Congress refused to seat those members until it drafted a plan for reforming and readmitting the Southern states.

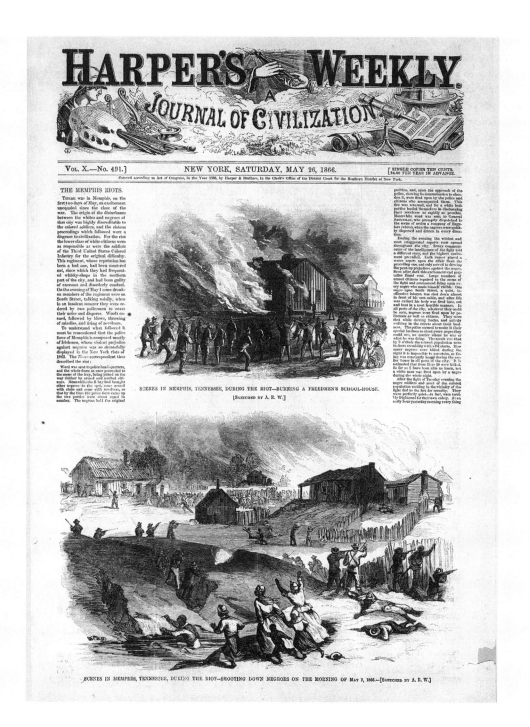

The May 26, 1866, issue of *Harper's Weekly* shows scenes of the riots in Memphis, Tennessee, on May 2, 1866. At top is the burning of a Freedmen's schoolhouse; below is the shooting of African Americans. *The Library of Congress.*

A 1868 political cartoon by Thomas Nast entitled "This is a white man's government." The cartoon depicts three kinds of white voters—an Irishman, a Southerner, and a Northern businessman—joining together over a fallen African American soldier. *The Library of Congress.*

"THIS IS A WHITE MAN'S GOVERNMENT."

" We regard the Reconstruction Acts (so called) of Congress as usurpations, and unconstitutional, revolutionary, and void."—*Democratic Platform.*

Congress formed a Joint Committee on Reconstruction that interviewed more than a hundred witnesses on the political climate of the South. The committee concluded that Congress should guard against future Southern rebellions by imposing certain conditions on the ex-Confederate states before bringing them back into the Union. The *Report of the Joint Committee on Reconstruction* reads, in part:

Whether legally and constitutionally or not, they did, in fact, withdraw from the Union and made themselves subjects to another government of their own creation. And they only yielded [stopped] when they were compelled [forced] by utter exhaustion to lay down their arms [weapons] … expressing no regret, except that they had no longer the power to continue the desperate struggle.

On March 2, 1867, Congress approved the first Reconstruction Act. It divided the South into five military districts, each one headed by a Union general. Each state was required to draft a new state constitution at a convention open to African American and white delegates alike (except high-ranking ex-Confederate officials). African American and white men alike would get to vote on it. The states would also have to approve the Fourteenth Amendment to the Constitution, a measure ensuring citizenship and equal rights for African Americans (see Chapter 9). Then they could be readmitted to the Union. (Tennessee was exempt from this entire process, as it had been readmitted in 1866 after approving the Fourteenth Amendment.)

The terms angered many Southern whites. Congress was forcing them to scrap their old governments, give African American men the vote, and allow ex-slaves to hold state office even though some ex-Confederates could not. The act also raised numerous questions for those Southerners, as noted in *The Civil War and Reconstruction*. "Of itself the reconstruction act accomplished nothing except to create puzzlement, confusion, and resentment in the South." It did not explain how the constitutional conventions would be run, or which ex-Confederates would be barred from the process, or whether they could get a pardon to hold office.

Things to remember while reading the first Reconstruction Act:

- The bloody, racial riots in Memphis and New Orleans, along with other reports of attacks on Southern African Americans, led many to conclude that Johnson's plan for rebuilding the South was not working. Under the president's plan, former Confederate officials were returning to power, whites were passing discriminatory laws, and African Americans were powerless without the vote. Above all, African Americans were not safe in many parts of the South, where white police officers often took part in the riots instead of stopping them.

- Abolitionists such as Douglass said African Americans would remain oppressed by their former masters unless they could vote, shape laws, and run for elected office.

- The process of bringing the former Confederate states back into the Union prompted a major debate. Southerners believed they should resume their former place in the country and send their congressmen back to Washington, D.C. But many Northerners wanted to reshape the South—take ex-Confederate leaders out of power, give African Americans a greater say in government—before letting the states return to the Union.

First Reconstruction Act of 1867

*WHEREAS no legal State governments or **adequate** protection for life or property now exists in the **rebel** States of Virginia, North Carolina, South Carolina, Georgia, Mississippi, Alabama, Louisiana, Florida, Texas, and Arkansas; and whereas it is necessary that peace and good order should be enforced in **said** States until loyal and **republican** State governments can be legally established: Therefore,*

*Be it enacted, That said rebel States shall be divided into military districts and made subject to the military authority of the United States as **hereinafter prescribed**, and for that purpose Virginia shall constitute the first district; North Carolina and South Carolina the second district; Georgia, Alabama, and Florida the third district; Mississippi and Arkansas the fourth district; and Louisiana and Texas the fifth district.*

*SEC. 2. That it shall be the duty of the President to assign to the command of each of said districts an officer of the army, not below the rank of brigadier-general, and to **detail** a **sufficient** military force to enable such officer to perform his duties and enforce his authority within the district to which he is assigned.*

*SEC. 3. That it shall be the duty of each officer assigned as **aforesaid**, to protect all persons in their rights of persons and property, to **suppress insurrection**, disorder, and violence, and to punish, or cause to be punished, all disturbers of the public peace and criminals; and to this end he may allow local civil **tribunals** to take*

Adequate: Sufficient.

Rebel: Former Confederate.

Said: Previously mentioned.

Republican: A type of government in which elected officials represent the people.

Hereinafter: From here forward.

Prescribed: Ordered.

Detail: Assign.

Sufficient: Large enough.

Aforesaid: Previously mentioned.

Suppress: Put down.

Insurrection: Uprising.

Tribunals: Courts.

jurisdiction of and to try offenders, or, when in his judgment it may be necessary for the trial of offenders, he shall have power to organize military commissions or tribunals for that purpose, and all interference under **color** of State authority with the exercise of military authority under this act, shall be null and void.

SEC. 4. That all persons put under military arrest **by virtue** of this act shall be **tried** without unnecessary delay, and no cruel or unusual punishment shall be inflicted, and no sentence of any military commission or tribunal hereby authorized, affecting the life or liberty of any person, shall be **executed** until it is approved by the officer in command of the district, and the laws and regulations for the government of the army shall not be affected by this act, except in so far as they conflict with its **provisions:** Provided, That no sentence of death under the provisions of this act shall be carried into effect without the approval of the President.

SEC. 5. That when the people of any one of said rebel States shall have formed a constitution of government in **conformity** with the Constitution of the United States in all respects, framed by a convention of delegates elected by the male citizens of said State, twenty-one years old and upward, of whatever race, color, or **previous condition,** who have been resident in said State for one year previous to the day of such election, except such as may be **disfranchised** for participation in the rebellion or for **felony** at common law, and when such constitution shall provide that the **elective franchise** shall be enjoyed by all such persons as have the qualifications herein stated for electors of delegates, and when such constitution shall be **ratified** by a majority of the persons voting on the question of ratification who are qualified as electors for delegates, and when such constitution shall have been submitted to Congress for examination and approval, and Congress shall have approved the same, and when said State, by a vote of its legislature elected under said constitution, shall have adopted the amendment to the Constitution of the United States, proposed by the Thirty-ninth Congress, and known as article fourteen, and when said article shall have become a part of the Constitution of the United States said State shall be declared entitled to representation in Congress, and senators and representatives shall be admitted there from on their taking the oath prescribed by law, and then and thereafter the **preceding** sections of this act shall be **inoperative** in said State: Provided, That no person excluded from the privilege of holding office by said proposed amendment to the Constitution of the United States, shall be eligible to election as a member of the convention to frame a constitu-

Jurisdiction: Authority.

Color: Appearance.

By virtue: Because.

Tried: Put through a trial.

Executed: Carried out.

Provisions: Rules.

Conformity: Agreement.

Previous condition: Prior work status, such as slavery.

Disfranchised: Barred from voting or holding office.

Felony: Crime.

Elective franchise: Right to vote.

Ratified: Approved.

Preceding: Earlier.

Inoperative: Out of use.

tion for any of said rebel States, nor shall any such person vote for members of such convention.

*SEC. 6. That, until the people of said rebel States shall be by law admitted to representation in the Congress of the United States, any civil governments which may exist therein shall be deemed **provisional** only, and in all respects subject to the **paramount** authority of the United States at any time to **abolish**, modify, control, or **supersede** the same; and in all elections to any office under such provisional governments all persons shall be entitled to vote, and none others, who are entitled to vote, under the provisions of the fifth section of this act; and no persons shall be eligible to any office under any such provisional governments who would be disqualified from holding office under the provisions of the third article of said constitutional amendment.*

Provisional: Temporary.

Paramount: Supreme.

Abolish: End.

Supersede: Overrule.

What happened next ...

Johnson vetoed the bill, describing it as "utterly [totally] destructive to those great principles of liberty and humanity for which our ancestors ... have shed so much blood and expended [spent] so much treasure [money]." He said the bill replaced the laws of the South with the will of a military ruler: "Everything is a crime which he chooses to call so," Johnson said in the veto message, "and all persons are condemned whom he pronounces guilty." He also objected that the bill placed all people of the South under "the most abject [bleak] and degrading slavery," by forcing African Americans and whites alike to vote a certain way in order to rejoin the Union. Johnson concluded:

> The military rule which it [the bill] establishes is plainly to be used, not for any purpose of order or for the prevention of crime, but solely as a means of coercing [forcing] the people into the adoption of principles and measures to which it is known that they are opposed, and upon which they have an undeniable right to exercise their own judgment.

Congress gathered the two-thirds majority necessary to overturn the veto and make the measure law. A couple of weeks later, on March 23, 1867, Congress told the Union generals to start gathering the votes to call a constitutional convention in each state. When Johnson's attorney general, Henry Stanbery (1803–1881), raised questions about the generals' powers under the first Reconstruction Act, Congress passed another act in July 1867 that reinforced the generals' authority over the state governments, giving them power to remove state officials from their posts. When a majority of Alabama voters defeated their state constitution by refusing to cast their ballots, Congress passed another Reconstruction measure in March 1868, allowing state constitutions to be approved by a majority of the people who actually vote, not by a majority of all registered voters.

The disqualification of high-ranking ex-Confederates, and the addition of African American voters, meant that former slaves outnumbered whites at the ballot box. According to *Reconstruction: After the Civil War,* among the 10 Southern states covered by the Reconstruction acts, about 703,400 registered voters were African American and about 660,000 were white. Many of these new African American voters lacked political experience or even the ability to read, but they were determined to learn and participate. Former South Carolina slave Beverly Nash summed up the desire of many: "We may not understand it at the start, but in time we shall learn to do our duty." Many joined political clubs and attended political meetings. In fact, as noted in *The Negro in the Reconstruction of Florida,* "Negroes became so interested in politics that crops were neglected." The Freedmen's Bureau told the men to never "lose an hour from their labor to attend a political meeting," as their friends could always fill them in later.

Some whites reacted violently to the entry of African Americans into local politics, particularly in areas where African American voters became the majority. A group of

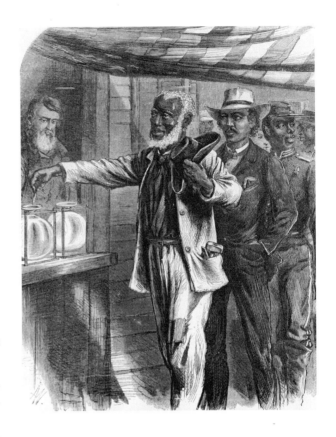

African American men—an elderly craftsman, a civilian, and a soldier—wait in line to vote for the first time.
The Library of Congress.

African American men in Calhoun, Georgia, wrote a letter in August 1867 asking for military protection in their town as the fall elections approached. Their letter, reprinted in *Trouble They Seen: The Story of Reconstruction in the Words of African Americans,* described the racial violence in their community:

> There has been houses broken open, windows smashed and doors broken down in the dead hours of the night, men rushing in, cursing and swearing and discharging [firing] their Pistols inside the house. Men have been knocked down and unmercifully beaten and yet the authorities [local police] do not notice at all. We would open a school here, but are almost afraid to do so, not knowing that we have any protection for life or limb.

Did you know ...

• Two months after the war ended, Johnson privately suggested that Mississippi governor William Sharkey (1798–1873) give voting rights to African Americans "who can read the Constitution of the United States in English and write their names" and to those who own property worth at least $250. The president believed this would prevent Congress from pushing for voting rights for all African American men, and the Southern states would have to be readmitted. But Sharkey ignored the advice.

• Johnson later tried to weaken Congress's Reconstruction plan by replacing the generals in a couple of Southern military districts. He named new commanders who were less interested in interfering with local officials who were mistreating African Americans.

• In many Southern communities before the Civil War, it was a crime to teach a slave how to read. Some whites used that as an argument after the war to deny African Americans the vote: After all, they argued, most African Americans did not know how to read.

Consider the following ...

• What was the significance of the 1866 riots in Memphis and New Orleans?

• Do you think it was a good idea to put Union troops back in the South after the Civil War?

• How would the Reconstruction governments differ from the Southern state governments before the war?

For More Information

Foner, Eric. *Reconstruction: America's Unfinished Revolution.* New York: Harper & Row, 1988.

Franklin, John Hope. *Reconstruction: After the Civil War.* Chicago: University of Chicago Press, 1961.

Randall, J. G., and David H. Donald. *The Civil War and Reconstruction.* Lexington, MA: D. C. Heath and Co., 1961.

"The Reconstruction Acts: 1867." *About Texas: Texas State Library and Archives Commission.* http://www.tsl.state.tx.us/ref/abouttx/secession/reconstruction.html (accessed on September 20, 2004).

Report of the Joint Committee on Reconstruction of the First Session Thirty-Ninth Congress. Washington, DC: Government Printing Office, 1866.

Richardson, Joe M. *The Negro in the Reconstruction of Florida, 1865–1877.* Tallahassee: Florida State University, 1965.

Sterling, Dorothy, ed. *The Trouble They Seen: The Story of Reconstruction in the Words of African Americans.* New York: Da Capo Press, 1994.

 **11**

Charles Sumner

Excerpt from "Argument for the Impeachment of President Johnson"

Delivered in May 1868; reprinted on *From Revolution to Reconstruction ... and What Happened Afterwards* (Web site)

A fierce enemy of Andrew Johnson tells why the president should be impeached

"Slavery has been our worst enemy, assailing all, murdering our children, filling our homes with mourning, and darkening the land with tragedy; and now it rears its crest anew, with Andrew Johnson as its representative."

When the assassination of Abraham Lincoln (1809–1865; served 1861–65) in April 1865 propelled Andrew Johnson (1808–1875; served 1865–69) to the presidency, Northerners thought they had a strong ally in the man who once declared that "treason must be made infamous, and traitors must be impoverished." During the American Civil War (1861–65), Johnson had been the only Southern member of Congress to keep his seat while his colleagues left for the Confederacy. When Union troops took control of the Tennessee capital of Nashville in 1862, Lincoln sent Johnson to serve as military governor of his home state, which remained under Confederate attack. Johnson's Southern ties and Democratic Party roots made him a logical running mate in 1864 for Lincoln, a Northern Republican president who sought to reunite a deeply divided nation.

Lincoln's death came just a week after the Confederate troops surrendered at the Appomattox, Virginia, courthouse, leaving Johnson with the monumental task of rebuilding the country after the Civil War. Many in the North wanted to punish the South, whom they blamed for starting the bloody conflict. Johnson also wanted to punish the traitors, but he did not see all of his fellow Southerners as the enemy.

Johnson was a tailor by trade, a self-taught man who grew up too poor to attend school. His wife, Eliza, taught him how to read. Throughout his life, he was suspicious of the rich upper class. He blamed the Southern plantation owners—many of them arrogant and dependent on slave labor—for starting the Civil War. He saw the vast majority of Southerners, working men like him, as good people who were dragged into a horrible conflict.

Johnson's sympathy for most Southerners and his racist attitude toward the African American slaves freed by the war were at odds with Congress's postwar plans for the South. The "Radical Republicans" who controlled Congress wanted to take land, voting rights, and elected offices away from the white men who participated in the "rebellion" against the North and give those rights and privileges to the newly freed slaves. Johnson objected: That would unfairly punish the Southern working families while placing democracy in the hands of African Americans who, Johnson believed, were intellectually unfit for the task. The Republicans grew angry when Johnson allowed former Confederates to return to elected office in the Southern states.

Within a year of taking office, the president was on a collision course with Congress. He vetoed a bill extending the life of the Freedmen's Bureau, the agency that provided assistance and education to the freed slaves (see Chapter 4). He vetoed the Civil Rights Bill of 1866, a measure allowing African Americans the same basic rights as whites to buy and sell land, enter into contracts, file lawsuits, and conduct other business (see Chapter 8). He vetoed the Reconstruction Acts that carved the South into five military districts, each one monitored by a commanding officer who could get involved with local issues (see Chapter 10). But in all three cases, Congress gathered a two-thirds majority to override Johnson's vetoes, allowing these measures to become law.

A fiery man with strong convictions and a stronger sense of pride, Johnson took his frustrations to the people. As described in *High Crimes & Misdemeanors: The Impeachment and Trial of Andrew Johnson,* Johnson was solid in his belief that they would back him against a "factious [divided], dom-

Charles Sumner. *Courtesy of the National Archives and Records Administration.*

ineering, tyrannical [authoritarian] Congress." He toured the country by train and gave harshly worded speeches at every stop. To a crowd in Cleveland, Ohio, Johnson called Congress a "common gang of cormorants [vicious sea birds] and bloodsuckers (who) have been fattening upon the country for the past four or five years." The speaking tour, known as the "Swing Around the Circle," drew hecklers and embarrassing newspaper accounts at nearly every stop. The Republican governors in Ohio, Indiana, and Illinois did not even greet the president as he passed through their states.

Johnson further stunned his friends and enemies alike with his unscripted remarks in February 1866 to a group of Democratic supporters gathered at the White House. The president called his opponents "traitors" and compared himself to the persecuted Jesus Christ, as noted in *The Struggle for Equality.* Johnson even suggested his leading enemies— U.S. representative Thaddeus Stevens (1792–1868) of Pennsylvania, U.S. senator Charles Sumner (1811–1874) of Massachusetts, and antislavery advocate Wendell Phillips (1811–1884)—were planning to assassinate him. "If my blood is to be shed because I vindicate [defend] the Union and the preservation of this government in its original purity and character, let it be shed," Johnson told the crowd.

As relations between Johnson and Congress grew more hostile, Secretary of War Edwin Stanton (1814–1869) became a central figure. A holdover from Lincoln's administration, Stanton supported Congress's military Reconstruction plan for the South. He stayed in close contact with Johnson's enemies in Congress, even though he answered to the president as a member of the Cabinet (the president's inner circle of advisors).

Members of Congress knew Stanton had become a threat to Johnson, and they feared the president would try to remove him. To protect their ally Stanton, Congress passed the Tenure of Office Act in March 1867. The measure barred the president from removing anyone in his cabinet without the Senate's approval. Predictably, Johnson vetoed the bill, and Congress overrode his veto.

Johnson believed the act was unconstitutional. It gave Congress too much power over the workings of the executive (presidential) branch of government, he thought. He was confident the U.S. Supreme Court would strike it down, but Johnson would have to challenge the law in order to get the issue to court. As a more practical matter, the president could not function with a Cabinet member who challenged his policies and conspired with his congressional foes.

In August 1867, Johnson sent a memo asking Stanton to resign, but Stanton refused. The president suspended Stanton, then tried to replace him with General Lorenzo Thomas (1804–1875), but Stanton refused to leave his office. In the meantime, Johnson also replaced three commanding officers in the Southern military districts (the areas where Union forces enforced Congress's Reconstruction plans) with more laid-back officers who would not interfere as local whites mistreated African Americans.

HARPER'S WEEKLY.
JOURNAL OF CIVILIZATION

VOL. XII.—No. 587.] NEW YORK, SATURDAY, MARCH 28, 1868. [SINGLE COPIES, TEN CENTS. $4.00 PER YEAR IN ADVANCE.

GEORGE T. BROWN, SERGEANT-AT-ARMS OF THE SENATE, SERVING THE SUMMONS ON PRESIDENT JOHNSON.—SKETCHED BY T. R. DAVIS.—[SEE PAGE 195.]

The cover of the March 28, 1868, issue of *Harper's Weekly* shows George T. Brown (left), sergeant of arms of the U.S. Senate, serving an impeachment summons to President Andrew Johnson (right), while Johnson's secretary, Col. W. G. Moore, looks on in the background. *The Library of Congress.*

Congress was alarmed by Johnson's juggling of key officials. The president was undermining Congress's Reconstruction efforts by trying to place more lenient men in power. Congress began to discuss impeachment, a two-step process outlined in the Constitution to remove the president from office (see box). The process starts in the House of Representatives, where members vote on whether to formally charge the president with misconduct. If the president is formally accused, or impeached, by the House, the Senate holds a trial to decide whether to vote him out of office.

What Is Impeachment?

The authors of the Constitution outlined a course of action for removing the president, vice president, or other officials who are guilty of "treason, bribery, or other high crimes and misdemeanors," as stated in Article 2, section 4, of the Constitution. The process starts in the House of Representatives with a majority vote to formally accuse, or "impeach," an official of some offense. The matter goes to trial in the Senate, where the senators serve as jurors. If at least two-thirds of the senators vote for conviction, the official is removed from office.

Congress has fleshed out the process over the years. The House Judiciary Committee starts by holding hearings, taking testimony, and drafting possible charges. The committee then makes a recommendation to the full House of Representatives. If the House votes to impeach, several of its members serve as prosecutors, or "managers," when the case goes to the Senate. Defense attorneys represent the accused official.

Andrew Johnson was the first of two presidents to be impeached; Bill Clinton (1946–; served 1993–2001) was the second. He was impeached in 1998 on charges that he lied under oath about having a relationship with White House intern Monica Lewinsky (1973–). Like Johnson, Clinton was a Southern Democrat at odds with a Republican Congress, and many questioned whether the charges were politically motivated. As with Johnson, Clinton was acquitted in the Senate.

Experts still debate what qualifies as "high crimes and misdemeanors." The framers of the Constitution added the catchall phrase to cover dangerous acts that might not involve treason or bribery. Some scholars take the phrase to literally mean criminal violations of the law, while others suggest a broader interpretation that covers an abuse of power. In reality, then–U.S. representative (and future president) Gerald Ford (1913–; served as president 1974–77) of Michigan noted in 1970, "An impeachable offense is whatever a majority of the House of Representatives considers it to be at a given moment in history."

At the urging of Representative Stevens, one of the leading Radical Republicans, the House of Representatives voted in February 1868 to bring impeachment charges against Johnson. A committee then drafted the eleven specific charges. Nine of them stemmed from Johnson's alleged violation of the Tenure of Office Act. The tenth charge accused the president of attacking the reputation of Congress in his speeches during the "Swing Around the Circle" tour by train. The eleventh charge summarized the other ones in more general terms. As noted in *The Presidency of Andrew Johnson*, the purpose of this last charge "was to induce senators who might have qualms about specific charges against Johnson to vote him guilty on general grounds."

The case presented to the Senate, which sits as the jury in an impeachment trial, did not focus on the details of the Tenure of Office Act. It became a debate over Johnson's performance as president. As quoted in *High Crimes & Misdemeanors: The Impeachment and Trial of Andrew Johnson,* U.S. representative John A. Logan (1826–1886) of Illinois, one of the officials acting as prosecutor in the case, told the Senate: Johnson's "great aim and purpose has been to subvert [overthrow] law, usurp [seize] authority, insult and outrage Congress, reconstruct the rebel states in the interests of treason, (and) insult the memories and resting places of our heroic dead."

As the six-week trial neared its end in May 1868, Senator Sumner rose to make his arguments for Johnson's removal from office. The powerful Radical Republican was one of Johnson's archrivals. He had been waiting for this day to come.

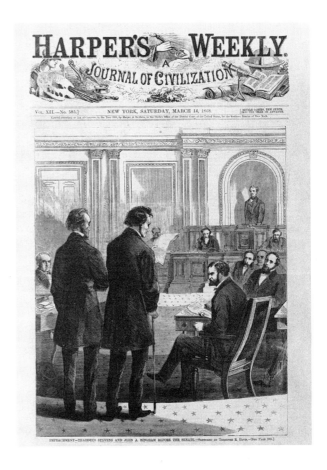

IMPEACHMENT—THADDEUS STEVENS AND JOHN A. BINGHAM BEFORE THE SENATE.—Sketched by Theodore R. Davis.—(See Page 165.)

In this cover of the March 14, 1868, issue of *Harper's Weekly,* Thaddeus Stevens and John A. Bingham stand before the Senate at the Andrew Johnson impeachment hearings. *The Library of Congress.*

Things to remember while reading an excerpt from "Argument for the Impeachment of President Johnson":

- Johnson was loyal to the North during the Civil War, and he spoke harshly about the "traitors" who created the Confederacy. But he was a Southerner, too, and he did not view all Southerners as the enemy. He blamed the rich plantation owners for starting the war. He opposed Congress's Reconstruction policies because he thought they were too harsh on everyday white Southerners. Unlike the Northerners who controlled Congress, Johnson did not support equal rights for African Americans.

- Although the impeachment charges mainly revolved around Johnson's attempts to replace his secretary of war, the debate during the trial focused on Johnson's performance as president. He had angered most Republicans in Congress by opposing their Reconstruction efforts. By his actions, critics said, Johnson was supporting the rebels.

- Sumner was one of the leading abolitionists (opponents of slavery) of his time. He viewed slavery as a great evil, and believed the work of the Civil War was not complete until African Americans were given equal footing with whites.

Excerpt from "Argument for the Impeachment of President Johnson"

*This is one of the last great battles with slavery. Driven from these legislative chambers, driven from the field of war, this **monstrous power** has found a refuge in the **executive mansion**, where, in utter disregard of the Constitution and laws, it seeks to exercise its ancient, far-reaching **sway**. All this is very plain. Nobody can question it. Andrew Johnson is the **impersonation** of the **tyrannical** slave power....*

*Not to **dislodge** (him) is to leave the country a **prey** to one of the most hateful tyrannies of history. Especially is it to surrender the Unionists of the Rebel states to violence and bloodshed. Not a month, not a week, not a day should be lost. The safety of the republic requires action at once. The lives of innocent men must be rescued from sacrifice....*

*Slavery has been our worst enemy, **assailing** all, murdering our children, filling our homes with mourning, and darkening the land with tragedy; and now it rears its **crest** anew, with Andrew Johnson as its representative. Through him it assumes once more to rule the republic and to impose its cruel law....*

*The formal accusation is founded on certain recent **transgressions**, **enumerated** in articles of impeachment, but it is wrong to sup-*

Monstrous power: Slavery.

Executive mansion: White House.

Sway: Influence.

Impersonation: Imitation.

Tyrannical: Oppressive.

Dislodge: Remove.

Prey: Victim.

Assailing: Attacking.

Crest: Head.

Transgressions: Violations.

Enumerated: Listed.

pose that this is the whole case. It is very wrong to try this impeachment merely on these articles. It is **unpardonable** to haggle over words and phrases when, for more than two years, the tyrannical **pretensions** of this offender, now in evidence before the Senate … have been **manifest** in their terrible, **heartrending** consequences.…

This **usurpation**, with its brutalities and indecencies, became manifest as long ago as the winter of 1866, when, being President, and bound by his oath of office to preserve, protect, and defend the Constitution, and to take care that the laws are faithfully executed, he took to himself legislative powers in the reconstruction of the Rebel states; and, in carrying forward this usurpation, **nullified** an act of Congress, intended as the cornerstone of Reconstruction, by virtue of which Rebels are excluded from office under the government of the United States; and, thereafter, in **vindication** of this misconduct, uttered a scandalous speech in which he openly charged members of Congress with being assassins, and mentioned some by name. Plainly he should have been impeached and expelled at that early day. The case against him was complete.…

More than one person was appointed **provisional** governor who could not take the oath of office required by act of Congress. Other persons in the same **predicament** were appointed in the revenue service. The effect of these appointments was disastrous. They were in the nature of notice to Rebels everywhere, that participation in the rebellion was no bar to office. If one of their number could be appointed governor, if another could be appointed to a confidential position in the Treasury Department, then there was nobody on the **long list of blood** who might not look for **preferment**. And thus all offices from governor to **constable** were handed over to a disloyal **scramble.**

Rebels crawled forth from their retreats. Men who had hardly **ventured** to expect their lives were now candidates for office, and the rebellion became strong again. The change was felt in all the **gradations** of government, whether in states, counties, towns, or villages. Rebels found themselves in places of trust, while the truehearted Unionists, who had watched for the coming of our flag and ought to have enjoyed its protecting power, were driven into hiding places. All this was under the **auspices** of Andrew Johnson. It was he who **animated** the wicked crew. He was at the head of the work. Loyalty everywhere was **persecuted**. White and black, whose only offense was that they had been true to their country, were insulted, abused, murdered. There was no safety for the loyal man except within the flash of our **bayonets**. The story is as authentic as hideous.…

Unpardonable: Not excusable.

Pretensions: Claims.

Manifest: Apparent.

Heartrending: Heartbreaking.

Usurpation: Seizure of power.

Nullified: Made legally invalid.

Vindication: Defense.

Provisional: Temporary.

Predicament: Difficult situation.

Long list of blood: The group of Southern soldiers who killed Union troops during the war.

Preferment: Promotion.

Constable: Policeman.

Scramble: Climb for a prize.

Ventured: Acted in a risky way.

Gradations: Levels.

Auspices: Guidance.

Animated: Brought to life.

Persecuted: Punished.

Bayonets: Detachable blades used on rifles.

Laws enacted by Congress for the benefit of the colored race, including that great statute for the establishment of the Freedman's Bureau, and that other great statute for the establishment of civil rights, were first attacked by his veto; and, when finally passed by the requisite majority over his veto, were treated by him as little better than dead letters, while he boldly attempted to prevent the adoption of a constitutional amendment by which the right of citizens and the national debt were placed under the guarantee of **irrepealable** law.

During these **successive** assumptions, usurpations, and tyrannies, utterly without **precedent** in our history, this deeply guilty man ventured upon public speeches, each an offense to good morals, where, lost to all shame, he appealed in **coarse** words to the coarse passions of the coarsest people, scattering **firebrands** of **sedition**, inflaming anew the rebel spirit, insulting good citizens, and, with regard to officeholders, announcing in his own characteristic phrase that he would "kick them out"—the whole succession of speeches being from their brutalities and indecencies in the nature of a "criminal exposure of his person," **indictable** at common law, for which no judgment can be too severe. But even this revolting transgression is aggravated when it is considered that through these utterances the cause of justice was **imperiled** and the **accursed** demon of civil feud was **lashed** again into **vengeful** fury.

All these things from beginning to end are plain facts, already recorded in history and known to all. And it is further recorded in history and known to all, that, through these **enormities**, any one of which is enough for condemnation, while all together present an **aggregation** of crime, untold **calamities** have been brought upon our country; disturbing business and finance; diminishing the national revenues; postponing **specie** payments; dishonoring the Declaration of Independence in its grandest truths; **arresting** the restoration of the Rebel states; reviving the dying rebellion, and instead of that peace and reconciliation so much longed for, **sowing** strife and wrong, whose natural fruit is violence and blood.

For all these, or any one of them, Andrew Johnson should have been impeached and expelled from office. The case required a statement only, not an argument. Unhappily this was not done. As a **petty** substitute for the judgment which should have been pronounced, and as a **bridle** on presidential tyranny in "kicking out of office," Congress enacted a law known as the Tenure of Office Act, passed March 2, 1867, over his veto by the vote of two-thirds of

Irrepealable: Unable to be overturned.

Successive: Series of.

Precedent: Prior example.

Coarse: Harsh.

Firebrands: People who stir passions.

Sedition: Rebellion.

Indictable: Able to be accused of an offense.

Imperiled: Put in danger.

Accursed: Under a curse.

Lashed: Whipped.

Vengeful: Seeking revenge.

Enormities: Wicked acts.

Aggregation: Total sum.

Calamities: Disasters.

Specie: Coin money, such as gold.

Arresting: Stopping.

Sowing: Spreading.

Petty: Unimportant.

Bridle: Restraint.

both houses. And in order to prepare the way for impeachment, by removing certain **scruples** of technicality, its violation was expressly declared to be a high misdemeanor.

The President began at once to **chafe** under its restraint. Recognizing the act and following its terms, he first suspended Mr. Stanton from office, and then ... made an attempt ... to oust [Secretary of War Edwin] Stanton.... Meanwhile, [General Philip] Sheridan in Louisiana, [General John] Pope in Alabama, and [General Dan] Sickles in South Carolina, who, as military commanders, were carrying into the **pacification** of these states all the energies which had been so brilliantly displayed in the war, were pursued by the same **vindictive** spirit.

They were removed by the President, and rebellion throughout that whole region clapped its hands. This was done in the exercise of his power as commander in chief. At last, in his **unappeased** rage, he openly violated the Tenure of Office Act so as to bring himself under its judgment by the defiant attempt to remove Mr. Stanton from the War Department, without the consent of the Senate, and the appointment of Lorenzo Thomas, adjutant general of the United States, as secretary of war **ad interim.**

The Grand Inquest of the nation, which had slept on so many enormities, was awakened by this open defiance. The **gauntlet** was flung into its very chamber, and there it lay on the floor. The President, who had already claimed everything for the executive with **impunity,** now rushed into conflict with Congress on the very ground selected in advance by the latter. The field was narrow, but sufficient. There was but one thing for the House of Representatives to do. Andrew Johnson must be impeached, or the Tenure of Office Act would become a dead letter, while his tyranny would receive a letter of **license,** and impeachment as a remedy for wrongdoing would be **blotted** from the Constitution.

Scruples: Doubts.

Chafe: Become irritated.

Pacification: Process of making peace.

Vindictive: In the spirit of revenge.

Unappeased: Not satisfied.

Ad interim: Interim.

Gauntlet: Challenge.

Impunity: Free from punishment.

License: Permission.

Blotted: Erased.

What happened next ...

The Senate voted May 16, 1868, on the eleventh article of impeachment, the general summary of charges against Johnson. The senators voted thirty-five to nineteen in favor of conviction—one vote short of the two-thirds majority re-

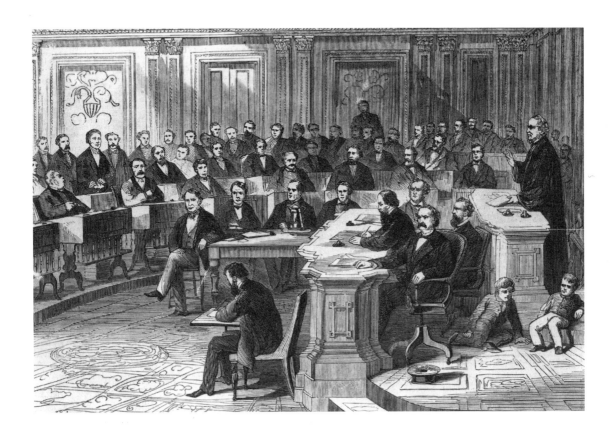

The impeachment of President Andrew Johnson, May 16, 1868. *The Library of Congress.*

quired to remove Johnson from office. After votes on two other impeachment charges on May 26 turned out the same way, the Senate ended the proceedings. Stanton resigned his post as secretary of war, finally allowing the president to replace him.

All of the Democrats in the Senate sided with Johnson, but the president could not have kept his seat without support from seven Republicans. He earned their backing, in part, by toning down his harsh comments about Congress and allowing General Ulysses S. Grant (1822–1885) to oversee the military districts in the South without the president's interference. Several Republican senators, such as William Pitt Fessenden (1806–1869) of Maine and James W. Grimes (1816–1872) of Iowa, did not think Congress had valid legal reasons to remove Johnson. They feared removing him would place the country in upheaval, and they thought the next man in line for the presidency—U.S. senator Benjamin Wade (1800–1878) of Ohio, the president of the Senate—was

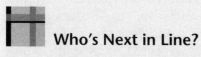

Who's Next in Line?

The impeachment of President Andrew Johnson raised an interesting question: Who would take his place if he was removed from office? Johnson had no vice president. At that time, the U.S. Constitution did not provide a way for a new vice president to be appointed after the previous one became president. So when Johnson took office after the assassination of Abraham Lincoln, he had no back-up.

The Presidential Succession Act, passed by Congress in 1792, placed the Senate president and the speaker of the House of Representatives next in line for the presidency, after the vice president. That act almost came into play during Johnson's impeachment, as the presidency would have passed to Senate president Benjamin Wade of Ohio if Johnson was convicted. But that created a tremendous conflict, as senators vote on whether to remove an impeached president from office. By casting a vote to convict Johnson, Wade was essentially voting to put himself in the oval office. That situation prompted Congress to revisit the succession policy in 1886, with an act that removed members of Congress from the list

of people in line for the White House. Instead, the presidency would pass to members of the cabinet (the secretary of state, secretary of the treasury, and so on) in the order those posts were created.

But that was not the last word. Congress passed a new succession act in 1947 that placed the Speaker of the House of Representatives and the president of the Senate back in line, after the vice president. The members of the cabinet followed. The Twenty-fifth Amendment to the U.S. Constitution, ratified in 1967, allowed a president to appoint a new vice president, with the approval of both chambers of Congress. The measure got its first test a few years later. In October 1973, Vice President Spiro Agnew (1918–1996) resigned amid accusations of wrongdoing as a Maryland county executive and governor, and President Richard Nixon (1913–1994; served 1969–74) appointed U.S. representative Gerald Ford (1913–) of Michigan as Agnew's replacement. When the Watergate scandal prompted Nixon to resign ten months later, Ford became the nation's first fully appointed president.

too extreme (see box). "I cannot agree to destroy the harmonious working of the Constitution for the sake of getting rid of an unacceptable president," Grimes said.

But their votes came at a cost. None of the seven Republicans who sided with Johnson was reelected. One of them, U.S. senator Edmund G. Ross (1826–1907) of Kansas, was physically attacked by an angry mob when he returned home.

Although the trial did not remove Johnson from the White House, it left him powerless for the last nine-and-a-half months of his presidency. Congress continued to overturn his vetoes. His written messages to Congress, including his final State of the Union speech, were placed in the written record without being read aloud to a Senate that refused to listen. His hopes of running for reelection on the Democratic Party ticket were dead.

Did you know ...

- Sumner was brutally beaten in 1856 by U.S. representative Preston Brooks (1819–1857) of South Carolina, a slavery supporter who was insulted by one of Sumner's antislavery speeches, in which he mocked Brooks's uncle, proslavery U.S. senator Andrew Butler (1796–1857) of South Carolina, accusing him of taking "a mistress"—slavery. Brooks attacked Sumner on the Senate floor with a gold-handled cane. Sumner spent four years recovering in Europe.

- Johnson returned to Washington, D.C., in March 1875 as a U.S. senator—the only former president to do so. (Former president John Quincy Adams [1767–1848] also returned to Congress, but as a U.S. representative.) By all accounts, it was an astonishing political comeback for the once-unpopular ex-president. But it was short-lived: Johnson died that July after suffering two strokes.

- Perhaps the greatest accomplishment of Johnson's administration was the $7.2 million purchase of Alaska, an area rich in gold and oil. The deal removed Russia from North America, and was the only time Russia voluntarily gave up land.

- Recovering from a possible bout with typhoid, Johnson downed three glasses of whiskey before his 1865 inauguration as vice president under Lincoln. His speech turned into a drunken tirade, causing the *New York World* to lament "that one frail life stands between this insolent [disrespectful] clownish creature and the presidency!" When Lincoln's assassination made Johnson the president about a month later, his aides persuaded him not to hold another public inauguration ceremony.

- One of the votes to convict Johnson in the impeachment trial came from U.S. senator Benjamin Wade of Ohio, the man who would become president if Johnson was removed.

- The Supreme Court ruled in 1926 that the Tenure of Office Act was unconstitutional, as Johnson had argued decades earlier. Some of the Republicans who pushed for impeachment later admitted that their efforts were based more on anger toward Johnson than any notion that he had committed a crime.

Consider the following ...
- Do you think Johnson should have been removed from office?

- Can you think of ways in which the president and Congress could have compromised?

- What would the South be like today if Congress did not override Johnson's vetoes on key Reconstruction programs?

For More Information

Castel, Albert. *The Presidency of Andrew Johnson.* Lawrence: University Press of Kansas, 1979.

"Charles Sumner: Opinion on the Trial of Andrew Johnson, 1868." *From Revolution to Reconstruction ... and What Happened Afterwards.* http://odur.let.rug.nl/~usa/D/1851-1875/reconstruction/ch_sumner. htm (accessed on September 20, 2004).

"Finding Precedent: The Impeachment of Andrew Johnson." *HarpWeek.* http://www.impeach-andrewjohnson.com (accessed on September 20, 2004).

McPherson, James M. *The Struggle for Equality.* Princeton, NJ: Princeton University Press, 1964.

Smith, Gene. *High Crimes & Misdemeanors: The Impeachment and Trial of Andrew Johnson.* New York: McGraw-Hill, 1985.

Trefousse, Hans L. *Andrew Johnson: A Biography.* New York: W. W. Norton & Company, 1989.

"The Trial of Andrew Johnson, 1868." *EyeWitness to History.* http://www.eyewitnesstohistory.com/john.htm (accessed on September 20, 2004).

Hiram Revels

Excerpt from "On the Readmission of Georgia to the Union"
Delivered on March 16, 1870; reprinted on *U.S. Senate* (Web site)

*An African American senator speaks up about the
readmission of a state*

"They bear toward their former masters no revengeful thoughts, no hatreds, no animosities."

In two short years after the American Civil War (1861–65), the African American men of the South had gone from working as slaves to casting ballots as freedmen. It was an astonishing development in Southern society, outmatched only by the fact that African American men could also hold elected office and make laws alongside their former masters. Historians estimate about two thousand African Americans held federal, state, and local offices in the decade after Southern African American men were given the right to vote under the Reconstruction Act of 1867 (see Chapter 10). During that time period, the South sent two African American men to the Senate and fourteen more to the House of Representatives. About eight hundred African Americans served as state legislators, and hundreds more held local offices ranging from city councilman to sheriff.

It was an exciting opportunity—and a tremendous responsibility—for African Americans. Robert Brown Elliott (1842–1884), an African American attorney from South Carolina, remembered how "everything was still" when he rose to give his first speech in 1871 as a member of the U.S. House of Representatives. His supporters quietly hoped he would perform well. Those who thought African Americans had no place in Congress secretly hoped Elliott would embarrass himself. "I shall never forget that day," Elliott said, in a passage reprinted in *Black Voices from Reconstruction*. "I cannot, fellow-citizens, picture to you the emotions that filled my mind." Elliott wound up serving nearly two terms in Congress and was known for a speech he gave in support of the Civil Rights Act, in which he proclaimed, "What you give to one class you must give to all."

Indeed, the political pioneers like Elliott faced criticism at every step. African American officials were often dismissed as ignorant and illiterate (unable to read or write), even though some had attended school and traveled around the country. Edward King (1848–1896), author of the 1875 book *The Great South: A Record of Journeys*, described the African American officials he met in Mississippi as "worthy, intelligent, and likely to progress." At the same time, he wrote, the white men of Louisiana "will not admit that the negro is at all competent to legislate for him, or to vote with him on matters of common importance to white and black." Some of those African American officials, particularly in local offices, were indeed illiterate—but so were many of the whites in those communities.

Some Southern whites also suspected African American politicians were only interested in helping their race, possibly at the expense of whites. But in most cases, historians say, African American officials worked for measures that would benefit both races. For example, they pushed hard for public education systems, a first in many Southern states. "If the whites would prove that they are willing to extend to others the rights which they desire for themselves, they would be met in the same spirit," said Robert DeLarge (1842–1874), one of the African Americans who helped rewrite South Carolina's state constitution, as quoted in *Black Voices from Reconstruction*. "If they will come forward … they will find us ready to meet them."

Perhaps the most damaging stereotype was that of the clueless and corrupt African American official, as portrayed in the 1874 book, *The Prostrate State*, by James Shepherd Pike (1811–1882; see Chapter 13). In his historically questionable

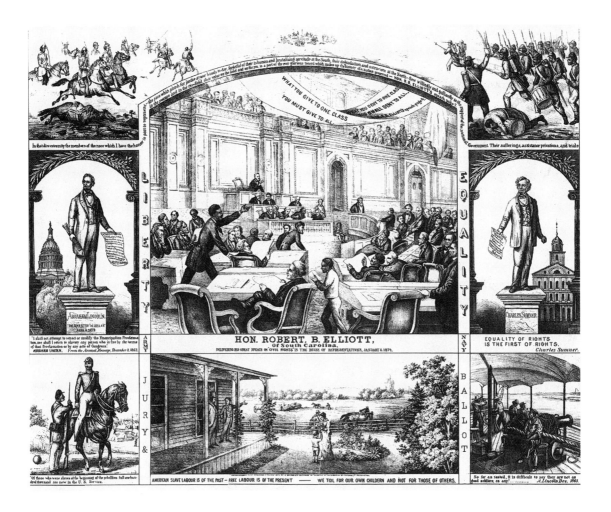

HON. ROBERT. B. ELLIOTT,
Of South Carolina.
DELIVERING HIS GREAT SPEECH ON CIVIL RIGHTS IN THE HOUSE OF REPRESENTATIVES, JANUARY 6, 1874.

Civil War and civil rights scenes. U.S. representative Robert B. Elliott's famous speech before the House of Representatives in favor of the Civil Rights Act; Civil War scenes of African American troops in action; a statue of Abraham Lincoln; and Charles Sumner holding the "Bill of Rights." *The Library of Congress.*

account of the African American–led South Carolina legislature, Pike wrote that lawmakers refurbished the capitol with $480 clocks and $650 chandeliers, renovated their apartments with Belgian carpets, and voted to reimburse the Speaker of the House $1,000 for a lost horse racing bet—all with taxpayer dollars. But there is limited evidence of such corruption among African American officials. The documented cases of corruption in Mississippi, for example, involved a white Republican who pocketed $7,251 from a local hospital, and a white Democrat who embezzled $315,612 from the state treasury, according to *Reconstruction in the South*.

For the most part, white Southerners resented the fact that African Americans were able to vote and hold office. Adding to their bitterness, many whites were barred from doing the same because they had been active participants in the "rebellion" against the North. A group of white men in Georgia decided to do something about it. As required for readmission into the Union, Georgia rewrote its state constitution in 1868 with the help of African American delegates, and elected a new legislature that included thirty-two African American members. But when the legislature met that summer, the white members kicked out their African American colleagues. The white Democratic majority—which included some ex-Confederates whom Congress had barred from office—passed a measure saying no man with more than one-eighth "African blood" could hold office.

A drawing of Hiram Revels from the February 19, 1870, issue of *Harper's Weekly*.

The move infuriated the African American legislators and their white Republican supporters. Henry McNeal Turner (1834–1915), an African Methodist Episcopal Church minister elected to the Georgia legislature, scolded the white lawmakers before leading the procession of African Americans out of the capitol. "I am here to demand my rights, and to hurl thunderbolts at the men who would dare to cross the threshold of my manhood," Turner said in a speech reprinted in *Reconstruction: Opposing Viewpoints*. Nowhere in the history of the world, Turner said, were millions of freed people governed by laws without having a say in how those laws were made. Plus, Turner asked: "How can a white man represent a colored constituency, if a colored man cannot do it?"

Congress pressured Georgia to readmit those African American legislators, but the dispute resurfaced in 1870 when Congress debated a bill to bring Georgia back into the Union. The bill included an amendment that could have allowed Georgia to exclude other African Americans from office. Although he had been sworn into office only three weeks earlier, U.S. senator Hiram R. Revels (1827–1901), the first African

American member of Congress, felt compelled to speak up. He had faced those same prejudices upon his swearing-in, when some members of Congress argued that Revels was not eligible for office because he had not been a U.S. citizen for at least nine years (African Americans were not recognized as citizens until the passage of the Civil Rights Act of 1866).

Born to freed slaves in North Carolina, Revels attended Knox College in Illinois and became a minister for the African Methodist Episcopal Church before the Civil War. Once the war broke out, Revels helped recruit African American soldiers for the Union army and served as a chaplain, or religious counselor, for an African American regiment. In his first speech in Congress, Revels reminded his colleagues of the sacrifice of those African American troops who helped turn the tide of the war. He also described the good will of the slaves who did not mistreat the Southern women and children after the white men went to war for the Confederacy. Surely the African American race had proved its trustworthiness to cast a ballot and hold elected office, Revels said.

Things to remember while reading an excerpt from "On the Readmission of Georgia to the Union":

- The 1867 Reconstruction Act of Congress gave African American men the right to vote and run for elected office. The same act barred certain ex-Confederates from doing the same, creating bitterness among whites who were exiled from the political process.

- African American officials faced suspicions that they were incompetent, corrupt, or only looking out for their own race. On the whole, however, historians say those stereotypes were untrue. Many African American officials were illiterate, but then again, so were many whites in the South, which largely lacked a system of public schools.

- In order to be readmitted to the Union, Georgia approved a new state constitution and elected a new legislature with input from African American voters. Thirty-two African American men were elected to the legislature, but their white colleagues kicked them out of

A League of Their Own

As soon as Congress gave African American men the ballot under the Reconstruction Act of 1867, the ex-slaves became a Southern political force some seven hundred thousand members strong. The Republican Party, which had pushed for African Americans' rights, quickly tapped into this new political base with "Union League" clubs. These secret societies for African Americans were part ritual and part propaganda (material distributed by supporters or opponents of a cause with the intent of swaying readers to their side), aimed at gaining African Americans' support for Republican candidates on election day.

The Union League meetings began with mysterious initiation rituals performed in the dark, creating a sense of intrigue that drew new members to the club. At the meetings, members heard political speeches, read newspaper articles aloud, debated current issues, organized parades and barbecues, and even prepared the banners for such celebrations. In some areas, the league helped build schools, collect funds to care for sick members, and organize strikes for higher pay. At its peak, the Union League had between two hundred thousand and three hundred thousand members. "This hothouse atmosphere of political mobilization made possible a vast expansion of black leadership ... that had emerged between 1864 and 1867," as noted in *Reconstruction: America's Unfinished Revolution.*

Not only did the Union League clubs vow to support Republican candidates, but many arranged group outings to the polls so African Americans could vote safely without being attacked or intimidated by whites. Often the clubs sparked the creation of African American militias that drilled for self-defense purposes. All of this activity made white Southerners very nervous, however. Some feared the African Americans were meeting and training to attack whites. In his book *The South During Reconstruction,* historian E. Merton Coulter argued the Union League taught African Americans "to hate their white neighbors."

Other historians believe the groups had a more positive purpose, however. In his book *White Terror: The Ku Klux Klan Conspiracy and Southern Reconstruction,* historian Allen W. Trelease found "almost no evidence" linking the Union League to racial violence against whites. "As a matter of fact it had a moderating [calming] effect more often than not, preaching a respect for democratic processes and obedience to the law even in the face of violence by the opposition," Trelease wrote. Nonetheless, the Union League clubs became a frequent Klan target—arousing so much hostility that Republican leaders decided it was better to just disband the clubs after the presidential election of 1868.

the assembly. Congress debated whether to allow Georgia back into the Union in a way that could allow the exclusion of African American officials.

Excerpt from "On the Readmission of Georgia to the Union"

*Mr. President, I rise at this particular **juncture** in the discussion of the Georgia bill with feelings which perhaps never before entered into the experience of any member of this body. I rise, too, with **misgivings** as to the **propriety** of lifting my voice at this early period after my admission into the Senate. Perhaps it were wiser for me, so inexperienced in the details of senatorial duties, to have remained a **passive** listener in the progress of this debate; but when I remember that my term is short, and that the issues with which this bill is **fraught** are momentous in their present and future influence upon the well-being of my race, I would seem **indifferent** to the importance of the hour and **recreant** to the high trust imposed upon me if I hesitated to lend my voice on behalf of the loyal people of the South....*

*I am well aware, sir, that the idea is **abroad** that an **antagonism** exists between the whites and blacks, that that race which the nation raised from the **degradation** of slavery, and **endowed** with the full and **unqualified** rights and privileges of citizenship, are intent upon power, at whatever price it can be gained....*

*Certainly no one possessing any personal knowledge of the colored population of my own or other states need be reminded of the **noble** conduct of that people under the most **trying** circumstances in the history of the **late** war, when they were beyond the protection of the federal forces. While the confederate army pressed into its ranks every white male capable of bearing **arms**, the mothers, wives, daughters, and sisters of the southern soldiers were left defenseless and in the power of the blacks, upon whom the chains of slavery were still **riveted**; and to bind those chains the closer was the real issue for which so much life and property was sacrificed.*

*And now, sir, I ask, how did that race act?... They waited, and they waited patiently. In the absence of their masters they protected the virtue and **chastity** of defenseless women. Think, sir, for a moment, what the condition of this land would be today if the slave*

Juncture: Moment.

Misgivings: Doubts.

Propriety: Appropriateness.

Passive: Inactive.

Fraught: Filled.

Indifferent: Unconcerned.

Recreant: Disloyal.

Abroad: In circulation.

Antagonism: Hostility.

Degradation: Humiliation.

Endowed: Provided.

Unqualified: Unrestricted.

Noble: Honorable.

Trying: Difficult.

Late: Recent.

Arms: Guns.

Riveted: Fastened.

Chastity: Virginity.

population had risen in **servile insurrection** against those who month by month were fighting to **perpetuate** that institution which brought to them all the evils of which they complained. Where would have been the security for property, female chastity, and childhood's innocence?

... Mr. President, I maintain that the past record of my race is a true **index** of the feelings which today **animate** them. They bear toward their former masters no revengeful thoughts, no hatreds, no **animosities.** They aim not to elevate themselves by sacrificing one single interest of their white fellow-citizens. They ask but the rights which are theirs by God's universal law, and which are the natural outgrowth, the logical **sequence** of the condition in which the legislative **enactments** of this nation have placed them. They **appeal** to you and to me to see that they receive that protection which alone will enable them to pursue their daily **avocations** with success and enjoy the liberties of citizenship on the same footing with their white neighbors and friends.....

And here let me say further, that the people of the North owe to the colored race a deep obligation which it is no easy matter to fulfill. When the federal armies were **thinned** by death and disaster, and **somber** clouds overhung the length and breadth of the Republic, and the very air was **pregnant** with the rumors of foreign interference—in those dark days of defeat, whose memories even yet haunt us as an ugly dream, from what source did our nation in its seeming death **throes** gain additional and new-found power? It was the **sable** sons of the South that **valiantly** rushed to the rescue, and but for their **intrepidity** and **ardent** daring many a northern fireside would miss today **paternal counsels** or a brother's love.

Sir, I repeat the fact that the colored race saved to the noble women of New England and the middle states men on whom they lean today for security and safety. Many of my race, the representatives of these men on the field of battle, sleep in the countless graves of the South. If those quiet resting-places of our honored dead could speak today what a mighty voice, like to the rushing of a mighty wind, would come up from those **sepulchral** homes! Could we resist the **eloquent** pleadings of their appeal?

... And now, sir, I protest in the name of truth and human rights against any and every attempt to **fetter** the hands of one hundred thousand white and colored citizens of the state of Georgia. Sir, I now leave this question to the consideration of this body, and I wish my last words upon the great issues involved in the bill

Servile: Slave-like.

Insurrection: Uprising.

Perpetuate: Continue.

Index Indication.

Animate: Inspire.

Animosities: Hostilities.

Sequence: Result.

Enactments: Acts.

Appeal: Make an urgent request.

Avocations: Activities.

Thinned: Reduced.

Somber: Gloomy.

Pregnant: Filled.

Throes: Agony.

Sable: Black.

Valiantly: Bravely.

Intrepidity: Boldness.

Ardent: Passionate.

Paternal: Fatherly.

Counsels: Advice.

Sepulchral: Burial.

Eloquent: Well-spoken.

Fetter: Bind.

Solemn: Formal.

Earnest: Serious.

*before us to be my **solemn** and **earnest** demand for full and prompt protection for the helpless loyal people of Georgia.*

What happened next ...

Revels lost the argument: Congress readmitted Georgia with the controversial amendment intact. But Congress required Georgia to ratify the Fifteenth Amendment to the U.S. Constitution, which guaranteed all African American men had the right to vote (see Chapter 16). Congress also forced the state to readmit the African American members of its legislature.

African Americans continued to face obstacles at all levels of public office. Although they often held positions such as mayor or justice of the peace, African Americans had the hardest time becoming sheriffs, a job widely regarded as the most important one in the county. Historian Vernon L. Wharton counts fewer than a dozen African Americans who served as sheriffs anywhere in Mississippi during Reconstruction. It was the last role Southern whites wanted to give to an African American man. "Law enforcement implied domination, and as [one white official] said, the white race was 'not in the habit of being dominated by the colored race,'" Wharton wrote in "The Negro in Mississippi Politics."

Once elected, African American officials faced the threat of violence from the Ku Klux Klan or other white supremacist groups. Jonathan C. Gibbs (1827–1874), an African American Methodist minister who served as Florida's secretary of state from 1868 to 1873, was praised by a Jacksonville paper as "a good example of what education will make of his race," according to *The Negro in the Reconstruction of Florida*. Yet his brother found Gibbs sleeping in the attic with a "considerable ... arsenal" (stockpile of weapons) for fear of the Klan, which had threatened to kill him, historian Joe M. Richardson wrote. When he suddenly died after giving a passionate speech at a Republican meeting, some people suspected the forty-eight-year-old Gibbs had been poisoned.

Although Southern whites would complain of being under "Negro rule," the term was misleading. True, in 1867, African American voters outnumbered whites in the South 703,400 to 660,000. But the South Carolina legislature was the only place where African American officials outnumbered whites, and only for a brief time. By the early 1870s, white supremacist groups (those who believe that whites are superior and should be in charge) were succeeding in intimidating African Americans from voting or running for office. African American lawmakers did not disappear after Reconstruction—North Carolina, for instance, had an African American congressman, George H. White (1852–1918), as late as 1901—but they depended on white legislators to get anything accomplished.

Blanche K. Bruce (1841–1898), an African American planter who represented Mississippi in the U.S. Senate, later defended the work of African American officials during Reconstruction. "We began our political career under the disadvantages of the inexperience in public affairs that generations of enforced bondage had entailed upon our race," Blanche said in an 1877 speech, reprinted in *200 Years: A Bicentennial Illustrated History of the United States.* But he said there was no sign that African American leaders were "oppressive" toward whites. And the new state constitutions written with African American men's help "were more in harmony with the spirit of the age and the genius of our free institutions than the obsolete laws" they replaced.

Did you know ...

- Revels was appointed to the Senate seat previously held by Jefferson Davis (1808–1889), the man who left Congress to become president of the Confederacy. Revels finished the last fourteen months of Davis's term, then returned to Mississippi in 1871 where he was named president of Alcorn College, the state's first African American college.

- Former slave John Roy Lynch (1847–1939) went to Washington, D.C., in 1873 as the first African American member of the House of Representatives from Mississippi. He was also the last African American representative from Mississippi until 1987.

- Although no African Americans were elected governor during Reconstruction, P. B. S. Pinchback (1837–1921) served as acting governor of Louisiana for about a month during the impeachment trial of Governor Henry Clay Warmoth (1842–1931) in 1872 and 1873. That made Pinchback the country's first African American governor, and the only African American to hold that position until 1990.

Consider the following …

- Do you think Southern whites would have been more accepting of African American officials if all ex-Confederates were allowed to vote? Or would that have made it harder for African American candidates to get elected?

- Why did certain whites resent African American officials? How did they try to keep African Americans out of power?

- How did Revels make the case for allowing African Americans the right to participate in politics?

For More Information

Coulter, E. Merton. *The South During Reconstruction*. Baton Rouge: Louisiana State University Press, 1947.

Foner, Eric. *Reconstruction: America's Unfinished Revolution*. New York: HarperCollins Publishers, 1988.

King, Edward. *The Great South: A Record of Journeys*. Hartford, CT: American Publishing Company, 1875. Also available at *University of North Carolina at Chapel Hill Libraries*. http://docsouth.unc.edu/nc/king/king.html#p89 (accessed on September 20, 2004).

Revels, Hiram R. "On the Readmission of Georgia to the Union." *U.S. Senate*. http://www.senate.gov/artandhistory/history/resources/pdf/RevelsGeorgia.pdf (accessed on September 20, 2004).

Richardson, Joe M. *The Negro in the Reconstruction of Florida*. Tallahassee: Florida State University, 1965.

Smith, John David. *Black Voices from Reconstruction*. Gainesville: University Press of Florida, 1997.

Stalcup, Brenda, ed. *Reconstruction: Opposing Viewpoints*. San Diego: Greenhaven Press, 1995.

Trelease, Allen W. *White Terror: The Ku Klux Klan Conspiracy and Southern Reconstruction*. Baton Rouge: Louisiana State University Press, 1971.

200 Years: A Bicentennial Illustrated History of the United States. Washington, DC: U.S. News & World Report, 1973.

Wharton, Vernon L. "The Negro in Mississippi Politics." In *Reconstruction in the South.* Lexington, MA: D. C. Heath and Company, 1972.

James Shepherd Pike

Excerpt from **The Prostrate State**
Published in 1874; reprinted on *Making of America Books* (Web site)

*A Reconstruction-era journalist provides an inaccurate account
of the African American politician*

"Seven years ago these men were raising corn and cotton under the whip of the overseer. To-day they are raising points of order and questions of privilege. They find they can raise one as well as the other. They prefer the latter. It is easier, and better paid...."

To the white Southerners who lost the American Civil War (1861–65), nothing was more humiliating than the idea of their former slaves casting ballots and holding elected office. They argued that African Americans, particularly the illiterate (unable to read or write) ex-slaves who had no education, were too ignorant to vote or rule wisely. They also held racist views that African Americans would never be equal to whites. When Congress gave Southern African American men the ballot under the Reconstruction Act of 1867 (see Chapter 10), one angry South Carolinian declared that, "I shall never cast another vote so long as I live," James L. Roark wrote in *Masters without Slaves*. Another man in Tennessee said that "to be governed by my former slaves was an ignominy [disgrace] which I should not and would not endure."

Indeed, the ex-slaves had a lot to learn. But many of them were eager to do so. They poured into newly created freedmen's schools to learn how to read. They attended political meetings to learn about the candidates and the upcoming elections. Not surprisingly, they threw their support behind the Republican Party, the party that had pushed for their freedom and political rights. Party supporters made sure to remind African Americans of this, as described in *High Crimes & Misdemeanors: The Impeachment and Trial of Andrew Johnson*:

> In Selma, Alabama, a man arose in front of the polling place and held up the blue ticket denoting the conservative [Democratic] slate. "No land!" he shouted. "No mules! No votes! Slavery again!" Then he held up the red Radical [Republican] ticket. "Forty acres of land! A mule! Freedom! Votes! Equal of a white man!"

Some Southerners say the party went a step further to intimidate African Americans to vote for Republican candidates. "They [African Americans] had been industriously drilled into believing that if they did not vote the republican ticket they would be placed back in slavery or deported to Africa," ex-Confederate soldier William Robert Houghton (1842–1906) wrote in his brotherhood memoirs, *Two Boys in the Civil War and After.*

The same act of Congress that gave Southern African American men the vote took it away from certain ex-Confederates. By the end of 1867, African American voters outnumbered white voters in the South, about 703,400 to 660,000. Some of those whites were so disgusted by the changing political tide that they boycotted, or abandoned, the elections altogether. Numerous African Americans were elected to offices ranging from city councilman to congressman, and almost immediately they faced opposition (see Chapter 12). The white members of the Georgia legislature expelled their newly elected African American colleagues in 1868, and countless African American officials were threatened or attacked by the Ku Klux Klan and other white supremacist groups (those who believe that whites are superior and should be in charge; see Chapter 15).

The South Carolina legislature quickly drew the nation's attention as the only assembly in which African American members outnumbered whites. When the legislature convened (gathered) in 1868, African Americans held seventy-eight seats in the House of Representatives and ten seats in the Senate. Whites held only forty-six seats in the House of Representatives, although they had twenty-one seats in the Senate. While these numbers would change slightly over the years, African Americans held a majority in the legislature

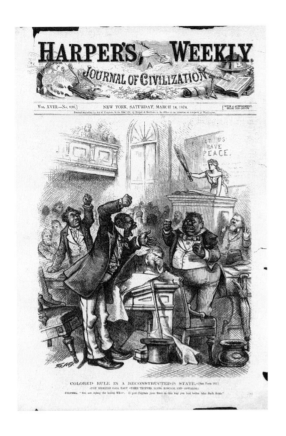

HARPER'S WEEKLY.
A JOURNAL OF CIVILIZATION

Vol. XVIII.—No. 898.] NEW YORK, SATURDAY, MARCH 14, 1874. ["THREE DOLLARS A YEAR.]

COLORED RULE IN A RECONSTRUCTED(?) STATE.—[See Page 237.]

This *Harper's Weekly* political cartoon by Thomas Nast, entitled "Colored rule in a reconstructed state," shows members of the South Carolina legislature arguing in the House, with Columbia (symbolically representing the United States) scolding them. *The Library of Congress.*

until 1874. "When negro domination had ... been established," H. H. Chalmers wrote in 1881 in "The Effects of Negro Suffrage," "there ensued a scene of incompetence, profligacy [wastefulness], and pillage [robbing], the like of which has never disgraced the annals [historical accounts] of any English-speaking people."

At least that was the picture painted by journalist James Shepherd Pike (1811–1882) in his 1874 book, *The Prostrate State.* The title itself suggested whites lying prostrate, or face-down, as a conquered people. Although he was a northern Republican who opposed slavery, Pike did not support equal rights for African Americans. At one point, he thought freed slaves should be sent to another country or placed on their own reservation. His racist views are reflected in *The Prostrate State,* where he described South Carolina's African American legislators as clueless and corrupt. In various passages, Pike wrote that lawmakers refurbished the capitol with $480 clocks and $650 chandeliers, renovated their apartments with Belgian carpets, and voted to reimburse the Speaker of the House $1,000 for a lost horse racing bet—all with taxpayer dollars.

The outrageous account was widely read but far from objective, as noted in *Reconstruction: America's Unfinished Revolution.* Pike "had long held racist views," and the journalist had published similar commentaries about African American officials before he ever visited South Carolina. Furthermore, Pike "acquired much of his information from interviews with white Democratic leaders and seems to have spoken with only one black Carolinian."

But Pike's readers did not know that. They believed what he wrote, and urged others to read the book. As noted in "The Effects of Negro Suffrage," if Pike's "book could be put into the hands of all our people, it would give them a

RADICAL MEMBERS

OF THE FIRST LEGISLATURE AFTER THE WAR

SOUTH CAROLINA

Dusenberry	Mayes	Demars	Rivers	Mileford	Smith	Swails
McKinlay	Jillson	Brodie	Duncan	White	Pettengill	Perrin
Dickson	Lomax	Hayes	BOOZER	Barton	Hyde	James
Wilder	Jackson	Cain	Smythe	Boston	Lee	Johnston
Hoyt	Thomas	Maxwell	Wright	Shrewsbury	Simonds	Wimbush
Randolph	Webb	Martin	MOSES	Mickey	Chesnut	Hayes
Harris	Bozeman	Cook	Sancho	Henderson	McDaniel	Farr
	Tomlinson	Miller	Sanders	Hewell	Williams	Meade
	Wright *		Nuckles	Hayne	Gardiner	Thompson
				Mobley		Rainey
				Hudson		
				Nash		
				Carmand		

* Afterwards associate Justice of the Supreme Court of the State

COPYRIGHT, 1878, BY MERCER BROWN.

Members of the first South Carolina legislature following the Civil War. *The Library of Congress.*

more truthful idea of the reconstruction era" than any other books of the time.

Things to remember while reading an excerpt from *The Prostrate State:*

- As part of the Reconstruction Act of 1867, Congress gave Southern African American men the right to vote and run for office. The same act barred certain ex-Confederates from doing the same. For many Southern whites, it was the worst humiliation they could imagine.

- South Carolina was the only state in which African Americans held a majority of the seats in the legislature. It drew national attention as an example of what could be expected of African American officials.

- Although Pike's book was widely read, historians question its accuracy. Pike held racist views and had published similar commentaries on African American officials before visiting South Carolina. It also appears that most of Pike's tales of the South Carolina legislature came from Democrats who opposed African Americans' rights, and that the journalist only spoke to one African American resident while writing his book.

Excerpt from The Prostrate State

*In the place of this **aristocratic** society stands the **rude** form of the most ignorant democracy that mankind ever saw, **invested** with the functions of government. It is the **dregs** of the population **habilitated** in the robes of their intelligent **predecessors**, and **asserting** over them the rule of ignorance and corruption, through the **inexorable** machinery of a majority of numbers. It is barbarism overwhelming civilization by physical force. It is the slave rioting in the halls of his master, and putting that master under his feet. And, though it is done without **malice** and without **vengeance**, it is nevertheless done.... Let us approach nearer and take a closer view. We will enter the House of Representatives. Here sit one hundred and twenty-four members. Of these, twenty-three are white men, representing the remains of the old civilization.... There they sit, grim and silent. They feel themselves to be but loose stones, thrown in to partially obstruct a current they are powerless to resist. They say little and do little as the days go by. They simply watch the rising tide, and mark the **progressive** steps of **inundation**.... He **comports** himself with a dignity, a **reserve**, and a **decorum**, that command **admiration**. He feels that the iron hand of Destiny is upon him. He is gloomy, **disconsolate**, hopeless....*

*This dense negro crowd they confront do the debating, the squabbling, the law-making, and create all the **clamor** and disorder of the body. These twenty-three white men are but the observers,*

Aristocratic: Upper class.

Rude: Primitive.

Invested: Empowered.

Dregs: Most worthless part.

Habilitated: Clothed.

Predecessors: Those who held office before them.

Asserting: Forcing.

Inexorable: Unchangeable.

Malice: Evil intent.

Vengeance: Revenge.

Progressive: Series of.

Inundation: Flooding.

Comports: Carries.

Reserve: Silence.

Decorum: Proper way.

Admiration: Respect.

Disconsolate: Distressed.

Clamor: Loud outcries.

the enforced **auditors** of the dull and clumsy imitation of a **deliberative** body, whose appearance in their present capacity is at once a wonder and a shame to modern civilization.

Deducting the twenty-three [white] members referred to, who comprise the entire strength of the opposition, we find one hundred and one remaining. Of this ... ninety-four are colored, and seven are their white **allies.** Thus the blacks outnumber the whole body of whites in the House more than three to one.... The **Speaker** is black, the Clerk is black, the door-keepers are black, the little **pages** are black, the chairman of the Ways and Means [committee] is black, and the **chaplain** is coal-black.... It must be remembered, also, that these men, with not more than half a dozen exceptions, have been themselves slaves, and that their ancestors were slaves for generations....

One of the things that first strike a casual observer in this negro assembly is the **fluency** of the debate, if the endless chatter that goes on there can be dignified with this term. The leading topics of discussion are all well understood by the members, as they are of a practical character, and appeal directly to the personal interests of every legislator, as well as to those of his constituents. When an **appropriation** bill is up to raise money to catch and punish the Ku-klux, they know exactly what it means. They feel it in their bones. So, too, with educational measures. The free school comes right home to them; then the business of arming and drilling the black militia....

But the old **stagers** admit that the colored **brethren** have a wonderful **aptness** at legislative proceedings. They are "quick as lightning" at **detecting points of order,** and they certainly make **incessant** and extraordinary use of their knowledge.... The talking and the interruptions from all quarters go on with the utmost **license.**...

But underneath all this shocking **burlesque** upon legislative proceedings, we must not forget that there is something very real to this **uncouth** and **untutored** multitude. It is not all **sham,** nor all burlesque. They have a genuine interest and a genuine **earnestness** in the business of the assembly which we are bound to recognize and respect, unless we would be accounted shallow critics. They have an earnest purpose, born of a conviction that their position and condition are not fully assured, which lends a sort of dignity to their proceedings.... The whole thing is a wonderful **novelty** to them as well as to observers. Seven years ago these men were raising corn and cotton under the whip of the overseer. To-day they are raising points of order and **questions of privilege.** They find they can raise one as well as the other. They prefer the **latter.** It is easier, and bet-

Auditors: Listeners.

Deliberative: Thoughtful.

Allies: Supporters.

Speaker: Leader of the assembly.

Pages: Assistants.

Chaplain: Clergyman serving the assembly.

Fluency: Flowing words.

Appropriation: Spending.

Stagers: Players.

Brethren: Brothers.

Aptness: Skill.

Detecting: Finding.

Points of order: Questions of procedure.

Incessant: Endless.

License: Freedom.

Burlesque: Comedy.

Uncouth: Crude.

Untutored: Untaught.

Sham: Fraud.

Earnestness: Seriousness.

Novelty: Unusual sight.

Questions of privilege: Procedural issues.

Latter: Second one.

Jubilee: Celebration.

*ter paid.... It means escape and defense from old oppressors. It means liberty. It means the destruction of prison-walls only too real to them. It is the sunshine of their lives. It is their day of **jubilee**. It is their long-promised vision of the Lord God Almighty.*

What happened next ...

Some journalists took issue with Pike's portrayal, offering their own accounts of the educational and economic improvements occurring in South Carolina. But for the most part, Pike's account was accepted as a true picture. As noted in *Reconstruction: America's Unfinished Revolution,* "despite its many inaccuracies, *The Prostrate State* not only helped make South Carolina a byword for corrupt misrule but reinforced the idea that the cause lay in 'negro government.'" Other newspapers and magazines followed with similar articles—so even people who never heard of *The Prostrate State* read similar articles in *Scribner's, Harper's,* or the *Atlantic Monthly.*

Decades later, former South Carolina governor Daniel H. Chamberlain (1835–1907) argued that the African American–dominated legislature was part of the "wide reign of corruption and general misrule" of the era. In "Reconstruction in South Carolina," Chamberlain pointed to the numbers: The state debt rose from $1 million in 1868 to $17.5 million in 1872. The cost of holding the annual legislative session rose from $20,000 before the war to $617,000 in 1871. The congressional act that gave the ballot to seventy-eight thousand African American men in South Carolina was "a frightful experiment," Chamberlain concluded. "Ought it not to have been as clear then as it is now that good government, or even tolerable administration, could not be had from such an aggregation of ignorance and inexperience and incapacity?"

But in his book *Black Reconstruction in America,* African American civil rights leader W. E. B. Du Bois (1868–1963) explained that such numbers are only part of the story. Southern legislators faced the costly task of rebuilding roads, bridges, and other facilities destroyed by the war. In many cases, they were also building their first public schools across the state. They had to raise millions of dollars in taxes and borrow millions more to accomplish the work. Northern bankers charged unusually high interest, or borrowing fees, on the money because of the risky political climate in the South, Du Bois wrote. Those high interest rates, charged as a percentage of the borrowed money, were so high that "If there were outstanding in 1874 twenty or even thirty millions of [dollars] of debt, it is unlikely that this represented more than ten millions in actual cash delivered," wrote Du Bois.

At the same time, many Southern whites resented the way this money was being raised and spent. Because most taxes were collected on businesses, banks, and machinery—something few African Americans had—most of the tax burden fell on whites. Yet some of the new budget items, such as the $900,000 public school system, would benefit African Americans (as well as whites). Some whites refused to pay taxes, which only caused the legislature to raise more taxes to make up the shortfall, Du Bois claimed.

Du Bois argued that the true legacy of African American legislators can be found in the South Carolina constitution, which was largely written by African American delegates. Aside from creating a statewide public school system, the constitution did away with debtors' prisons and allowed men to vote even if they did not own property. "The constitution was written in good English and was an excellent document," Du Bois wrote. But the other work of South Carolina's African American lawmakers has been distorted, in part, because "little effort has been made to preserve the records of Negro effort and speeches, actions, work and wages, homes and families," Du Bois contended. "Nearly all this has gone down beneath a mass of ridicule and caricature [mockery], deliberate omission and misstatement."

Did you know ...

- According to *The Prostrate State,* the African American legislators bought themselves elegant porcelain "spittoons," or containers for spitting the juices from chewing tobacco. The spittoons instantly became a symbol of the alleged extravagance of the South Carolina legislature.

- In some Southern counties, the African American men who were appointed to oversee the new school districts were illiterate. They signed official documents with an "X," the symbol used when a person cannot write his or her own name.

- Before the Civil War, Southern whites paid taxes on the slaves they owned, as slaves were considered property. But once slavery was abolished, or outlawed, Southern states could no longer collect such a tax. To make up for the lost revenue, they raised taxes on land and businesses.

Consider the following ...

- If you were a Northerner in the 1870s reading *The Prostrate State,* how would you feel about requiring Southern states to give African American men the right to vote and run for office?

- Can you find three examples of racist language in the *Prostrate State* excerpt?

- Why is *The Prostrate State* considered an inaccurate account of the South Carolina legislature?

For More Information

Chalmers, H. H. "The Effects of Negro Suffrage." *North American Review* (February 1881): pp. 239–48. http://etext.lib.virginia.edu/toc/modeng/public/ChaEffe.html (accessed September 20, 2004).

Chamberlain, Daniel H. "Reconstruction in South Carolina." *In Reconstruction in Retrospect: Views from the Turn of the Century.* Baton Rouge: Louisiana State University Press, 1969.

Du Bois, W. E. B. *Black Reconstruction in America.* New York: Harcourt, Brace and Co., 1935. Reprint, New York: Maxwell Macmillan International, 1992.

Foner, Eric. *Reconstruction: America's Unfinished Revolution.* New York: HarperCollins Publishers, 1988.

Houghton, William Robert, and Mitchell Bennett Houghton. *Two Boys in the Civil War and After.* Montgomery, AL: Paragon Press, 1912. Also available at *University of North Carolina Chapel Hill Libraries.* http://docsouth.unc.edu/houghton/menu.html (accessed on September 20, 2004).

Pike, James Shepherd. *The Prostrate State: South Carolina Under Negro Government.* New York: D. Appleton and Company, 1874. Also available at *Making of America Books.* http://www.hti.umich.edu/cgi/t/text/text-idx?c=moa;idno=AFK4119.0001.001 (accessed on September 20, 2004).

Roark, James L. *Masters without Slaves: Southern Planters in the Civil War and Reconstruction.* New York: W. W. Norton & Company, 1977.

Smith, Gene. *High Crimes & Misdemeanors: The Impeachment and Trial of Andrew Johnson.* New York: McGraw-Hill, 1985.

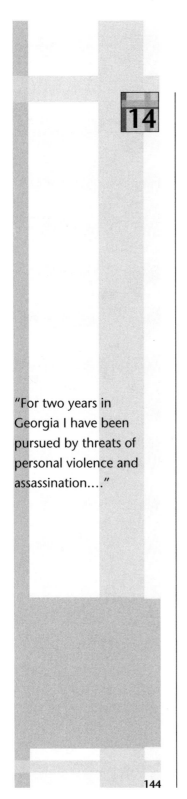

Rufus B. Bullock

Excerpt from Letter from Rufus B. Bullock, of Georgia, to the Republican Senators and Representatives, in Congress Who Sustain the Reconstruction Acts

Published in May 21, 1870; reprinted on *Making of America Books* (Web site)

A Georgia governor describes what it is like to be a loyal supporter of Reconstruction in the sometimes hostile South

"For two years in Georgia I have been pursued by threats of personal violence and assassination...."

Perhaps no figure was hated as much as the "carpetbagger" during the postwar years in the South. The term referred to Northerners who went to the South during or after the American Civil War (1861–65) with so few belongings they could fit them all in an old-fashioned traveling bag made of carpet. They were Republicans, viewed as opportunists who pressed for civil and voting rights for African Americans in order to further their own political careers. Indeed, many of them would become governors or congressmen in their newly adopted states, with the support of African American voters.

The carpetbaggers' very presence was a reminder of the South's crushing defeat at the hands of the North. Most Southerners could accept losing the war, but they could not accept the dramatic postwar changes, in which African Americans were allowed to own land, vote, and even hold elected office. "Well we might and did forgive the wrongs of war," Virginia soldier David Emmons Johnston (1845–1917) wrote in his 1914 memoirs, *The Story of a Confederate Boy in the Civil War*, "but how were we to overlook and forget the outrageous and shameful things done in the name of restoration of civil government, by the carpetbagger, Northern political pest and pirate...."

The men who had been labeled carpetbaggers clearly felt the animosity. Albion W. Tourgée (1838–1905), an Ohio native and Union soldier who served as a Superior Court judge in North Carolina after the war, described Southern attitudes toward carpetbaggers in his 1880 book, *A Fool's Errand, by One of the Fools.*

> To the Southern mind [carpetbagger] meant ... a creature of the conqueror, a witness of their defeat, a mark of their degradation.... They hissed his name through lips hot with hate, *because* his presence was hateful to that dear, dead Confederacy which they held in tender memory.... He was to all that portion of the South ... not only an enemy, but the representative in miniature of all their enemies.

Often these outsiders were accused of corruption, not exactly an uncommon occurrence in the fast-growth years after the war (see Chapter 17). Sometimes they were accused of offering bribes to get into office, accepting bribes from railroads and other industries, or pocketing some of the state treasury as taxes reached new, painful highs. In Mississippi, one tax increased fourteen-fold from 1869 to 1874, as noted in *Kemper County Vindicated and A Peep at Radical Rule in Mississippi.* "These [carpetbagger] legislators, having little or no property interest in the State, manifested on every occasion the most bitter feelings against the white people who owned all the property and paid all the taxes."

Yet many historians believe carpetbaggers have been unnecessarily criticized. As noted in "Carpetbaggers Reconsidered" in *Reconstruction in the South,* most of these Northerners arrived well before Southern African American men got the right to vote under the 1867 Reconstruction Acts (see Chapter 10), meaning they could not have come to use African Americans for their personal gain. They came because the postwar South was a land of economic opportunity, where they could buy land at cheap prices, raise a crop, or start a business venture. Nor were they penniless men who could fit all of their belongings in a single bag: Brothers Albert T. and Charles Morgan, for instance, left Wisconsin for Mississippi, where they poured $50,000 into a lumber business. Tourgée went to

Rufus B. Bullock. *The Library of Congress.*

North Carolina with $5,000 to start his own nursery business.

But most of these newcomers' ventures failed. Drought and pests killed the crops, and in some areas, Southerners boycotted Yankee businesses (especially those owned by former Union soldiers). Most of the Northerners returned home. Those who stayed behind turned to politics, searching for a way to make the state more prosperous and friendly to business. They believed the state would be stronger in the long run with a free African American work force that could vote. As noted in "Carpetbaggers Reconsidered" in *Reconstruction in the South,* these Northerners believed "they had a right and a duty to be where they were and to do what they did. This was now their home, and they had a stake in its future as well as the future of the country as a whole."

Rufus B. Bullock (1834–1907) is sometimes not counted among the carpetbagger governors because he moved from New York to Georgia in 1857 or 1859, a couple of years before the Civil War started. But in many ways he fits the mold. Economic opportunities drew him South, where he laid telegraph and railroad lines. He turned to politics after the war, after learning the banks would not lend money to his business until Georgia was readmitted to the Union. He supported the Republican plan for Reconstruction—including the measures to open the ballot box and elected offices to African Americans—as the best way to mend Georgia's war-ravaged economy. And his efforts as governor would make him a hated figure among many white Southerners, who would accuse him of using millions of dollars in railroad bonds to enrich his friends.

In this 1870 letter to Congress, Bullock describes the difficulties he faced as a member of the delegation that drafted a new Georgia state constitution, and later as governor.

Under the Reconstruction Acts (a congressional plan for re-making Southern society after the Civil War), high-ranking ex-Confederates could not vote on the new state constitution; and the Fourteenth Amendment (see Chapter 9) barred them from voting or holding office. At the same time, Congress required the Southern states to give African American men the ballot. The Georgia legislature elected in 1868 included the state's first African American members—as well as some former Confederates who should have been barred from office. The white majority of the legislature kicked out the African American members, arguing the right to vote did not necessarily mean the right to hold office. It was a recipe for racial strife, pitting white Southerners against African Americans and the carpetbaggers who pushed for their rights.

Bullock drafted his letter to Congress for a couple of reasons. He wanted more federal troops stationed in Georgia to make sure the federal rules for Reconstruction were followed. He also wanted to fire back at his critics—including some Democrats in Congress—who fueled the investigations into his alleged corruption. Most of all, he wanted to let Congress know what it was like to be a loyal supporter of Reconstruction in the sometimes hostile South.

Things to remember while reading an excerpt from *Letter from Rufus B. Bullock, of Georgia, to the Republican Senators and Representatives, in Congress Who Sustain the Reconstruction Acts:*

- The South was a land of economic opportunity during and after the Civil War, with cheap land and cities in need of new businesses. This drew thousands of Northerners, called "carpetbaggers," to the South, where they later became politically active as Republicans pushing for African Americans' rights.

- Most white Southerners resented the carpetbaggers, suspecting these Northerners were simply using African Americans to get elected to office and line their own pockets (which turned out to be true in some cases). Most Southern whites also opposed the postwar changes—new laws allowing African Americans to own land, vote, and hold elected office—that carpetbaggers enforced.

- In order to be readmitted to the Union, the Southern states had to write new state constitutions. Congress required the states to include African American men in the constitutional conventions and give them the right to vote, while excluding ex-Confederates from the conventions and the polls.

Excerpt from Letter from Rufus B. Bullock, of Georgia, to the Republican Senators and Representatives, in Congress Who Sustain the Reconstruction Acts

*On the 4th day of July, 1867, a convention met in Atlanta to organize a Republican party in our State.... That convention resolved to **sustain** the reconstruction acts of Congress, and to **endeavor** to establish a government for the State under and by virtue of those acts. It was a small beginning, and the men who participated in that organization were surrounded by all the **malignity** of rebel hate, inflamed and embittered by the **endorsement** of the colored men so **lately** their slaves. And the little band who thus bravely met were threatened on all sides and their lives were by no means secure.*

*In November of the same year an election was had to decide by a vote whether a convention under the reconstruction acts should be called, and at the same time for the election of delegates to the convention should its call be **ratified**. In this election the Republicans of the State were successful. The convention was called, and during the winter of 1867–'8 a constitution was framed in which there is no sign of **proscription**, no **test oaths**, no **disfranchisement**. All men of sound mind, who have not been convicted of a felony, and who are twenty-one years of age and residents of the State, are under it entitled and to hold office....*

*Under and by virtue of the [Reconstruction] act of June 25, 1868 [which readmitted Georgia to the Union], the General Assembly **convened** on the 4th of July of the same year. Among those elected by the opposite party [Democrats] were at least thirty [former Confederates] who were especially prohibited by the act of June 25, and by previous acts, from holding office, they being disquali-*

Sustain: Uphold.

Endeavor: Attempt.

Malignity: Evil influence.

Endorsement: Support.

Lately: Recently.

Ratified: Approved.

Proscription: Banning certain voters.

Test oaths: Loyalty pledges required of some ex-Confederates.

Disfranchisement: Taking the vote away from certain people.

Convened: Met.

fied by the 3d section of the fourteenth amendment.... Notwithstanding this presentation of facts, however, the commanding general **deemed** it wise to make no objection to those members **retaining** their seats, and the Legislature this organized in violation of the law, having gone through the form of adopting the conditions then required in the reconstruction acts, the State, by military order, was **remanded** to the civil government thus established.

In September of the same year this legislative organization excluded from their seats some twenty-eight of its members, who were of African descent.

At this point the **contest** originating from the **enfranchisement** of the colored men was renewed with all its bitterness. While the question of this **expulsion** was being considered by the Legislature, I, in an official communication, impressed upon them, in the strongest terms which I was capable of using, the great wrong which was about to be **perpetrated,** and, of course, thereby stimulated a renewal of our political **animosities. Earnest** appeals were made to me by frightened and discouraged Republicans to **acquiesce in** this outrage, and offers of high political **preferment** and advancement were indirectly **tendered** to me by the opposite party to **effect** the same object, accompanied by threats of the **vengeance** that would be visited upon me if I did not accept their terms....

If away out on the **confines** of civilization a settler is threatened in his cabin by a prowling band of Indians, troops are at once moved, money is lavishly spent, and the whole country is aroused for his protection; but, on the other hand, if white and African American friends of the Union are whipped and murdered in the South by prowling bands of disguised **Kuklux,** the President is prevented from granting protection because the laws do not authorize him; and when men or delegations come to the capital from the South to plead with Congress for help and for their rights, haste is made to put them under "investigation" with the vain hope that the lies of the interested rebels may have some foundation in fact.... While we risk our lives and our property, will you aid in taking from us that which is dearer than all these—our good name and our reputation?

... The most **atrocious** lies and **insinuations** have been telegraphed from Washington to different parts of the country, and circulated among members of **both houses,** to the effect that I have attempted to influence the votes of Senators by offers of Georgia bonds or money, and every possible means had been employed to create prejudice against myself and the Republican party of Georgia....

Deemed: Believed.

Retaining: Keeping.

Remanded: Sent back.

Contest: Dispute.

Enfranchisement: Voting rights.

Expulsion: Removal.

Perpetrated: Committed.

Animosities: Hostilities.

Earnest: Serious.

Acquiesce in: Consent to.

Preferment: Recognition.

Tendered: Offered.

Effect: Bring about.

Vengeance: Revenge.

Confines: Boundaries.

Kuklux: Ku Klux Klan, a white supremacist group.

Atrocious: Cruel.

Insinuations: Rumors.

Both houses: Senate and House of Representatives.

*These **infamous** lies have a common origin, and have been **coined** and well put into circulation by men who **hypocritically** pretend to belong to the Republican party, but who are, and have been, acting in concert with the rebel Democracy in Georgia.*

*For two years in Georgia I have been pursued by threats of personal violence and assassination, and, during that period, my friends have believed my life was in danger. For two years I have been pursued by the most **villainous slanders** that rebel **ingenuity** could invent, charging corruption in office, personal immorality, and in every way **impeaching** my character as a man and an officer. One after another these slanders have been worn out and abandoned only to be renewed in some other form. Every attempt to sustain any one of them, and in every instance, has proved an utter and shameless failure....*

Whatever else may happen to me, I shall leave the office of Governor of Georgia with clean hands, and without having performed any act for which my children or my friends shall have occasion to blush, but with my private fortune greatly diminished by the heavy expenses which I have been subjected to sustain myself and the loyal men of Georgia....

What happened next ...

Bullock quietly resigned as governor in October 1871 and fled to New York after learning his Democratic enemies planned to impeach him (attempt to remove him from office for charges of wrongdoing). Specifically, Bullock borrowed millions of dollars in bonds, and critics said he used the money to make his railroad industry friends rich. In reality, Bullock used the money to rebuild some of the railroad lines destroyed during the war, improve the schools, and move the capital from Milledgeville to Atlanta—all facts presented at an 1874 trial in which Bullock was cleared of any wrongdoing. Bullock stayed in Atlanta after his trial and became a successful businessman, serving as president of the Atlantic Cotton Mills and director of the Union Pacific Railroad. He

---

Infamous: Scandalous.

Coined: Invented.

Hypocritically: Not sincerely.

Villainous: Evil.

Slanders: Lies.

Ingenuity: Cleverness.

Impeaching: Discrediting.

returned to Albion, New York, as his health was failing in 1903, and he died four years later.

Carpetbagger officials in other states would face the same suspicions of corruption, as the Southern states borrowed millions of dollars and raised millions more in new taxes after the war. But reality supported the need for these debts: Rebuilding the postwar South was expensive. Roads and railroad lines had to be rebuilt. So did government buildings in certain devastated cities. Many Southern states found themselves building their first public schools. While there were some corrupt officials who found ways to enrich themselves along the way, historians believe they were few, and they were not all carpetbaggers.

In fact, carpetbaggers deserve credit for some of the positive features in the new Southern state constitutions, as noted in the article "Carpetbagger Constitutional Reform in the South Atlantic States, 1867–68," from the 1961 issue of *Journal of Southern History.* The North Carolina constitution guaranteed all residents a public education, and the constitutions in Virginia, North Carolina, and South Carolina prohibited officials from requiring people to own property in order to vote—all measures championed by carpetbaggers. These new constitutions also protected homeowners from losing their property for unpaid taxes, and they made taxes the same throughout the state.

But the carpetbaggers would face resistance, and often violence, for supporting civil and political rights for African Americans. That was an unforgivable act in the minds of many white Southerners, and carpetbaggers would pay the price. Some were killed, or their family members murdered, or their homes burned to the ground (see Chapter 15). In the decades that followed, they would be painted as the villains of Reconstruction. "'Carpetbagger' was only a word," historian Richard Nelson Current concluded in his book, *Those Terrible Carpetbaggers,* but it "stuck and continues to stick."

Did you know ...

- Bullock was mentioned a couple of times in Margaret Mitchell's epic Civil War novel, *Gone with the Wind.* Of Bullock's election to governor in 1868, Mitchell wrote:

"If the capture of Georgia by [Union general William Tecumseh] Sherman had caused bitterness, the final capture of the state's capitol by the Carpetbaggers, Yankees, and negroes caused an intensity of bitterness such as the state had never known before.... And Rhett Butler was a friend of the hated Bullock!"

- After Bullock left office, more than 130 years would pass before Georgia elected another Republican governor—Sonny Perdue (1946–), in 2002.

Consider the following ...

- How did Bullock make his case for more federal troops in Georgia? Do you think they were needed?

- What was it like to be a carpetbagger in the South?

- Do you think newcomers from the North should have been allowed to participate in Southern politics and run for office?

For More Information

Bullock, Rufus B. *Letter from Rufus B. Bullock, of Georgia, to the Republican Senators and Representatives, in Congress Who Sustain the Reconstruction Acts.* Washington, DC: Chronicle Print, 1870. Also available at *Making of America Books.* http://www.hti.umich.edu/cgi/t/text/text-idx?c=moa;idno=AFJ9485.0001.001 (accessed on September 20, 2004).

Current, Richard Nelson. "Carpetbaggers Reconsidered." In *Reconstruction in the South.* Lexington, MA: D. C. Heath and Company, 1972.

Current, Richard Nelson. *Those Terrible Carpetbaggers: A Reinterpretation.* New York: Oxford University Press, 1988.

Johnston, David Emmons. *The Story of a Confederate Boy in the Civil War.* Portland, OR: Glass & Prudhomme Co., 1914. Also available at *University of North Carolina Chapel Hill Libraries.* http://docsouth.unc.edu/johnstond/menu.html (accessed on September 20, 2004).

Lynch, James D. *Kemper County Vindicated and A Peep at Radical Rule in Mississippi.* New York: E. J. Hale & Son, 1879.

Scroggs, Jack B. "Carpetbagger Constitutional Reform in the South Atlantic States, 1867–1868." *Journal of Southern History* (1961).

Tourgée, Albion W. *A Fool's Errand, by One of the Fools.* New York: Fords, Howard, & Hulbert, 1880.

John Paterson Green

Excerpt from Recollections of the Inhabitants, Localities, Superstitions, and KuKlux Outrages of the Carolinas
Published in 1880; reprinted on *Documenting the American South* (Web site)

A former slave recounts his experiences with the Ku Klux Klan

15

S tarted as a secret society for ex-Confederates, the Ku Klux Klan did not remain a secret for long. In a few short years, the white-hooded Klansmen became the most notorious band of terrorists in the postwar South, known for lynching African Americans, shooting "carpetbaggers," and torching freedmen's schools. Their goal was obvious: To defeat any efforts to elevate African Americans to the political or social equal of whites. That meant keeping African Americans away from polling places, chasing African Americans out of elected office, and running off the so-called carpetbaggers, Northern Republicans who came South and ran for office with promises to support African American rights (see Chapter 14).

The group actually had fairly innocent beginnings. Six young Confederate soldiers, having just returned to their hometown of Pulaski, Tennessee, created the secret society in 1866 to launch minor pranks—almost like a college fraternity. "Ku Klux" came from the Greek word *kuklos,* meaning circle or band. "The origin of the order had no political significance," one of those founders, John C. Lester, later wrote in *Ku Klux Klan: Its Origin, Growth, and Disbandment.* "It was at

"The bull-whip and rawhide were also instruments of their torture, and made to produce arguments which none dared refute...."

Ku Klux Klan members, in a drawing from the December 19, 1868, issue of *Harper's Weekly*.

first purely social and for our amusement." Members had elaborate initiation rituals, exotic titles like Grand Cyclops and Grand Turk, and bizarre pointy-hat costumes they wore comically at fairs while communicating with each other using children's whistles.

In time, their pranks—and their ranks—grew. Members wore ghost-like robes and made nighttime visits to African Americans, claiming to be dead Confederate soldiers seeking revenge. Just to spook the ex-slaves, the Klansmen would appear to drink tremendous amounts of water (which was actually poured into bags underneath their costumes), saying it was their first thing to drink since their last battle. But, as William Garrott Brown wrote in *Reconstruction in Retrospect,* this "purposeless fooling" soon led to "the Klan's inevitable discovery that mystery and fear have [power] over the African mind." For Southern whites who resented the new rights being exercised by African Americans, the Klan became a way to intimidate the freedmen.

The South was brimming with racial tension in the years after the American Civil War (1861–65). Not only had the war freed the slaves, but Congress had given Southern African American men the vote under the Reconstruction Act of 1867 (see Chapter 10). At the same time, Congress forbade high-ranking ex-Confederates from voting or holding office. In any given Southern town, the white community leaders were barred from the polls while their former slaves cast ballots and ran for office. "It seems astounding," historian Brown wrote, that Congress did not foresee that white men "so circumstanced would resist, and would find some means to make their resistance effective."

John Brown Gordon (1823–1904), a Confederate general linked to the Klan in Georgia, described the group as "purely a peace police organization," during his 1871 testimony to Congress, reprinted in *Reconstruction: Opposing Viewpoints.* After the war freed the slaves, Gordon testified, whites lived in fear of being attacked by African Americans, particularly as Northern carpetbaggers "organized" African Americans to push for their rights. Gordon continued:

Men were in many instances afraid to go away from their homes and leave their wives and children, for fear of outrage. Rapes were already being committed in the country.... It was therefore necessary, in order to protect our families from outrage and preserve our own lives, to have something that we could regard as a brotherhood—a combination of the best men in the country, to act purely in self-defense, to repel the attack in case we should be attacked by these people.

But this rationalization had little basis in fact, according to historians. Although freed by the war, most African Americans still relied on whites for a living, as noted in *White Terror: The Ku Klux Klan Conspiracy and Southern Reconstruction.* "Seldom were Negroes willing to stand up to a white man and resist or defy him to his face; those who did automatically incurred the wrath of the white community, and risked their lives." In proportion to their population, African Americans committed fewer murders than whites, and usually their victims were other African Americans. "Certainly black men were more often the victims than the perpetrators of racial violence."

The violence from the Klan—and other white supremacist groups (those who believe that whites are superior and should be in charge) such as the Knights of the White Camellia, the Pale Faces, and the White Brotherhood—was aimed at preventing African Americans from voting, so that white Southern Democrats could return to office. "Klansmen repeatedly attacked Negroes for no other stated offense than voting, or intending to vote, the Republican ticket," as noted in *White Terror: The Ku Klux Klan Conspiracy and Southern Reconstruction*. In Arkansas, more than three hundred Republicans, including U.S. representative James M. Hinds (1833–1868), were killed in 1868 by Klansmen. That same year, the Klan killed more than one thousand people in Louisiana. And similar attacks in Georgia helped the Democratic Party reclaim various offices in the 1870 elections. "The Klan became in effect a terrorist arm of the Democratic party, whether the party leaders as a whole liked it or not." Klan defenders, such as Gordon, blamed such violence on Klan imposters acting without the group's support.

The Carolinas were a hotbed of Klan activity, so much so that President Ulysses S. Grant (1822–1885; served 1869–77) sent federal troops into nine South Carolina counties in October 1871 to quiet the violence. The following year, former slave John Paterson Green (1845–1940) left Hudsonville, South Carolina, with two other African American families in search of a new town with better opportunities for African Americans. Born in North Carolina, Green escaped from his master as a child and fled to western Ohio, where he learned to read and write. After the war, Green wrote in *Recollections of the Inhabitants, Localities, Superstitions, and KuKlux Outrages of the Carolinas,* he "returned to the Sunny South with a burning zeal to do something … for the common good."

Green's book describes his travels with Jones, an ex-slave who had extensive knowledge about the local towns, and the other African American family members looking to relocate. In the following passage, Green describes the Klan's destruction.

Things to remember while reading an excerpt of *Recollections from the Inhabitants, Localities, Superstitions, and KuKlux Outrages of the Carolinas:*

- Although originally founded as a "purely social" secret society for ex-Confederate soldiers, the Ku Klux Klan quickly became a terrorist organization that used intimidation and violence against freed African Americans and the white Northerners who supported African Americans' rights.

- Klan defenders said the group was needed to protect whites from attacks by African Americans. But historians say those fears were greatly exaggerated; African Americans were more often the victims—not the perpetrators—of racial violence.

- The Klan's violence had a political goal: Prevent African Americans from voting or holding office so that white Southern Democrats could return to power. To achieve that goal, the Klan also targeted white Republicans who supported civil and voting rights for African Americans.

Excerpt from Recollections of the Inhabitants, Localities, Superstitions, and KuKlux Outrages of the Carolinas

*We had only proceeded a short distance further on our way, when we were confronted by the charred remains of what had been a dwelling house. "What's that?" I asked for the hundredth time, addressing Jones. "That," said he, "is the work of the Ku-Klux-Klan. The man who lived there was nominated for an office of **inconsiderable** importance; but being a "Yankee" and for that reason displeasing to his Democratic neighbors, he was warned to leave the country; and failing to **heed** the notice, he was taken from his house one night by a body of masked men, given a coat of tar and feathers, and twenty-four hours in which to make his escape. After that treatment he hesitated no longer, but left for parts unknown, glad enough to be spared his life. On the following night his house, with all its contents, were burned to the ground, and left in the condition you now see it."*

*Further inquiry only tended to strengthen the truth of Jones' statement; not only this but the additional fact that throughout the region we were then **traversing**, there was a thoroughly organized association of men under the name given above. The Ku-Klux-Klan was an organization **conceived** in sin, and born in **iniquity**; based not so much upon any wrongs or oppression that its members were actually suffer-*

Inconsiderable: Trivial.

Heed: Pay attention to.

Traversing: Crossing.

Conceived: Formed.

Iniquity: Wickedness.

ing at the hands of the members of the newly organized government of the State, as upon an imagined violence done to "all their **preconceived** opinions and prejudices...." One of those opinions was that the South ought to have been left alone to **secede** from the Union of these States, and not restrained by the vigorous North; hence a violence had been done the South in restraining her. Another opinion was that, after having been **scourged** back into the line of States, South Carolina ought to have been given loose reins to reconstruct herself, and make her own laws; even though their tendency were such as to crush out every spark of civil life from the freedmen, deprive them of their newly **acquired** political privileges, and **relegate** them to the condition of "corn-field darkies," with **overseers** to crack their whips over their heads, and not even a master to say them nay. Violence had been done to their "preconceived opinions" by denying them this privilege, and to cap the climax, their "preconceived prejudices" had been violated by permitting "corn-field darkies and army **sutlers**" to hold offices of **emolument** and trust, notwithstanding the fact they utterly refused to **fraternize** with them even politically, and reap a portion of the benefits **accruing** therefrom. There was no reasonable cause of complaint existing on the part of the people of that State that could not have been adjusted by lawful means entirely within their power and under their control; and that, in any one of our more considerate States of the North would have been modified without resort to violence and **incendiarism.** Not so with these **impulsive** people, however. "Their preconceived opinions and prejudices" had been violated, and now, just as when the Republican party of the North had violated them by electing Abraham Lincoln to the Presidential chair, nothing short of blood would wipe out the stain....

The objects of the Klan, as have been already hinted at, were to banish the so-called "carpet-baggers" from the State, restore the freedmen to positions of **serfdom** under their former masters, and regain control of the government of the State. They carried a knife in one hand and a torch in the other, while in their belt they wore a revolver. The bull-whip and **raw-hide** were also instruments of their torture, and made to produce arguments which none dared refute. In their **expeditions** they spared neither age, sex nor color, and the reputation of being a "black republican" was all that was needed to place one under the ban of their condemnation....

As time wore on **apace** their opposition increased in **virulence**, and assumed a more open form. About six months later direct opposition in the nature of Ku-Klux outrages began to be felt and heard from. In the adjoining county a white Republican was summoned to

Preconceived: Pre-formed.

Secede: Withdraw.

Scourged: Whipped.

Acquired: Obtained.

Relegate: Assign.

Overseers: Supervisors.

Sutlers: Men who sell goods to the military.

Emolument: Reward.

Fraternize: Associate in a friendly way.

Accruing: Collecting.

Incendiarism: Fiery destruction.

Impulsive: Easily excitable.

Serfdom: Slavery.

Raw-hide: A whip made of cow skin.

Expeditions: Marches.

Apace: At a fast pace.

Virulence: Deadliness.

his door one night by the usual alarm; he went accompanied by his wife and daughter, and instead of welcoming a neighbor or friend who had come to perform a friendly errand, they were confronted by a band of Ku-Klux, who, without any word of warning or even opportunity of making his peace with his God, shot him down like a dog....

The question is sometimes asked: "Why don't the freedmen fight?" If our readers will for a moment consider that these men were, from their **infancy**, taught to fear and obey white men; that they are uneducated and unsophisticated, while their former masters are educated and shrewd; that while the white men of the South were educated to the use of the rifle and the shot-gun, the freedmen were kept in ignorance of their use; and further, that in many instances the freedmen are without leaders, they will appreciate the condition of these poor men with their unfortunate surroundings....

Ku Klux Klan member attacking a black family, from the February 24, 1872, issue of *Harper's Weekly.*

Infancy: Earliest stage.

The First Grand Wizard

Regarded as a brilliant lieutenant general for the Confederacy during the Civil War, Nathan Bedford Forrest (1821–1877) commanded a different force during Reconstruction: the Ku Klux Klan. As Klan groups began forming in various parts of Tennessee in 1866 to intimidate ex-slaves and harass the so-called carpetbaggers (Northern whites who entered Southern politics), the Klansmen realized they needed a strong leader to unite their efforts. They found an ideal Grand Wizard in Forrest, a respected Confederate cavalry man who had defeated a Union force twice as large as his own in 1864 at the Battle of Brice's Crossroads. Forrest also had a reputation for racial brutality, stemming from the 1864 capture of Fort Pillow, where Forrest's troops killed nearly two hundred African American Union soldiers *after* seizing the west Tennessee fort.

It appears Forrest joined the Klan in late 1866 or early 1867, although (like most Klansmen) he publicly denied his involvement with the group at the time. Still, he defended the Klan's purpose as a "protective, political, military organization," according to an interview with the *Cincinnati Commercial,* reprinted in *Nathan Bedford Forrest: A Biography.* Once the Klan became active, Forrest told the newspaper, bands of black men "quit killing and murdering our people." But if the Tennessee militia start attacking the Klan, Forrest added, "there will be war, and a bloodier one than we have ever witnessed."

Forrest served as Grand Wizard, or the top leader of the Klan, until 1869, when he issued an order essentially disbanding the organization. In that order, Forrest suggested the violent actions of a few members had taken the Klan away from its original "patriotic" purpose to pro-

What happened next ...

Green and his companions reached their destination of Magnolia, North Carolina, and found the once-prosperous city still in ruins from the war. "Gloom and despondency seemed to brood over the forsaken place," Green wrote. The group decided to return to Hudsonville, just long enough to pack all of their belongings for a move to the North. "We had breathed the pure atmosphere of the free North for so long a time that the prejudices and customs peculiar to that locality [the Carolinas] could illy [scarcely] be brooked [endured] by us," Green wrote.

In response to the violent outbursts in the South, Congress passed the Ku Klux Klan Act of 1871, which al-

Confederate major general Nathan Bedford Forrest, founder of the Ku Klux Klan and leader of the Klan from 1866 to 1869. © *Corbis.*

tect white people. He ordered each member to burn his costumes and masks, and said no further "demonstrations" could be held without the approval of top leaders.

Forrest was done with the Klan and, it seems, everything the Klan represented.

In the last years of his life, Forrest grew more receptive to African Americans' rights and less tolerant of violence toward African Americans. When a group of masked white men kidnapped and murdered several African American men in 1874 from a jail in Trenton, Tennessee, Forrest said that if he had the power, "he would capture and exterminate the white marauders [raiders] who disgrace their race by this cowardly murder of negros," according to an account reprinted in *Nathan Bedford Forrest: A Biography.* "Forrest ... had plainly tired of the race struggle, as well as his own reputation as Fort Pillow's Butcher and the Klan's great wizard," wrote biographer Jack Hurst. Older and wiser, Forrest realized the South would only heal when the two races made peace with each other.

lowed the federal government to prosecute people who "go in disguise" to threaten or attack any person. The act also allowed the president to use the military against such groups, as Grant did in South Carolina. A federal grand jury determined at least eleven murders and more than six hundred whippings had occurred at the hands of Klansmen in a single South Carolina county. "The most vigorous [forcible] prosecution of the parties implicated in these crimes is imperatively [urgently] demanded," the grand jury concluded in a report reprinted in *Reconstruction: Opposing Viewpoints.* "That without this [prosecution] there is great danger that these outrages will be continued, and that there will be no security to our fellow citizens of African descent."

Prosecutors from the U.S. Department of Justice put a couple dozen Klansmen on trial in South Carolina. Most of them pleaded guilty and went to prison, although up to two thousand more fled the state to escape prosecution, as noted in *Reconstruction: America's Unfinished Revolution*. Hundreds more Klansmen were charged in North Carolina. And nearly seven hundred more faced trials in Mississippi, although most of them received little more than a warning not to resume their Klan activities.

By the mid-1870s, the Klan had all but disappeared. Some historians credit the Grant administration's newly created Department of Justice, and particularly Attorney General Amos Akerman (1821–1880), for shutting down the Klan. Others point to an 1869 order from Grand Wizard Nathan Bedford Forrest (1821–1877), a former Confederate general from Tennessee, disbanding the Klan (see box). "The Order of the Ku Klux Klan is in some localities being perverted from its original honorable and patriotic purposes," and public opinion was turning against masked organizations, Forrest wrote in the order, as cited in *Invisible Empire: The Story of the Ku Klux Klan, 1866–1871*. For whatever reason, the Klan went into a half-century hibernation, stirring again in the 1920s for another reign of terror that would last through the Civil Rights Movement of the 1950s and 1960s.

Yet some viewed the Klan as a group of necessity. It arose when Southern whites needed a way to control the African Americans just freed from slavery. It disappeared when those whites regained control of their state governments, often through voter intimidation efforts. "The important work of the Klan was accomplished in regaining for the whites control over the social order and in putting them in a fair way to regain political control," as noted in *Ku Klux Klan: Its Origin, Growth, and Disbandment*. "In some States this occurred sooner than in others. When the order accomplished its work it passed away."

Did you know ...

- Forrest Gump, the title character in the 1994 movie starring Tom Hanks (1956–), was named after Nathan Bedford Forrest, a former Confederate general and the first Grand Wizard of the Klan.

- Forrest, a former Confederate general from Tennessee, had a reputation from the Civil War as a brave leader, but one who was very violent. The most famous example of his temper was in an incident known as the Fort Pillow Massacre, a battle in which hundreds of Union troops—many of them black—were killed. Later reports indicated that many of them were trying to surrender, but that Forrest approved of the killings.

- The Department of Justice was created in 1870, during Reconstruction, to handle lawsuits on behalf of the federal government. Before then, the attorney general was a one-man department who gave legal advice to the president and Congress, but the workload had grown too great for one person. Armed with extra attorneys in the newly created Department of Justice, Grant had the manpower to prosecute the Ku Klux Klan.

- Perhaps the most commonly associated Klan symbol— the burning cross—was not used by the original Klan.

A scene from the Fort Pillow Massacre. Here, Confederate cavalryman, led by Nathan Bedford Forrest, kill unarmed black Union soldiers after the surrender of Fort Pillow in Tennessee. *Getty Images.*

The men who revived the Klan in the late 1910s or early 1920s created the haunting symbol.

Consider the following …

- Why was the Ku Klux Klan created?

- What were the Klan's tactics? What were they trying to accomplish?

- Why did the Klan essentially disappear by the mid-1870s?

For More Information

Brown, William Garrott. "The Ku Klux Movement." In *Reconstruction in Retrospect*. Baton Rouge: Louisiana State University Press, 1969.

Foner, Eric. *Reconstruction: America's Unfinished Revolution*. New York: HarperCollins Publishers, 1988.

Green, John Paterson. *Recollections of the Inhabitants, Localities, Superstitions, and KuKlux Outrages of the Carolinas*. Cleveland, OH, 1880. Also available at *Documenting the American South: University of North Carolina Chapel Hill*. http://docsouth.unc.edu/southlit/green/green.html (accessed on September 20, 2004).

Horn, Stanley F. *Invisible Empire: The Story of the Ku Klux Klan, 1866–1871*. Montclair, NJ: Patterson Smith, 1939. Reprint, New York: Haskell House, 1973.

Hurst, Jack. *Nathan Bedford Forrest: A Biography*. New York: A. A. Knopf, 1993.

Lester, J. C., and D. L. Wilson. *Ku Klux Klan: Its Origin, Growth, and Disbandment*. New York: Da Capo Press, 1973.

Stalcup, Brenda, ed. *Reconstruction: Opposing Viewpoints*. San Diego: Greenhaven Press, 1995.

Trelease, Allen W. *White Terror: The Ku Klux Klan Conspiracy and Southern Reconstruction*. Baton Rouge: Louisiana State University Press, 1971.

Fifteenth Amendment to the U.S. Constitution

Ratified by the required three-fourths of states on February 17, 1870
Reprinted on *GPO Access: Constitution of the United States* (Web site)

African American men gain the right to vote

Once the slaves were freed by the North's victory in the American Civil War (1861–65), white abolitionist (slavery opponent) William Lloyd Garrison (1805–1879) thought his work was done. At the May 1865 meeting of the American Anti-Slavery Society, Garrison urged the group to disband and celebrate its success. Frederick Douglass (1817–1895), a leading African American abolitionist, said that would be a huge mistake. "Slavery is not abolished [ended] until the African American man has the ballot," said Douglass, as recorded in *Reconstruction: America's Unfinished Revolution.* After a heated debate, members decided to keep the group and replace Garrison, who had been the society's president.

The squabble underscored a larger debate: What did it mean to end slavery? Some people, including many white Northerners, thought it was enough to simply outlaw the practice of owning slaves. Others, such as Douglass, recognized that African Americans would remain powerless and mistreated—a condition similar to slavery—unless they had the right to vote for people who would protect their interests.

"The right of citizens of the United States to vote shall not be denied ... on account of race, color, or previous condition of servitude."

Whites gave several reasons for denying the ballot to African Americans. Most of the freed slaves had little or no education, the whites argued, so how could they make an informed decision at election time? Some whites, such as U.S. representative Benjamin M. Boyer (1823–1887) of Pennsylvania, also believed African Americans were "by nature inferior in mental caliber [ability], and lacking that vim [energy], pluck [courage], and pose of character which give force and direction to human enterprise," according to a speech reprinted in *Reconstruction: Opposing Viewpoints*. In a separate speech reprinted in the same book, Douglass dismissed that argument:

> It is said that we are ignorant; I admit it. But if we know enough to be hung [for crimes], we know enough to vote. If the negro knows enough to pay taxes to support the Government, he knows enough to vote—taxation and representation should go together. If he knows enough to shoulder a musket and fight for the flag, fight for the Government, he knows enough to vote.

The question of African American suffrage, or granting African Americans the right to vote, was almost as controversial in the North as in the South. White voters in Connecticut, Minnesota, and Wisconsin defeated proposals in 1865 to give African Americans the ballot in those states. Their counterparts in the South did not have that choice, however. The 1867 Reconstruction Act by Congress (see Chapter 10) required the ex-Confederate states to give African American men the ballot, while taking it away from certain members of the "rebellion" against the North. In an 1868 letter to Congress, reprinted in *Reconstruction: Opposing Viewpoints,* the Democratic Party of South Carolina summed up the feelings of many white Southerners: "A superior race … is put under the rule of an inferior race—the abject [degraded] slaves of yesterday, the flushed [excited] freedmen of to-day. And think you that there can be any just, lasting reconstruction on this basis?"

The Fourteenth Amendment (see Chapter 9), which required states to give African Americans the same legal treatment as whites, did not specifically grant voting rights to African American men. It simply said that states could lose some of their seats in the House of Representatives based on the number of men turned away from the polls. The careful

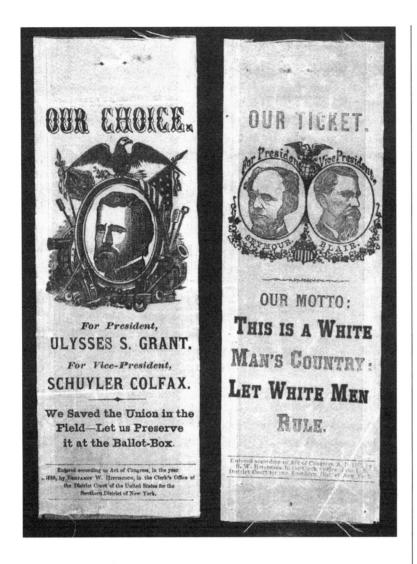

Campaign ribbons from the 1868 election. Left, ribbon for Republican presidential and vice presidential candidates Ulysses S. Grant and Schuyler Colfax. Right, ribbon for Democratic candidates Horatio Seymour and Francis Preston Blair Jr. Much of the Seymour-Blair campaign highlighted white supremacy. © David J. & Janice L. Frent Collection/Corbis.

language was aimed at the South, where denying the ballot to the large African American population would mean losing dozens of congressional seats. The North was largely off the hook, because its African American population was so small that denying them the vote would scarcely affect its number of congressional districts, which are based on population.

Then came the presidential election of 1868. Ulysses S. Grant (1822–1885; served 1869–77), the Union general who led the North to victory in the Civil War, seemed like a strong Republican candidate. Out of nearly 6 million ballots cast, however, Grant won by only three hundred thousand votes. It was safe to assume the 450,000 African American voters in that election supported Grant over Democrat Horatio Seymour (1810–1886), whose running mate, Francis Preston Blair Jr. (1821–1875), made racist remarks throughout the campaign. That meant the African American vote had decided the presidential election in Grant's favor. "This election showed how essential it was that the Negro vote be secured permanently for the Republican Party," in the North as well as the South, as pointed out in *The South During Reconstruction*. Failure to protect the African American vote could mean losing the White House to a Democrat in 1872.

At the same time, there was a group of so-called Radical Republicans who had long pushed for giving African Americans the same rights as whites. They recognized that the 1868 election results would bring the rest of the Republicans on board for their cause, albeit for political reasons. As pointed out in *The Presidency of Andrew Johnson,* "It would be too cynical to say that the Republicans were devoid [lacking] of idealism in thus conferring the vote on the Negro. On the other hand it is naive to claim that their main motive was anything other than political self-preservation."

Congress drafted the Fifteenth Amendment in 1869, using short, simple language that mirrored the Thirteenth Amendment, which outlawed slavery (see Chapter 2). Yet the words were carefully chosen. Voting rights could not be denied "on account of race, color, or previous condition of servitude." But states could pass laws denying the vote to foreign-born residents, as California would do with the Chinese, and some Northern states would do to European immigrants. The wording also left the door open for literacy tests, poll taxes, and other barriers the Southern states would later use to turn African American voters away from the polls.

Things to remember while reading the Fifteenth Amendment:

- After the Civil War, whites in the North and South alike were divided on the issue of African American suffrage. Some thought it was enough to simply outlaw slavery. Others argued African Americans would remain in a powerless state similar to slavery if they did not have the right to vote for people who would safeguard their interests.

- Southern states were already required to give African American men the vote, under the Reconstruction Act passed by Congress in 1867. After the African American vote decided the 1868 presidential election in Grant's favor, however, Republicans realized the need to constitutionally secure the voting rights for all African Americans, in the North and South alike.

- The Fifteenth Amendment was drafted to prevent discrimination against African American voters because of their skin color. But it was left intentionally vague, to allow western and northern states to turn immigrants away from the polling places.

Fifteenth Amendment to the U.S. Constitution

*Section 1. The right of citizens of the United States to vote shall not be denied or **abridged** by the United States or by any State on account of race, color, or **previous condition of servitude**.*

*Section 2. The Congress shall have power to enforce this **article** by appropriate legislation.*

Abridged: Limited.

Previous condition of servitude: Former status as a slave.

Article: Provision of the Constitution.

What happened next ...

Congress approved the amendment, and the necessary three-fourths of the states ratified it by March 30, 1870—in plenty of time to ensure African American men could participate in the 1872 presidential election. Once again, abolitionist William Lloyd Garrison was ready to celebrate. "Nothing in all history [could match] this wonderful, quiet, sudden transformation of four millions of human beings from ... the auction-block to the ballot-box," said Garrison, as quoted in *Reconstruction: America's Unfinished Revolution*. This time, the members of the American Anti-Slavery Society followed his suggestion to disband the group in March 1870, their mission accomplished.

"The Result of the Fifteenth Amendment," oval image showing a parade held in Baltimore, Maryland, on May 19, 1870. *The Library of Congress.*

But the victory was a temporary one. The removal of Union troops from the South in 1877, and a series of court rulings overturning some pieces of Reconstruction legislation, allowed some whites to chip away at African Americans' rights. Once the 1896 Supreme Court ruling *Plessy v. Ferguson* allowed "separate but equal" racially segregated facilities, some Southern states went one step further and passed literacy tests or poll taxes to prevent African Americans from voting. By then, the Northern states had lost their zeal to interfere in what they viewed as a Southern issue.

The Fourteenth and Fifteenth Amendments remained in the Constitution, however, as "sleeping giants," amendments that would have far-reaching legal implications once they were "reawakened" by the civil rights cases of the 1950s and 1960s. Those amendments would provide the basis for ending segregation and outlawing the barriers that had been used to keep African Americans away from the ballot box. Yet only the unique conditions of the post–Civil War era could have paved the way for these amendments that, decades later, would "give the American Negro the ultimate promise of equal civil and political rights," as noted in *The Era of Reconstruction*.

Did you know ...

- Some leaders of the women's suffrage movement opposed the Fifteenth Amendment, resenting the fact that unschooled African American men would get the ballot while educated white women would not. Another half century would pass before women would get the vote under the Nineteenth Amendment to the Constitution.

- The Twenty-fourth Amendment to the Constitution, ratified in 1964, outlawed the use of polling taxes. The Civil Rights Act of 1965 outlawed the use of literacy tests for voters.

- With the tax and literacy obstacles removed, about a quarter million African Americans registered to vote by the end of 1965. The following year, more than half of the African American adults had registered to vote in nine of the thirteen Southern states.

Consider the following ...

- Why was the Fifteenth Amendment necessary, when Congress had already passed Reconstruction Acts requiring the ex-Confederate states to give African American men the ballot?

- Look carefully at the wording of the Fifteenth Amendment. Aside from literacy tests and polling taxes, can you think of other ways officials could have discriminated against voters without violating the amendment?

- What made the Fifteenth Amendment a "sleeping giant?"

For More Information

Castel, Albert. *The Presidency of Andrew Johnson*. Lawrence: University Press of Kansas, 1979.

Coulter, E. Merton. *The South During Reconstruction*. Baton Rouge: Louisiana State University Press, 1947.

Foner, Eric. *Reconstruction: America's Unfinished Revolution.* New York: HarperCollins Publishers, 1988.

Stalcup, Brenda, ed. *Reconstruction: Opposing Viewpoints.* San Diego: Greenhaven Press, 1995.

Stampp, Kenneth M. *The Era of Reconstruction.* New York: Random House, 1965.

United States Government Printing Office. "Fifteenth Amendment— Rights of Citizens to Vote." *GPO Access: Constitution of the United States.* http://www.gpoaccess.gov/constitution/html/amdt15.html (accessed on September 20, 2004).

Edward Winslow Martin

Excerpt from "A Complete and Graphic Account of the Crédit Mobilier Investigation" from Behind the Scenes in Washington
Published in 1873; reprinted on *Making of America Books* **(Web site)**

Evidence mounts against the vice president of the United States

17

Ulysses S. Grant (1822–1885; served 1869–77), the Union general who led the North to victory in the American Civil War (1861–65), was pressed into politics by those seeking a fresh start after the troubled presidency of Andrew Johnson (1808–1875; served 1865–69) (see Chapter 11). Grant had never run for office, nor did he seek the presidency, but the war hero was nominated by the Republican Party in 1868 and won. His simple slogan, "Let us have peace," spoke to a weary nation still torn over race issues and the army occupation of the Southern states. In reality, however, the Grant administration would find itself embattled in some of the worst scandals in U.S. presidential history.

Grant was never personally implicated in (blamed for) any of the scandals, but the crooked ways of some of his closest associates would cloud his two terms in office. The general prized loyalty above all else, clinging to his friends with "hooks of steel," in the words of Major General Greenville M. Dodge (1831–1916), as quoted in the *Prologue* magazine article, "Grant, Babcock, and the Whiskey Ring." At times, it seems, Grant's loyalty blinded him to the faults of his friends.

"The people do not wish to believe him guilty; but they are appalled by the terrible mass of circumstantial evidence against him...."

Grant's brother-in-law, Abel Rathbone Corbin (1808–1881), was a player in the first disaster of Grant's presidency, the 1869 stock market panic known as "Black Friday." Businessmen Jay Gould (1836–1892) and James Fisk (1834–1872) hatched a get-rich-quick scheme to buy large amounts of gold, drive up the price, then sell for a huge profit. It was a daring plan, as gold in those days was not just an investment, but the backbone of the currency system. Corbin used his influence to make sure the president and the U.S. Treasury Department did not interfere with the plan until it was too late: Gould and Fisk made their profits, but many honest investors lost their fortunes as the gold price later plummeted.

It was the first of several scandals that would taint the administration. Secretary of the Treasury William Richardson (1821–1896) resigned in 1874, after officials learned that a man Richardson hired to collect back taxes was pocketing hundreds of thousands of dollars for himself. Secretary of War William W. Belknap (1829–1890) resigned in 1876 after officials learned he was accepting bribes from the man he appointed to a profitable Indian trading post in the Oklahoma territory. "Fighting scandal was practically a state of being in the Grant White House," as noted in *Prologue* magazine.

By no means was the corruption limited to the White House. In New York City, William Marcy "Boss" Tweed (1823–1878) charged the city $11 million for a courthouse that actually cost $3 million to build, pocketing the rest. In several cities, political powerbrokers bought the votes of poor immigrants with food or fuel. Congress gave vast tracts of valuable land to railroad or mining companies—often the very businesses in which members of Congress owned stock. And since U.S. senators were elected by the state legislatures at that time, the right bribes could even buy a seat in Congress.

In some ways, the corruption was simply a sign of the times. While the South was busy rebuilding entire cities destroyed by the war, the rest of the country was building personal and financial empires. Scores of settlers headed for the West to create new ranches and trading posts. Northern factories, built up by the war, churned out better goods for a cheaper price. Railroad companies began criss-crossing the country to transport materials and link once far-away places. The opportunities for striking it rich seemed endless, and the temptation to accept a few bribes or pocket some of the profits along the way was immense.

Schuyler Colfax, vice president during Ulysses S. Grant's first term; he was involved in the Crédit Mobilier scandal. *The Library of Congress.*

One of those tempting schemes would ultimately drag down Grant's first vice president, Schuyler Colfax (1823–1885), and taint the careers of several other congressmen. The Crédit Mobilier scandal was actually pretty simple: The Union Pacific railroad created a spinoff (smaller) company, called Crédit Mobilier, to build the nation's first transcontinental (coast-to-coast) railroad. The company would significantly overcharge the U.S. government for the work, charging $94 million for a railroad that actually cost about $44 million to build. The Crédit Mobilier stockholders would pocket the extra money as dividends, or profits from the stock.

To make sure the government did not raise questions about the high-priced railroad, the company bribed several key congressmen by selling them stock at favorable prices. U.S. representative Oakes Ames (1804–1873) of Massachusetts helped place the railroad stock in the hands of his colleagues, including Colfax, who was Speaker of the House of Representatives in the late 1860s. When the scandal broke in 1872, Ames provid-

The Golden Spike ceremony celebrating the completion of the first transcontinental railroad. *Getty Images.*

ed the damaging testimony before the Poland Committee (named after U.S. senator Luke Poland [1815–1887] of Vermont) linking the other congressmen to the scheme. Newspapers reported each day's stunning revelations of corruption at the highest levels of government, and ultimately it was revealed that public officials had pocketed about $33 million in taxpayer money from the overpriced railroad. Writing under the pen name of Edward Winslow Martin, contemporary author James Dabney McCabe (1842–1883) compiled the events in his 1873 book, *Behind the Scenes in Washington.*

Things to remember while reading an excerpt from "A Complete and Graphic Account of the Crédit Mobilier Investigation":

- Ulysses S. Grant was a moral man who campaigned on a promise to bring peace to the war-torn country. But his presidency was plagued by scandals involving some of his closest associates, including his first vice president, Schuyler Colfax.

- Railroad lines grew at an astonishing pace after the Civil War, aided by Congress, which gave vast tracts of land and generous construction contracts to the railroad companies. In some cases, congressmen owned stock in the very companies they were helping.

- The Union Pacific railroad company created a spinoff company, called Crédit Mobilier, to build the transcontinental railroad and overcharge the U.S. government for the work. The stockholders, including congressmen turning a blind eye to the corrupt scheme, would pocket millions of dollars in profits.

Excerpt from *"A Complete and Graphic Account of the Crédit Mobilier Investigation"*

When the charge was made that Mr. Colfax had been a purchaser of Crédit Mobilier stock from Mr. Ames, that gentleman denied it.... The substance of this sworn statement [before the Poland Committee investigating the scandal] may be thus stated in Mr. Colfax's own words:

*"I state explicitly, that no one ever gave, or offered to give me any shares of stock in the Crédit Mobilier or the Union Pacific Railroad. I have never received, nor had **tendered** to me any **dividends** in cash, stock, or bonds **accruing** upon any stock, in either of said organizations."*

*Mr. Ames had from the first included Mr. Colfax in his list of the Congressmen who had purchased stock from him. Upon Mr. Colfax's denial of the charge, he declared his ability to prove his **assertion**.*

*On the 24th of January, Mr. Ames testified that he had purchased twenty shares of Crédit Mobilier stock for Mr. Colfax, in December, 1867, at the request of that gentleman. Mr. Colfax not having the money at the time, Mr. Ames **advanced** it. Soon after this, there was an eighty per cent dividend declared in Union Pacific bonds. Mr. Ames stated that he had sold these, and had applied the proceeds to paying for the stock bought for Mr. Colfax, after **deducting** the **interest**. Mr.*

Tendered: Offered.

Dividends: Profits.

Accruing: Collecting.

Assertion: Claim.

Advanced: Loaned.

Deducting: Taking out.

Interest: Fee charged on loaned money.

A political cartoon by Thomas Nast showing two congressmen involved in the Crédit Mobilier scandal, James Brooks of New York (left) and Oakes Ames of Massachusetts. *The Granger Collection, New York. Reproduced by permission.*

Sergeant-at-Arms: The doorkeeper of Congress who provided banking and other services for members.

Emphatically: Strongly.

Sustained: Upheld.

Obliged: Compelled.

*Colfax then gave him a check on the **Sergeant-at-Arms** for $534.72, the balance of the purchase money. Mr. Ames further stated that in June there was a cash dividend on the Crédit Mobilier of $1200, which he gave to Mr. Colfax by a check payable to "S. C. or bearer," drawn on the Sergeant-at-Arms of the House.*

*Mr. Colfax **emphatically** denied Mr. Ames's statement, and declared that he had never received the $1200, or any of the stock or money to which Ames referred. The books of the Sergeant-at-Arms were produced, and exhibited to the Committee. It was found that in June, 1868, Mr. Ames had drawn a check on the Sergeant-at-Arms to "S. C. or bearer," and that this check had been paid to some one. This much of Mr. Ames's statement being **sustained**, Mr. Colfax found himself **obliged** to show that the check in question had not been paid to him....*

The Committee decided to examine the accounts of the First National Bank of Washington City, where Mr. Colfax's accounts were kept. The books were produced before the Committee on the 28th of

January [1873], and Mr. Colfax's account examined. [According to the committee,] "There appeared a credit of $1968.63, dated June 22, 1868, two days after the date of Ames's check to 'S. C.' on the Sergeant-at-Arms, and one day after that check was paid. This furnished only **presumptive** proof of the deposit of $1200, but all doubt was removed when the cashier produced a deposit ticket, bearing Mr. Colfax's signature, in which the $1968.63 was **itemized**, $1200 being cash, and the remainder **drafts** or checks...."

The **circumstantial** evidence against him [Colfax] was **appalling.** His best friends stood **aghast,** and pitied him from their very souls.

Mr. Colfax repeated his denials respecting the stock, and declared that he would show that the $1200 deposited by him was received from another source. If he could succeed in doing this, his **vindication** would be complete.... On the 11th of February [1873], he appeared before the Committee, accompanied by Judge Hale, whom he had retained as his **counsel,** and made a statement under oath that the $1200, which he had deposited in cash in the First National Bank of Washington, on the 22d of June, 1868, was composed of two sums, of $1000 and $200 respectively. The $1000, he stated, he had received from a Mr. George F. Nesbitt, of New York, who had written him a letter congratulating him upon his nomination for the Vice-Presidency, and enclosing a $1000 bill to be used for political purposes during the campaign. The sender of the gift, Mr. Nesbitt, died a few years ago, and the letter in which the money was sent had, Mr. Colfax stated, been destroyed. Mr. Colfax submitted the evidence of several members of his family in proof of the **reception** of Nesbitt's letter. They swore to a recollection of it, and stated the incidents connected with its reception. The other $200 Mr. Colfax stated was received from his step-father, Mr. Matthews, in payment of money borrowed from Mr. Colfax some time before. Mr. Colfax repeated his former denials concerning the stock and Ames's check.

This statement of Mr. Colfax was not accepted by the public as **satisfactory.** It amounted to this, in part: That a leading business man of New York had entrusted to the mail in a letter, a bill for $1000 dollars, without making any note of it, the man was dead, and the letter could not be found. Against this explanation was Oakes Ames's sworn statement, the proofs afforded by the books of the Sergeant-at-Arms, and the suspicious deposit of the exact amount of Ames's check....

Presumptive: Supposed.

Itemized: Listed as an individual item.

Drafts: Money orders.

Circumstantial: Suspicious, but not conclusive.

Appalling: Shocking.

Aghast: Horrified.

Vindication: Effort to clear his name.

Counsel: Attorney.

Reception: Act of receiving.

Satisfactory: Good enough.

U.S. representative Oakes Ames of Massachusetts, a key figure in the Crédit Mobilier scandal.
© Corbis/Bettmann.

Perjury: Lying under oath.

Precaution: Security measure.

Inclined: Led.

Note: Cash.

Unregistered: Not secured by the post office.

Cordially: Warmly.

*In order to get at the facts of the case, for it was clear to all that either Oakes Ames or Schuyler Colfax was guilty of **perjury**, a member of the Poland Committee made an investigation of Mr. Colfax's deposits in the First National Bank of Washington. He found that two checks or drafts from Mr. Nesbitt to Mr. Colfax had been deposited by the latter in 1868, one in April, and the other on the 13th of July, of that year. Each of these drafts was for $1000. This discovery did not help Mr. Colfax much. It showed that Mr. Nesbitt had twice sent Mr. Colfax the sum of $1000, and had taken the **precaution** to insure the money against loss by sending each sum in the form of a draft payable to Mr. Colfax's order. This very precaution **inclined** people to doubt that Mr. Nesbitt would have been so reckless as to send Mr. Colfax a thousand dollar **note** in an **unregistered** letter, only a short while before he took the precaution to send a similar sum by a draft....*

*There the case rests at present. Mr. Colfax has still before him the task of proving that he received $1000 from Nesbitt in June, and did not receive $1200 from Oakes Ames. He is still entangled in the terrible web of circumstantial evidence against him. That he may escape from it and vindicate himself is the wish of all good men. There is not a public man in America whose vindication would be more **cordially** hailed by the people. The people do not wish to believe him guilty; but they are appalled by the terrible mass of circumstantial evidence against him, and he must, in justice to himself, destroy this. It is the earnest wish of the writer, who has sought to present a simple statement of the facts of the case as far as they have been developed, that he may succeed.*

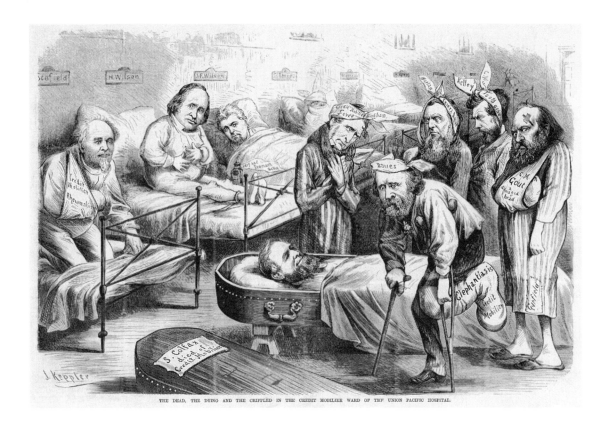

THE DEAD, THE DYING AND THE CRIPPLED IN THE CREDIT MOBILIER WARD OF THE UNION PACIFIC HOSPITAL.

What happened next ...

Some members of Congress wanted to get rid of Ames and Colfax by impeachment, a process of removing people from office for wrong-doing. But they backed off in both cases. Congress censured (formally criticized) Ames three months before his death in 1873. Colfax finished his term as vice president, but his political career was ruined. When Grant ran for reelection in 1872, Colfax was replaced by U.S. senator Henry Wilson (1812–1875) of Massachusetts—ironically, another official linked by Ames to the Crédit Mobilier scandal.

It would not be the last time the Grant administration faced a humiliating scandal. Grant's close friend and long-time assistant, Orville E. Babcock (1835–1884), was charged in 1875 as a member of the Whiskey Ring, an intricate conspiracy in which St. Louis alcohol distillers avoided paying millions of dollars in federal taxes on whiskey. Some of the profits from this scheme helped finance Grant's 1872 reelection campaign, bringing yet another scandal into the heart of the White

A political cartoon depicting politicians involved in the Crédit Mobilier affair as residents in a hospital ward; the coffin contains Vice President Schuyler Colfax, who was also involved in the scandal. © *Corbis.*

President Ulysses S. Grant.
AP/Wide World Photos. Reproduced by permission.

House. Grant once again displayed his undying loyalty to his friends—and, it seems, his obliviousness to their misdeeds—by testifying to Babcock's good character in a deposition that was read aloud at the sensational trial. It worked: Although other prominent members of the Whiskey Ring were convicted, Babcock was acquitted.

The scandals of the Grant administration distracted the president at a time when his attention was desperately needed: The South was torn by racial tensions, the West was the scene of various Indian wars, and the North was awhirl in economic expansion, partly fueled by the underpaid labor of European immigrants. The corruption also discouraged many African American voters who originally supported Republicans as the party that freed them. They saw the government give away millions of acres of land to railroad companies, even as officials denied land to African Americans starting their new lives, as noted in *Reconstruction: America's Unfinished Revolution*. Freedman Anthony Wayne asked, "Whilst Congress appropriated land by the million acres to pet railroad schemes ... did they not aid poor Anthony and his people starving and in rags?"

Did you know ...

- Grant often walked from the White House to the ornate Willard Hotel for an evening drink, a cigar, and a chance to relax. As people learned of his routine, however, they stopped by the hotel lobby to pitch a piece of legislation or ask the president for help. In time, these favor-seekers hanging around the hotel became known as lobbyists, a term still used today.

- Grant's testimony in the Whiskey Ring case was the first, and so far only, time a sitting U.S. president has voluntarily testified in a criminal trial.

- Born in Ohio to a family of modest means, Grant did not plan to enter the military. But his father enrolled him at the U.S. Military Academy at West Point, recognizing it as an opportunity to give his son a first-rate education at no cost to the family. Grant graduated from West Point as the finest horse-rider in his class, setting a high-jump record that lasted twenty-five years.

- Adding to the perceptions of a corrupt administration, Grant signed a bill in 1873 doubling his salary from $25,000 to $50,000 a year. According to biographer Richard Goldhurst, Grant "was outraged that people accused him of a salary grab."

Consider the following ...

- Why did members of Congress get drawn into the Crédit Mobilier scandal?

- Contrast the accounts given by Oakes Ames and Schuyler Colfax. Who would you believe, and why?

- How does the corruption of the Grant administration compare to modern-day political scandals?

For More Information

Foner, Eric. *Reconstruction: America's Unfinished Revolution*. New York: HarperCollins Publishers, 1988.

Goldhurst, Richard. *Many Are the Hearts: The Agony and the Triumph of Ulysses S. Grant*. New York: Reader's Digest Press, 1975.

Johannsen, Robert W. "Crédit Mobilier of America." *The American Presidency*. http://ap.grolier.com/article?assetid=0112820-00&template name=/article/article.html (accessed on September 20, 2004).

Martin, Edward Winslow. "A Complete and Graphic Account of the Crédit Mobilier Investigation." *Behind the Scenes in Washington*. New York: Continental Publishing Company, 1873. Also available at *Making of America Books*. http://www.hti.umich.edu/cgi/t/text/text-idx?c=moa;idno=AFJ8728.0001.001 (accessed on September 20, 2004).

Perret, Geoffrey. *Ulysses S. Grant: Soldier & President*. New York: Random House, 1997.

Rives, Timothy. "Grant, Babcock, and the Whiskey Ring." *Prologue: Quarterly of the National Archives and Records Administration* (Fall 2000). Also available at http://www.archives.gov/publications/pro

logue/fall_2000_whiskey_ring_1.html (accessed on September 20, 2004).

Simpson, Brooks D. *The Reconstruction Presidents.* Lawrence: University Press of Kansas, 1998.

James Rapier

18

Excerpt from his speech on the Civil Rights Bill of 1875
Given on June 9, 1874

A U.S. representative from Alabama talks about the discrimination he faces as a black man

The struggle for racial equality was a difficult and step-by-step battle in the years after the American Civil War (1861–65). In three hard-won constitutional amendments passed over a five-year period, African Americans were freed from slavery, granted citizenship and equal legal treatment, and given the right to vote (although this last amendment applied to men only). But in many aspects of everyday life, African Americans remained second-class citizens. African Americans and whites attended separate schools, worshipped in separate churches, and buried their dead in separate cemeteries. African Americans were limited to the least-desirable cars on any train, and often they were turned away from restaurants and hotels.

Charles Sumner (1811–1874), a U.S. senator from Massachusetts who led the Radical Republicans' push for racial equality, proposed a bill that would ban such discrimination in schools, churches, cemeteries, hotels, theaters, railroads, and other public facilities. Just as the earlier Civil Rights Act of 1866 (see Chapter 8) had barred local governments from passing discriminatory laws

"I feel this humiliation very keenly; it dwarfs my manhood, and certainly it impairs my usefulness as a citizen...."

Excerpt of the Civil Rights Bill of 1875

Whereas it is essential to just [righteous] governments we recognize the equality of all men before the law, and hold that it is the duty of government in its dealings with the people to mete [give] out equal and exact justice to all, of whatever nativity [birth], race, color, or persuasion, religious or political; and it being the appropriate object of legislation to enact great fundamental principles into law:

Therefore, Be it enacted, That all persons within the jurisdiction [authority] of the United States shall be entitled to the full and equal enjoyment of the accommodations, advantages, facilities, and privileges of inns, public conveyances [transportation] on land or water, theaters, and other places of public amusement; subject only to the conditions and limitations established by law, and applicable alike to citizens of every race and color, regardless of any previous condition of servitude.

Section 2. That any person who shall violate the foregoing [previous] section by denying to any citizen, except for reasons by law applicable to citizens of every race and color, and regardless of any previous condition of servitude, the full enjoyment of any of the accommodations, advantages, facilities, or privileges in said

section enumerated [listed], or by aiding or inciting such denial, shall for, every such offense, forfeit [surrender] and pay the sum of five hundred dollars to the person aggrieved [done wrong] thereby ... and shall also, for every such offense, be deemed guilty of a misdemeanor, and upon conviction thereof, shall be fined not less than five hundred nor more than one thousand dollars, or shall be imprisoned not less than thirty days nor more than one year....

Section 4. That no citizen possessing all other qualifications which are or may be prescribed by law shall be disqualified for service as grand or petit [trial] juror in any court of the United States, or of any State, on account of race, color, or previous condition of servitude; and any officer or other person charged with any duty in the selection or summoning of jurors who shall exclude or fail to summon any citizen for the cause aforesaid shall, on conviction thereof, be deemed guilty of a misdemeanor, and be fined not more than five thousand dollars.

Section 5. That all cases arising under the provisions of this act ... shall be renewable by the Supreme Court of the U.S., without regard to the sum in controversy....

against African Americans, this Civil Rights Bill would prohibit businesses from treating African Americans differently than whites (see box). The bill would also protect African American men's rights to sit on a jury. With Sumner on his death bed in the spring of 1874, the passage of the bill became his final wish.

The Senate passed the measure in May 1874—in part, out of respect for a dying colleague—but many doubted the House of Representatives would approve it. The bill faced opposition among white Northerners and Southerners alike, who viewed it as a step toward creating "social equality" among the races. Many whites feared the idea of racial intermingling: African Americans competing in white-dominated industries or marrying into white families. Those fears may have been exaggerated: "It is a wholesale falsehood to say that we wish to force ourselves upon white people," said P. B. S. Pinchback (1837–1921), an African American member of the Louisiana state senate, as quoted in *Reconstruction: After the Civil War.* Yet the white voters' fears weighed heavily on the congressmen, as they were all up for reelection in 1874.

James T. Rapier. *Fisk University Library. Reproduced by permission.*

The congressmen passionately debated the bill over the coming months, with the seven African American members of Congress detailing their own experiences of being thrown from trolleys or turned away from upscale restaurants. John Roy Lynch (1847–1939), an African American representative from one of the largest and wealthiest districts in Mississippi, described the discrimination he faced on every trip to Washington, D.C., in a speech reprinted in *The American Heritage History of the Confident Years:*

> I am treated, not as an American citizen, but as a brute. Forced to occupy a filthy smoking-car both night and day, with drunkards, gamblers, and criminals; and for what? Not that I am unable or unwilling to pay my way; not that I am obnoxious in my personal appearance or disrespectful in my conduct; but simply because I happen to be of a darker complexion.

U.S. representative James Rapier (1837–1883) of Alabama had a similar story to share. Rapier was born to a free African American family in Alabama and educated in Tennessee and Canada. He returned to the South during the Civil War, and was one of the ninety-six delegates who rewrote Alabama's state constitution after the war. Upon his 1872 election to Congress, Rapier lobbied for providing former plantation lands to African Americans and quality schools for all. Yet every trip to the capital brought fresh reminders of the discrimination he was trying to fight.

Things to remember while reading James Rapier's speech on the Civil Rights Bill:

- African Americans had been freed from slavery, granted citizenship and equal legal treatment, and given the right to vote (for men) under three constitutional amendments passed after the Civil War. But African Americans still faced discrimination in the private sector: train conductors put them in the least desirable cars, and the operators of some hotels and restaurants refused to serve them.

- The earlier Civil Rights Bill of 1866 barred local governments from passing discriminatory laws against African Americans. The later Civil Rights Bill, debated by Congress in 1874–75, would prevent businesses from treating African Americans differently than whites.

- In 1874, Congress had seven African American members—men who could vote and shape laws—yet even these men faced discrimination during their travels to the capital.

Excerpt from James Rapier's speech on the Civil Rights Bill of 1875

*I must confess it is somewhat embarrassing for a colored man to urge the passage of this bill, because if he exhibit an **earnestness** in the matter and express a desire for its immediate passage,*

Earnestness: Determination.

straightway he is charged with a desire for social equality, as explained by the **demagogue** and understood by the ignorant white man. But then it is just as embarrassing for him not to do so, for, if he remain silent while the struggle is being carried on around, and for him, he is **liable** to be charged with a **want** of interest in a matter that concerns him more than any one else, which is enough to make his friends desert his cause....

Let me cite a case. Not many months ago Mr. [Francis] Cardozo, treasurer of the State of South Carolina, was on his way home from the West. His route lay through Atlanta. There he made request for a **sleeping-berth.** Not only was he refused this, but was denied a seat in a first-class carriage, and the parties went so far as to threaten to take his life because he insisted upon his rights as a traveler. He was compelled, a most elegant and accomplished gentleman, to take a seat in a dirty smoking-car, along with the traveling **rabble,** or else be left, to the **detriment** of his public duties.

I **affirm,** without the fear of **contradiction,** that any white ex-convict (I care not what may have been his crime, nor whether the hair on the shaven side of his head has had time to grow out or not) may start with me to-day to Montgomery (Alabama), that all the way down he will be treated as a gentleman, while I will be treated as the convict. He will be allowed a berth in a sleeping-car with all its comforts, while I will be forced into a dirty, rough box with the drunkards, apple-sellers, railroad **hands,** and next to any dead that may be in transit, regardless of how far decomposition may have progressed....

And I state without the fear of being **gainsaid,** ... that there is not an inn between Washington and Montgomery, a distance of more than a thousand miles, that will accommodate me to a bed or meal. Now, then, is there a man upon this floor who is so heartless, whose breast is so void of the better feelings, as to say that this brutal custom needs no regulation? I hold that it does and that Congress is the body to regulate it....

Sir, I submit that I am **degraded** as long as I am denied the public privileges common to other men, and that the members of this House are correspondingly degraded by recognizing my political equality while I occupy such a humiliating position....

Mr. Speaker, nothing short of a complete acknowledgment of my manhood will satisfy me. I have no compromises to make, and shall unwillingly accept any....

Straightway: At once.

Demagogue: A leader who manipulates others' emotions.

Liable: Likely.

Want: Lack.

Sleeping-berth: Built-in bed on a train.

Rabble: Mob.

Detriment: Damage.

Affirm: Swear.

Contradiction: Argument.

Hands: Workers.

Gainsaid: Contradicted.

Degraded: Dishonored.

Unfurled: Flew.

Steamer: A steam-powered ship.

Keenly: Strongly.

Asylum: Refuge.

Misnomer: Wrong name.

Pariah: Outcast.

Prescribe: Order.

*Sir, in order that I might know something of the feelings of a freeman, a privilege denied me in the land of my birth, I left home last year and traveled six months in foreign lands [in Europe], and the moment I put my foot upon the deck of a ship that **unfurled** a foreign flag from its mast-head, distinctions on account of my color ceased. I am not aware that my presence on board the **steamer** put her off her course. I believe we made the trip in the usual time. It was in other countries than my own that I was not a stranger, that I could approach a hotel without the fear that the door would be slammed in my face. Sir, I feel this humiliation very **keenly;** it dwarfs my manhood, and certainly it impairs my usefulness as a citizen....*

*Mr. Speaker, to call this land the **asylum** of the oppressed is a **misnomer**, for upon all sides I am treated as a **pariah.** I hold that the solution of this whole matter is to enact such laws and **prescribe** such penalties for their violation as will prevent any person from discriminating against another in public places on account of color. No one asks, no one seeks the passage of a law that will interfere with any one's private affairs. But I do ask the enactment of a law to secure me in the enjoyment of public privileges....*

What happened next ...

Aware that the measure was unpopular with many voters, the House of Representatives postponed a vote on the Civil Rights Bill until after the 1874 elections. It would be a tough enough campaign, as the country was in the midst of an economic depression. Some whites had grown increasingly frustrated with the role of African American men as voters and public officials, and they decided intimidation and violence was the best way to keep African Americans out of politics. In various pockets of the South, white supremacist groups drove African Americans from their homes and assassinated Republican officials who supported equal rights (see Chapter 15). The tactics worked: the Democrats, the party of the white South, won a landslide victory in 1874.

Congress still had one last session in early 1875 before the new members were sworn in, and the Republicans realized they would soon lose control of Congress—and the post-war Reconstruction efforts. Before leaving, they added funding for Union troops in the South, beefed up efforts to fight voter intimidation, and gave the federal courts the power to handle more racial discrimination cases. They also approved the Civil Rights Bill after removing the passage that would have integrated schools, a move that made it easier for moderates to support the bill.

The Civil Rights Bill only fueled the resentments among white Southerners. In the Alabama community of Troy, for example, a group of whites passed a resolution strongly opposing the measure. They vowed to cut off all social interactions with the bill's supporters, whom they described as "the enemies of our race," according to the resolution reprinted in *The American Heritage History of the Confident Years*. To those whites, the bill threatened "the protection of our dearest and most sacred interests, our homes, our honor, the purity and integrity of our race," as well as the "peace and tranquility of the country."

An anti–African American political cartoon entitled "We Intend to Beat the Negro in the Battle of Life and Defeat Means One Thing—Extermination."
© *Corbis.*

Yet the bill was stronger on paper than in practice. The law offered sweeping statements on the rights of African Americans, but few specifics on how to enforce those rights. As noted in *Reconstruction: America's Unfinished Revolution,* "it left the initiative for enforcement primarily with black litigants [plaintiffs] suing for their rights in the already overburdened federal courts." Only a handful chose that route, and ultimately they lost.

The Supreme Court overturned the Civil Rights Bill in 1883, declaring the law unconstitutional. The amendments to the Constitution ended slavery and prohibited discriminatory laws against African Americans, but Congress cannot go beyond those measures to regulate "the conduct of individuals in society towards each other," Justice Joseph P. Bradley (1813–1892) wrote in the ruling, reprinted in *Reconstruction: Opposing Viewpoints.* Any discriminatory business

African Americans being discriminated against at the polls by members of the "White League." *The Library of Congress.*

"EVERY THING POINTS TO A DEMOCRATIC VICTORY THIS FALL."—Southern Papers.

practices should be addressed on the local level, through state laws or state courts, Bradley wrote.

The ruling was devastating to African Americans. The Reconstruction efforts were already unraveling, as the Union troops left the South shortly after the 1876 election and Democrats regained control of the local governments. The court's ruling signaled a final blow to the efforts to provide racial equality. Henry McNeal Turner (1834–1915), a bishop of the African Methodist Episcopal Church, blasted the ruling in a letter to the *Memphis Appeal* newspaper, reprinted in *Reconstruction: Opposing Viewpoints.* He wrote:

If the decision is correct, the United States constitution is a dirty rag, a cheat, a libel [damaging lie], and ought to be spit upon by every negro in the land. More, if the decision is correct and is accepted by the country, then prepare to return to Africa, or get ready for extermination.

The promise of equal rights would be replaced in 1896 by a new phrase: "separate but equal." That was the new standard set by the Supreme Court's ruling in *Plessy v. Ferguson,* which allowed railroads to provide separate cars for African Americans and whites, as long as those cars were comparable. Racial segregation remained legal under that ruling until the landmark 1954 *Brown v. Board of Education of Topeka* decision, in which the Supreme Court ordered a Kansas school district to do away with separate schools for African American and white students.

Did you know ...

- Rapier lost his congressional seat in 1876, after Alabama officials redrew the districts in a way that made whites the majority in all but one district. Although he remained active in Republican politics, he grew discouraged with the second-class treatment African Americans received in his home state. He urged African Americans to move to the western states, where they enjoyed greater freedoms than in the South. But he remained in Alabama, where he died in 1883 of tuberculosis (a fatal infection of the lungs).

- Some Southern whites were so opposed to the idea of sending whites to the same schools as African Americans, they vowed to shut down all schools if the Civil Rights Bill forced them to integrate. Fearing this would bring an end to the newly created public school systems—leaving the South unschooled and ignorant—the supporters of the Civil Rights Bill agreed to drop any mention of integrated schools.

- After the Supreme Court overturned the Civil Rights Bill, nearly three-quarters of a century would pass before Congress passed another civil rights measure, in 1957.

Consider the following ...

- Why did Rapier and others think the Civil Rights Bill was necessary?

- Why did some whites oppose the bill?

- How do you think the issue of discrimination in hotels, restaurants, public transportation, and other business-owned facilities should have been addressed?

For More Information

Andrist, Ralph K., ed. *The American Heritage History of the Confident Years.* New York: American Heritage/Bonanza Books, 1987.

Coulter, E. Merton. *The South During Reconstruction.* Baton Rouge: Louisiana State University Press, 1947.

Foner, Eric. *Reconstruction: America's Unfinished Revolution.* New York: HarperCollins Publishers, 1988.

Franklin, John Hope. *Reconstruction: After the Civil War.* Chicago: University of Chicago Press, 1994.

Stalcup, Brenda, ed. *Reconstruction: Opposing Viewpoints.* San Diego: Greenhaven Press, 1995.

Rutherford B. Hayes

Excerpt from his Inaugural Address
Given on March 5, 1877; reprinted on *Bartleby.com* **(Web site)**

*The winner of a controversial election officially
greets the nation as president*

19

Ohio governor Rutherford B. Hayes (1822–1893) went to bed election night believing he had lost the 1876 race for the presidency. Hayes, a Republican, seemed to hopelessly trail Democratic New York governor Samuel J. Tilden (1814–1886) in the electoral college, the group of state-selected delegates who actually pick the president. But Hayes's strongest supporters were not ready to give up. One of them, former U.S. congressman Daniel E. Sickles (1819–1914) of New York, sent urgent telegrams that night to Republican leaders in South Carolina, Louisiana, Florida, and Oregon, historian Ari Hoogenboom wrote in *The Presidency of Rutherford B. Hayes.* "With your state sure for Hayes, he is elected. Hold your state," the telegrams read. By three o'clock in the morning, Sickles heard back from Daniel H. Chamberlain (1835–1907), governor of South Carolina, where federal troops had been stationed for the past month to prevent the intimidation of African American voters. "All right," Chamberlain responded. "South Carolina is for Hayes. Need more troops. Communication with interior cut off by mobs."

"Only a local government which recognizes and maintains inviolate the rights of all is a true self-government...."

The First Florida Election Fiasco

The 1876 election was not just a battle for the White House. In Florida and several other Southern states, it was a struggle for the governor's mansion—and thus the political control of the state. Throughout the South, local Democrats were building up the political strength to vote out the unpopular Republican carpetbaggers, Northerners who supported the Reconstruction efforts to ensure equal rights for African Americans. That struggle in Florida pitted Republican governor Marcellus Lovejoy Stearns (1839–1891) against Democratic challenger George Franklin Drew (1827–1900).

With the stakes so high, it is not surprising that both sides tried to manipulate the outcome of the 1876 election in Florida. Ballots for the Democratic candidates were printed with Republican symbols to trick illiterate voters (those who could not read or write) who wanted to vote for the Republican candidate, as noted in Ari Hoogenboom's *The Presidency of Rutherford B. Hayes.* Both sides stuffed extra ballots into the boxes, and election officials delayed the results from faraway precincts so the numbers could be changed, if needed. In the 1888 book *Carpet-Bag Rule in Florida,* former state senator John Wallace described how many African American Republican voters followed instructions to "vote early and often":

> From the Georgia line to the capital [of Tallahassee] was a distance of twenty miles, with three or four precincts [election districts] between those points. They started early in the morning and

So began the contested election of 1876, an unusual chapter in American political history that would bring an end to Reconstruction (1865–77), the difficult efforts to reshape the South after the American Civil War (1861–65) with equal rights for ex-slaves. It would take months to untangle the election controversy, amid allegations of voter intimidation, ballot box-stuffing, and other charges (see box). In the meantime, Southern leaders used their votes as bargaining chips, offering their support in exchange for a new Reconstruction policy that would allow Southern whites to resume control of their states. Ultimately a panel of Supreme Court justices and congressmen would vote 8-7, along party lines, to reward the disputed votes in South Carolina, Louisiana, Florida, and Oregon to Hayes, giving the Republican the exact number of votes he needed to clinch the presidency.

voted at every precinct on that line of march to the capital, and each time the same man would vote under an assumed name. It can be fairly estimated that at least five hundred votes were secured in Leon county alone by this method.

In precincts overrun by fraud, the votes from the entire polling place were thrown out. The Republican officials in Florida threw out the right combination of precinct returns to give a nine-hundred-vote lead to Republican presidential candidate Rutherford B. Hayes. Those votes from Florida, along with disputed votes in South Carolina, Louisiana, and Oregon, clinched the presidency for Hayes. "With fraud rampant [widespread], it is impossible to determine who would have won a fair election," Hoogenboom wrote.

Ironically, Florida found itself at the center of another disputed presidential election in 2000, when Republican candidate George W. Bush (1946–) and Democratic challenger Al Gore (1948–) were separated by several hundred votes in the state that would decide the presidency. In a couple of counties, a confusing ballot design was blamed by thousands of Gore supporters who said they accidentally voted for another candidate. Contributing to the controversy were the "punch card ballots" in which voters used a metal-tipped pen to punch a hole next to their candidate's name. Officials debated how to count ballots that had not been entirely punched through, but only dented. Ultimately the dispute landed in the U.S. Supreme Court, which found in favor of Bush.

Born and raised on an Ohio farm, Hayes graduated from Harvard Law School and defended captured runaway slaves during the 1850s. He joined the Union army when the Civil War broke out, and he was wounded five times before his honorable discharge as a major general. After the war, he spent two years in Congress supporting the Radical Republican Reconstruction efforts to rebuild the South with equal rights for African Americans. Later, as governor of Ohio, he helped establish Ohio State University and secure the approval of the Fifteenth Amendment to the Constitution guaranteeing African American men had the right to vote (see Chapter 16).

At the 1876 Republican Party convention, Hayes originally ranked fifth among the men seeking the presidential nomination. But he became the compromise candidate, an acceptable second-choice among the party's various factions. Ethical and reform-minded, Hayes promised to be an

John Mercer Langston, an ex-slave who served in the U.S. Senate. *The Library of Congress.*

improvement over the scandal-ridden administration of President Ulysses S. Grant (1822–1885; served 1869–77), a fellow Republican (see Chapter 17). As part of his campaign, Hayes promised to give white Southerners greater control over their governments once it was clear the rights of African Americans would be respected.

Reconstruction was a bitter period for many in the South. Under the Reconstruction Act of 1867 (see Chapter 10), Congress gave Southern African American men the right to vote and hold office, but barred certain ex-Confederates from doing the same. Carpetbaggers, the name for Northerners who entered Southern politics, became hated figures as they pushed for African Americans' rights (and, according to suspicious Southerners, manipulated African American voters for their own gain; see Chapter 14). Some angry whites joined groups like the Ku Klux Klan (see Chapter 15), a group endorsing white supremacy, to intimidate African Americans from voting or holding office. This only lengthened the stay of federal troops sent to the South to try to maintain peace.

By 1876, much of the country had grown weary of Reconstruction. Most white Southerners still resented the federal presence in their states, and a growing number of Northerners felt the policy was too harsh. Hayes wanted a "peaceful Reconstruction" that would give white Southerners a greater hand in rebuilding their region while protecting the hard-won equal rights for African Americans. But the contested election of 1876 sped up his plans: In a behind-the-scenes deal referred to as the Compromise of 1877, the contested states threw their votes behind Hayes in return for promises that federal troops would be removed from the South.

John Mercer Langston (1829–1897), an ex-slave from Virginia who served one term in the U.S. Senate, believed Hayes's peaceful Reconstruction plan would be an "inestimable [countless] blessing" for African Americans, according to an 1877 speech reprinted in *Reconstruction: Opposing Viewpoints.* Langston believed the removal of federal troops would dissolve the hard feelings between African Americans and whites, allowing everyone to pursue their lives in peace. "Relieved from too pressing and absorbing political excitement, he [the African American man] will cultivate industry more thoroughly and advantageously, locate his family, educate his children, accumulate wealth, and improve himself in all those things which pertain to dignified life," Langston said.

But that feeling was hardly universal. Chamberlain, the South Carolina governor who pledged his state to Hayes, only to lose his own reelection, called Hayes's compromise an "overthrow" of the Reconstruction state governments, according to an 1877 speech reprinted in *Reconstruction: Opposing Viewpoints.* "It consists in the abandonment of … the colored race to the control and rule … of that class at the South which regarded slavery as a Divine Institution, which waged four years of destructive war for its perpetuation [continuation], which steadily opposed citizenship and suffrage [voting rights] for the negro.…"

Hayes knew the plan would be controversial. But after a decade of Reconstruction efforts that saw increasing resentment and violence, he was convinced it was time for a change. In his *Inaugural Address,* delivered three days after the contested election was officially called in his favor, Hayes hoped to reassure the South of his friendly intentions. He believed everyone would benefit under a government that made African Americans and whites equal partners, without the weight of federal intrusion. He hoped the rights of African Americans would remain protected under such an arrangement.

Things to remember while reading an excerpt from Hayes's *Inaugural Address:*

- After the Civil War, the South went through a tense Reconstruction period. Congress gave Southern African American men the right to vote and hold office, but

The inauguration of Rutherford B. Hayes. Chief Justice Morrison R. Waite administers the oath of office to Hayes on a flag-draped inaugural stand on the east portico of the U.S. Capitol. *The Library of Congress.*

barred certain ex-Confederates from doing the same. The presence of federal troops to enforce these changes only added to the feeling that the North was forcibly imposing a new order on the South.

- Hayes, a major general in the Union army during the war, opposed slavery and supported equal rights for African Americans. He wanted to make sure African Americans' rights to vote, hold office, and participate in society remained intact.

- A dispute over all the votes in South Carolina, Louisiana, and Florida, as well as one vote in Oregon, threw the 1876 election into chaos. While Hayes and his opponent, Samuel J. Tilden, both claimed the electoral college votes from those states, local leaders used the votes as bargaining chips. In a behind-the-scenes deal known as the Compromise of 1877, those states threw their support behind Hayes in exchange for a promise to remove federal troops from the South.

Excerpt from Hayes's Inaugural Address

Fellow-Citizens:

*We have assembled to repeat the public ceremonial, begun by Washington, observed by all my **predecessors,** and now a time-honored custom, which marks the **commencement** of a new term of the Presidential office. Called to the duties of this great trust, I proceed, in **compliance** with **usage,** to announce some of the leading principles, on the subjects that now chiefly **engage** the public attention....*

*Many of the **calamitous** efforts of the tremendous revolution which has passed over the Southern States still remain. The **immeasurable** benefits which will surely follow, sooner or later, the hearty and generous acceptance of the **legitimate** results of that revolution have not yet been **realized.** Difficult and embarrassing questions meet us at the **threshold** of this subject. The people of those States are still **impoverished,** and the **inestimable** blessing of wise, honest, and peaceful local self-government is not fully enjoyed. Whatever difference of opinion may exist as to the cause of this condition of*

Predecessors: Those who previously held the office.

Commencement: Beginning.

Compliance: Agreement.

Usage: Custom.

Engage: Occupy.

Calamitous: Disastrous.

Immeasurable: Endless.

Legitimate: Lawful.

Realized: Achieved.

Threshold: Beginning point.

Impoverished: Deprived.

Inestimable: Countless.

things, the fact is clear that in the progress of events the time has come when such government is the **imperative** necessity required by all the varied interests, public and private, of those States. But it must not be forgotten that only a local government which recognizes and maintains **inviolate** the rights of all is a true self-government.

With respect to the two distinct races whose **peculiar** relations to each other have brought upon us the **deplorable** complications and **perplexities** which exist in those States, it must be a government which guards the interests of both races carefully and equally. It must be a government which submits loyally and heartily to the Constitution and the laws—the laws of the nation and the laws of the States themselves—accepting and obeying faithfully the whole Constitution as it is.

Resting upon this sure and **substantial** foundation, the **superstructure** of **beneficent** local governments can be built up, and not otherwise. In **furtherance** of such obedience to the letter and the spirit of the Constitution, and in behalf of all that its **attainment** implies, all so-called party interests lose their apparent importance, and party lines may well be permitted to fade into **insignificance.** The question we have to consider for the immediate welfare of those States of the Union is the question of government or no government; of social order and all the peaceful industries and the happiness that belongs to it, or a return to **barbarism.** It is a question in which every citizen of the nation is deeply interested, and with respect to which we ought not to be, in a **partisan** sense, either Republicans or Democrats, but fellow-citizens and fellowmen, to whom the interests of a common country and a common **humanity** are dear.

The sweeping revolution of the entire labor system of a large portion of our country and the advance of four million people from a condition of servitude to that of citizenship, upon an equal **footing** with their former masters, could not occur without presenting problems of the **gravest** moment, to be dealt with by the **emancipated** race, by their former masters, and by the General Government, the author of the act of emancipation. That it was a wise, just, and **providential** act, **fraught** with good for all concerned, is not generally **conceded** throughout the country. That a moral obligation rests upon the National Government to **employ** its constitutional power and influence to establish the rights of the people it has emancipated, and to protect them in the enjoyment of those rights when they are **infringed** or **assailed,** is also generally admitted.

The evils which afflict the Southern States can only be removed or **remedied** by the united and **harmonious** efforts of both races,

Imperative: Urgent.

Inviolate: Unbroken.

Peculiar: Special.

Deplorable: Regrettable.

Perplexities: Uncertainties.

Substantial: Large.

Superstructure: Structure built on the foundation.

Beneficent: Good.

Furtherance: Promotion.

Attainment: Accomplishment.

Insignificance: Obscurity.

Barbarism: Brutality.

Partisan: Political.

Humanity: Humanness.

Footing: Position.

Gravest: Most serious.

Emancipated: Freed.

Providential: Divinely guided.

Fraught: Filled.

Conceded: Agreed.

Employ: Use.

Infringed: Violated.

Assailed: Attacked.

Remedied: Corrected.

Harmonious: Like-minded.

*actuated by motives of **mutual** sympathy and regard; and while in duty bound and fully determined to protect the rights of all by every constitutional means at the **disposal** of my Administration, I am sincerely anxious to use every legitimate influence in favor of honest and efficient local self-government as the true resource of those States for the promotion of the **contentment** and **prosperity** of their citizens. In the effort I shall make to accomplish this purpose I ask the **cordial** co-operation of all who **cherish** an interest in the welfare of the country, trusting that party ties and the prejudice of race will be freely surrendered in behalf of the great purpose to be accomplished. In the important work of restoring the South it is not the political situation alone that merits attention. The **material** development of that section of the country has been **arrested** by the social and political revolution through which it has passed, and now needs and deserves the considerate care of the National Government within the just limits prescribed by the Constitution and wise public economy.*

*But at the basis of all prosperity, for that as well as for every other part of the country, lies the improvement of the intellectual and moral condition of the people. Universal **suffrage** should rest upon universal education. To this end, **liberal** and permanent **provision** should be made for the support of free schools by the State governments, and, if need be, supplemented by legitimate aid from national authority.*

*Let me assure my countrymen of the Southern States that it is my **earnest** desire to regard and promote their truest interest—the interests of the white and of the colored people both and equally—and to put forth my best efforts in behalf of a civil policy which will forever wipe out in our political affairs the color line and the distinction between North and South, to the end that we may have not merely a united North or a united South, but a united country....*

Actuated: Put into action.

Mutual: Common.

Disposal: Availability.

Contentment: Happiness.

Prosperity: Success.

Cordial: Friendly.

Cherish: Hold dear.

Material: Business.

Arrested: Halted.

Suffrage: Voting rights.

Liberal: Generous.

Provision: Arrangements.

Earnest: Sincere.

What happened next ...

Not long after Hayes's speech, federal troops left the South. The move signaled "the peaceful lapse of the whole South into the control of whites," as noted in *Reconstruction in Retrospect: Views from the Turn of the Century.* While African American men still had the right to vote under the Fifteenth Amendment, Southern states came up with clever ways to

An editorial cartoon shows "Mrs. U.S." choosing to dance with 1876 election winner Rutherford B. Hayes, rather than the loser, Samuel Tilden. *The Granger Collection, New York. Reproduced by permission.*

keep African Americans away from the polls. Sometimes they put the polling places twenty or forty miles away from African American communities. Or they put the polling place in an area only reachable by boats, and had all boats out for repair on election day. Or a group of whites would stage time-consuming arguments at the polling places, ending just in time for the whites to cast their ballots before the precinct closed to the African Americans waiting in line behind them.

Southerners quickly learned these tricky methods worked. Unlike Klan violence against African American voters, these methods sparked little outrage in the North. In the meantime, the U.S. Supreme Court struck down the Civil Rights Act of 1875 (see Chapter 18), which had required restaurants, hotels, railroads, and other businesses to treat African Americans the same as whites. Reconstruction was unraveling, but there was little agreement in Washington about what—if anything—to do about it. By the late 1870s, Democrats and Republicans split control of Congress and the White House, and neither one had enough power to push through a new policy. As noted in *Reconstruction in Retrospect: Views from the Turn of the Century*, "the legislative deadlock had for its general result a policy of noninterference by the national government, and the whites were left to work out in their own way the ends they had in view."

Rutherford B. Hayes, winner of the 1876 presidential election. *The Library of Congress.*

Thousands of African Americans decided to try their luck elsewhere. In *A Narrative of the Negro*, Leila Amos Pendleton (1860–c. 1930) wrote that about sixty thousand African Americans left the South in 1879. Many went to Kansas, where the Kansas Freedman's Relief Association helped provide food, clothing, and other supplies until the newcomers got settled. "With the end of Republican power came the end of anything like justice to the Negro," Pendleton wrote. Nearly a century would pass before the civil rights movement of the 1950s and 1960s would resume the push for racial equality.

Did you know ...

- First lady Lucy Webb Hayes (1831–1889) was a devout Methodist who believed strongly in temperance, or the avoidance of alcohol. She refused to serve alcohol at any White House functions—earning her the nickname

"Lemonade Lucy"—which was applauded by other members of the temperance movement. The movement achieved its goal in 1919 with the Eighteenth Amendment to the Constitution prohibiting the manufacture and sale of liquor. The unpopular amendment was repealed in 1933 by the Twenty-first Amendment to the Constitution.

- Ballot box–stuffing was a common practice in the late 1800s because there were no rules about the size or shape of ballots. This allowed dishonest voters to make a dozen or so mini ballots out of tissue paper, then slip them into the large folded ballot they dropped in the ballot box. Officials had an impossible task of identifying the fake ballots, as some people claimed the tissue ballots were given to African American men so they could vote for the Democratic ticket without drawing attention to themselves. As noted in "The Undoing of Reconstruction," one South Carolina precinct saw 1,163 ballots cast in an 1878 election where only 620 voters existed. The first 620 ballots pulled out by a blindfolded man determined the winner.

- Daniel E. Sickles, the Republican who sparked the 1876 disputed election with his late-night telegrams to several key states, earned one other eyebrow-raising spot in history. In 1859, Sickles murdered Philip Barton Key (1818–1859), the son of "Star-Spangled Banner" lyricist Francis Scott Key (1779–1843), after learning the younger Key was having an affair with his wife. A jury found Sickles not guilty of murder, however, after his attorney argued Sickles was "temporarily insane"—the first successful use of that controversial defense.

Consider the following ...

- What did Hayes hope to accomplish by "peaceful Reconstruction?" Do you think his hopes were realistic?

- How did some whites prevent African Americans from voting?

- What kind of a Reconstruction policy would you recommend for the South after the Civil War?

For More Information

Dunning, William A. "The Undoing of Reconstruction." In *Reconstruction in Retrospect: Views from the Turn of the Century*. Baton Rouge: Louisiana State University Press, 1969.

Franklin, John Hope. *Reconstruction: After the Civil War*. Chicago: University of Chicago, 1961.

Hoogenboom, Ari. *The Presidency of Rutherford B. Hayes*. Lawrence: University Press of Kansas, 1988.

Pendleton, Leila Amos. *A Narrative of the Negro*. Washington, DC: Press of R. L. Pendleton, 1912. Also available at *Documenting the American South: University of North Carolina at Chapel Hill*. http://docsouth. unc.edu/pendleton/menu.html (accessed on September 20, 2004).

"Rutherford B. Hayes: Inaugural Address." *Bartleby.com*. http://www. bartleby.com/124/pres35.html (accessed on September 20, 2004).

Stalcup, Brenda, ed. *Reconstruction: Opposing Viewpoints*. San Diego: Greenhaven Press, 1995.

Wallace, John. *Carpet-Bag Rule in Florida*. Gainesville: University of Florida Press, 1964 [a facsimile reproduction of the 1888 edition].

Where to Learn More

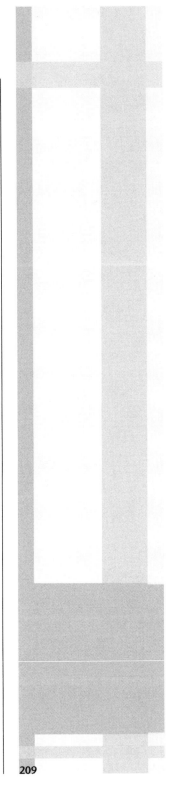

Books

Anthony, Susan B., Elizabeth Cady Stanton, and Matilda Joslyn Gage, eds. *History of Woman Suffrage*. New York: Fowler & Wells, 1881–1922. Reprint, Salem, NH: Ayer Co., 1985.

Appiah, Kwame Anthony, and Henry Louis Gates Jr., eds. *Africana: The Encyclopedia of the African and African American Experience*. New York: Basic Civitas Books, 1999.

Archer, Jules. *A House Divided: The Lives of Ulysses S. Grant and Robert E. Lee*. New York: Scholastic, 1995.

Ayers, Edward L. *The Promise of the New South: Life After Reconstruction*. New York: Oxford University Press, 1992.

Barney, William L. *The Civil War and Reconstruction: A Student Companion*. New York: Oxford University Press, 2001.

Benedict, Michael Les. *A Compromise of Principle: Congressional Republicans and Reconstruction, 1863–1869*. New York: Norton, 1974.

Berlin, Ira A., et al., eds. *Freedmen: A Documentary History of Emancipation, 1861–1867*. New York: Cambridge University Press, 1982.

Blassingame, John W., ed. *Slave Testimony*. Baton Rouge: Louisiana State University Press, 1977.

Cox, LaWanda C., and John H. Cox, eds. *Reconstruction, the Negro, and the New South*. New York: Harper & Row, 1973.

Crook, William H. *Through Five Administrations: Reminiscences of Colonel William H. Crook.* New York: Harper & Brothers, 1910.

Cruden, Robert. *The Negro in Reconstruction.* Englewood Cliffs, NJ: Prentice Hall, 1969.

Davis, Jefferson. *The Rise and Fall of the Confederate Government.* New York: D. Appleton, 1881. Reprint, New York: Da Capo Press, 1990.

Douglass, Frederick. *Escape from Slavery.* Edited by Michael McCurdy. New York: Knopf, 1994.

Douglass, Frederick. *My Bondage and My Freedom.* New York: Miller, Orton and Mulligan, 1855. Reprint, Urbana: University of Illinois Press, 1987.

Foner, Eric. *Reconstruction: America's Unfinished Revolution, 1863–1877.* New York: Harper & Row, 1988.

Foner, Eric. *A Short History of Reconstruction.* New York: Harper & Row, 1990.

Franklin, John Hope. *Reconstruction After the Civil War.* Chicago: University of Chicago Press, 1961.

Golay, Michael. *Reconstruction and Reaction: The Emancipation of Slaves, 1861–1913.* New York: Facts on File, 1996.

Jenkins, Wilbert L. *Climbing Up to Glory: A Short History of African Americans During the Civil War and Reconstruction.* Wilmington, DE: Scholarly Resources, 2002.

Josephson, Matthew. *The Robber Barons: The Great American Capitalists, 1861–1901.* New York: Harcourt, Brace and Company, 1934. Reprint, 1995.

Kirchberger, Joe H. *The Civil War and Reconstruction.* New York: Facts on File, 1991.

Litwack, Leon F. *Been in the Storm So Long: The Aftermath of Slavery.* New York: Vintage Books, 1979.

Litwack, Leon F., and August Meier, eds. *Black Leaders of the Nineteenth Century.* Urbana: University of Illinois Press, 1988.

Lynch, John Roy. *The Facts of Reconstruction.* New York: Neale Publishing Co., 1913. Reprint, Indianapolis: Bobbs-Merrill, 1970.

Mantell, Martin E. *Johnson, Grant and the Politics of Reconstruction.* New York: Columbia University Press, 1973.

McCulloch, Hugh. *Men and Measures of Half a Century: Sketches and Comments.* New York: C. Scribner's Sons, 1888. Reprint, New York: Da Capo Press, 1970.

McFarlin, Annjennette Sophie, ed. *Black Congressional Reconstruction Orators and Their Orations, 1869–1879.* Metuchen, NJ: Scarecrow Press, 1976.

McKittrick, Eric. L. *Andrew Johnson and Reconstruction.* Chicago: University of Chicago Press, 1960. Reprint, New York: Oxford University Press, 1988.

McPherson, James M. *The Struggle for Equality: Abolitionists and the Negro in the Civil War and Reconstruction*. Princeton, NJ: Princeton University Press, 1965.

Morris, Roy, Jr. *Fraud of the Century: Rutherford B. Hayes, Samuel Tilden, and the Stolen Election of 1876*. New York: Simon & Schuster, 2003.

Murphy, Richard W. *The Nation Reunited: War's Aftermath*. Alexandria, VA: Time-Life Books, 1987.

Oubre, Claude F. *Forty Acres and a Mule: The Freedmen's Bureau and Black Land Ownership*. Baton Rouge: Louisiana State University Press, 1978.

Patrick, Rembert W. *Reconstruction of the Nation*. New York: Oxford University Press, 1967.

Perman, Michael. *The Road to Redemption: Southern Politics, 1869–1879*. Chapel Hill: University of North Carolina Press, 1984.

Rehnquist, William H. *Centennial Crisis: The Disputed Election of 1876*. New York: Alfred A. Knopf, 2004.

Simpson, Brooks D. *The Reconstruction Presidents*. Lawrence: University Press of Kansas, 1998.

Smith, John David. *Black Voices from Reconstruction, 1865–1877*. Gainesville: University of Florida Press, 1997.

Stampp, Kenneth M. *The Era of Reconstruction: 1865–1877*. New York: Vintage Books, 1965.

Stephens, Alexander Hamilton. *Recollections of Alexander H. Stephens: His Diary Kept When a Prisoner at Fort Warren, Boston Harbour, 1865*. New York: Doubleday, 1910. Reprint, Baton Rouge: Louisiana State University Press, 1998.

Trefousse, Hans Louis. *Impeachment of a President: Andrew Johnson, the Blacks, and Reconstruction*. Knoxville: University of Tennessee Press, 1975. Reprint, New York: Fordham University Press, 1999.

Wagner, Margaret E., Gary W. Gallagher, and Paul Finkelman, eds. *Civil War Desk Reference*. New York: Simon & Schuster, 2002.

Wharton, Vernon L. *The Negro in Mississippi, 1865–1900*. New York: Harper & Row, 1965.

Woodward, C. Vann. *Reunion and Reaction: The Compromise of 1877 and the End of Reconstruction*. Boston: Little, Brown, 1951. Reprint, New York: Oxford University Press, 1991.

Web Sites

Civil War Archive. http://www.civilwararchive.com/intro.htm (accessed on September 13, 2004).

The Civil War Homepage. http://www.civil-war.net/ (accessed on September 13, 2004).

Douglass, Frederick. "Reconstruction." *The Atlantic Online.* http://www.theatlantic.com/unbound/flashbks/black/douglas.htm (accessed on July 19, 2004).

"Famous American Trials: The Andrew Johnson Impeachment Trial." *University of Missouri–Kansas City.* http://www.law.umkc.edu/faculty/projects/ftrials/impeach/impeachmt.htm (accessed on July 26, 2004).

Hoemann, George A. *Civil War Homepage.* http://sunsite.utk.edu/civil-war/ (accessed on September 13, 2004).

Library of Congress. "African American Odyssey." *American Memory.* http://memory.loc.gov/ammem/aaohtml/aohome.html (accessed on September 13, 2004).

Louisiana State University. *The United States Civil War Center.* http://www.cwc.lsu.edu/ (accessed on August 31, 2004).

Osborn, Tracey. "Civil War Reconstruction, Racism, the KKK, & the Confederate Lost Cause." *Teacher Oz's Kingdom of History.* http://www.teacheroz.com/reconstruction.htm (accessed on September 13, 2004).

"Reconstruction." *African American History.* http://afroamhistory.about.com/od/reconstruction/ (accessed on August 31, 2004).

"Reference Resources: Civil War." *Kidinfo.* http://www.kidinfo.com/American_History/Civil_War.html (accessed on August 31, 2004).

"US Civil War." *Internet Modern History Sourcebook.* http://www.fordham.edu/halsall/mod/modsbook27.html (accessed on August 31, 2004).

Index

Boldface indicates main
entries and their page
numbers; illustrations are
marked by (ill.).

B

O

P

slaves and, 12–13, 16, 70
Presidential Succession Act of 1792, 119
Presidential Succession Act of 1947, 119
Proclamation of Amnesty and Reconstruction of 1863, 67–68
Property
  African Americans as, 48
  slaves as, 14
  voting rights and, 151
The Prostrate State (Pike), 123–24, **134–43**
Provisional governments, 104
Public places, discrimination in, 185–86, 187–90
Public school systems
  Freedmen's Bureau and, 41, 42 (ill.)
  Hayes, Rutherford B., on, 203
  integration and, 193
  in Southern United States, 43
Punch card ballots, 197

R

Racial equality. *See* Equal rights
Racial riots, 97–98, 99 (ill.)
Racial segregation, 54–55, 170, 193
Racial tension, 155
Racial violence. *See* Violence
Racism, 18, 134, 136, 166
Radical Republicans, 84, 88, 109, 168
Railroads
  celebrating first transcontinental, 176 (ill.)
  corruption and, 175–79
  U.S. Congress and, 174, 177
Rapier, James, **185–94**, 187 (ill.)
Recollections of the Inhabitants, Localities, Superstitions, and KuKlux Outrages of the Carolinas (Green), **153–64**
Reconstruction
  African American politicians during, 122–25
  African Americans as governors during, 132
  as a bitter period, 198
  corruption during, 174

Douglass, Frederick, on, 49–52
  end of, 54
  Hayes, Rutherford B., peaceful plan for, 198, 199
  Johnson, Andrew, and, 46–47, 49, 68–69, 101, 106
  Joint Committee on, 47, 70, 71–72, 74, 100–101
  Lincoln, Abraham, plan for, 67–68
  questions concerning, 46
  Radical Republicans and, 109
  readmission of Southern states in, 53, 67–68, 98, 101, 102
  resentment over taxes during, 141
  Stephens, Alexander, on, 72–74
  tobacco label depicting, 71 (ill.)
  unraveling of, 203–5
  U.S. Congress's plan for, 47–48, 53, 68
Reconstruction Acts of 1867, 74, 84, 147
  First, 53, **97–107**, 137, 166
  state constitutions and, 103–4, 105
  Union generals' powers and, 105
"Reconstruction" (Douglass), **46–56**
"Reconstruction in South Carolina" (Chamberlain), 140
Regiments, Fifty-fourth Massachusetts, 55
Reid, Whitelaw, 24
  on former slaves and work, 64
  on Southern states and Constitutional rights, 69
  on white Southerners, 58
Relatives, searching for, 25–26, 29–30
Reminiscences of the Civil War (Gordon), **1–11**
Report of the Joint Committee on Reconstruction, 100–101
Republican Party convention, 1876, 197
Republicans. *See also* Moderate Republicans; Radical Republicans
  African American voters and, 168, 169, 182
  former slaves and, 134–35

after the Civil War, 2–3, 5, 9,
57–58, 60, 61, 63–64
debt in, 89, 93, 140–41, 151
elections, 105, 135
elections of 1876 in, 195–98
federal troops in, 74, 198, 201,
203
Hayes, Rutherford B., *Inaugural
Address* and, 199, 201–3
honoring war heroes, 9–10
Johnson, Andrew, Reconstruction plan and, 46–47, 49,
68–69, 101
lawlessness after the Civil War,
4
Lincoln, Abraham, Reconstruction plan for, 67–68
new social order, 3, 4–5
options for freed slaves, 26
political rights of former Confederates, 89
provisional governments, 104
public schools, 43
readmission to Union, 53,
67–68, 93, 98, 101, 102, 103,
148
Reconstruction as bitter period,
198
Reconstruction expenditures,
140–41
slaves in, 20
taxes in, 7, 141, 142, 151
Thirteenth Amendment and,
17
U.S. Congress's Reconstruction
plan for, 47–48, 49, 53
Spittoons, 141
Stanbery, Henry, 105
Stanton, Edwin, 19, 110–11, 117,
118
Stanton, Elizabeth Cady, 95
State constitutions
carpetbaggers and, 151
Reconstruction Acts of 1867
and, 103–4, 105
Reconstruction era South and,
53
South Carolina, 141
Thirteenth Amendment and,
17
States' rights, 50–51, 81
Stearns, Marcellus Lovejoy, 196

Stephens, Alexander, 67–76, 70
(ill.)
Stereotypes, of African American
politicians, 123–24, 126
Stevens, Thaddeus, 19, 87, 91,
110, 112, 113 (ill.)
Stock market panic (1869), 174
Stocks, Crédit Mobilier scandal
and, 175, 177–80
Stone, Kate, 58
Store owners, cheating African
Americans, 65
Sumner, Charles, 110 (ill.), 124
(ill.)
as abolitionist, 114
argument for impeachment
of Johnson, Andrew, 108–21
attacked by Brooks, Preston,
120
Johnson, Andrew, and, 110
racial equality and, 185–87
Supreme Court. *See* U.S. Supreme
Court
"Swing Around the Circle" tour,
110, 112

T

Taxes
African Americans and, 78
to fund Freedmen's Bureau, 42
in Mississippi, 145
poll, 54, 170, 171
in Reconstruction era South, 7,
141, 142, 151
Temperance, 205–6
Temporary insanity, 206
*Ten Years on a Georgia Planta-
tion Since the War* (Leigh),
57–66
Tennessee, 68, 69–70, 93
Tenure of Office Act (1867), 111,
116–17, 121
Terrorism, 78, 98, 153, 156–57,
162
Texas, First Reconstruction Act of
1867 and, 102
Thieves, 3, 4
Thirteenth Amendment, 12–21
*Thirty Years a Slave: From Bond-
age to Freedom* (Hughes),
22–33

V

W

African Americans in politics
and, 105–6, 123, 124–25,
134, 135, 137
Bullock, Rufus B., and, 146
carpetbaggers and, 144–45, 147
Civil Rights Bill of 1875 and,
191
First Reconstruction Act of
1867 and, 101
Freedmen's Bureau and, 40–41
Hayes, Rutherford B., and, 198
humiliation of, 61, 134, 137
Johnson, Andrew, view of, 109,
113
Ku Klux Klan and, 154
new social order, 3, 4–5
rebuilding without slaves, 4–5,
58, 61
Reconstruction era taxes and,
141
resentment of, 7–8, 124–25,
141, 191
in South Carolina legislature,
135–36
Union League and, 127
White supremacists
African American officials and,
130, 135
intimidation by, 131

violence from, 155–56
Wilson, Henry, 181
Wisconsin, African American suf-
frage in, 89, 166
Women
abolitionism and, 94–95
clothing of, 8
new roles for, 60–61
Women's rights
abolitionism and, 94–95
Douglass, Frederick, and, 55
Women's suffrage
abolitionism and, 95
Douglass, Frederick, and, 55
Fifteenth Amendment and, 171
Fourteenth Amendment and,
95–96

Y

Yulee, David, 69

Z

Zion School for Colored Children, 54 (ill.)

WEST ORANGE PUBLIC LIBRARY

3 3078 00396319 3